Reviews for Wo

The writer's attention to detail in sharing ... ... his life is both entertaining and inspiring. His ...... e Middle East provide valuable insight into America's involvement. — *Mardelle and James Manes, Educators*

It was not uncommon to hear the phrase "writes like an Engineer." The author has blown that negative theory out the window as he delves into an extraordinarily rich account of his life in a superbly researched and written book "Work Hard—Play Hard" with impressive clarity.— *Dimas M. Chavez, Author; worked for the Department of State, Bureau of Diplomatic Security, retired from the CIA and also severed as the Director of Security for AECOM providing support to the National Counterterrorism Center.*

This book is an American story, a great story. It begins with Skipper's life in the depression, his working through college, and his rise from a beginning engineer through to management in the pressure-driven rocket and arms-race world. While I worked with him in Iraq during the in-be-tween war years, we talked little about ourselves because of the ever-present hidden microphones and listening ears. From my position backing-up all the UN inspection disciplines with monitoring, I observed his effective positive impact on all the inspection efforts as well as his influence on the Iraqi engineers, who had the greatest respect for him. He was tough but fair, honest but took no BS, yet treated the Iraqis like human beings. His professionalism spread to the Chemical, Biological, and Nuclear inspection teams, as well as his missile team. A good leader as well as a good manager, he could think outside as well as inside the box and worked harder than the Iraqis or other UN inspectors. I think he was the force behind the success of the initial years of the UN inspection teams, and I observed a decrease in their effectiveness after he left Baghdad. His story explains to me why he has been so successful. It is a very enjoyable read yet provides many lessons for success. — *John A. Hollstein, Col USAFR Ret, BS, MBA-Harvard, JD.*

Work Hard

Play Hard

Ernest
"Skipper"
Colin

Copyright © 2020 Ernest "Skipper" Colin
Work Hard—Play Hard

CBA Publishing Services, LLC
www.cbapub.com
editor@cbapub.com

Editing and layout by John E. Carson and Christine M. Brown
Cover art and design by Anna Talyn

All rights reserved. No part of this book may be reproduced in any form or by any electronic means including storage and retrieval systems—except in the case of brief quotation embodied in critical articles and reviews—without express written consent from its author, except provided by the Unites State of America copyright law.

The events, locales and conversations were created from the author's memories of them. In order to maintain anonymity in some instances, only first names of individuals were used or changed except where publicly available or with permission.

First Edition 2020

ISBN: 978-0-578-67040-9

Dedication

In memory of my beloved parents
Dorothea Elizabeth and Ernest Wellwood Colin, Sr.

The two most important days in your life are
the day you are born and the day you find out why.

~Mark Twain

I haven't been everywhere, but it's on my list.

~Susan Sontag

Table of Contents

Preface

This book is about the adventures of Ernest Wellwood Colin, Jr., better known as "Skipper." The story must naturally begin with the varied relatives and their personalities that provided his foundation. First, his grandparents in Chapter I and II then parents and siblings in Chapters III and IV. All these unusual "characters" will be sprinkled throughout the rest of the story.

Various chapters repeat some of the characters' details or stories. Apologies in advance from the author.

Skipper's parents, Ernest Wellwood Colin, Sr. and Dorothea Elizabeth Hoier, were attractive extroverts; charming, hardworking, highly intelligent, musically talented, and lived life to the fullest. Many of their other characteristics were very different.

Dorothea was an educated intellect, an Episcopal nun for five years, nurse, and lived her life close to our Lord. She did not have any interest in material things except for a piano. Dorothea never met a stranger and would always see the good in people. An eternal optimist she could rationalize anything. She also possessed a high set of values, principles and knowledge which she attempted to lovingly pass on to her children. She worked as a nurse throughout her adult life.

Ernest, on the other hand, orphaned at age 12, did not go beyond the 10th grade, although he was a good student. He was a sailor with the stereotypical language and adventures. Ernest was not an enabler of bad behavior or shirking one's duty to family or country. He expected his children to be responsible, independent, self-reliant and accountable for their actions. Skipper was thankful for the lessons learned when reflecting decades later. Ernest was also a binge alcoholic. His behavior during binges was not something to write home about. He was at sea much of Skipper's first seven years. During WWII Ernest served as captain of several ships. He was rarely home until the end of the war which coincided with the end of Skipper's first grade. Dorothea had to endure much during these times but was always an anchor for their children.

Maternal grandparents, Thomas Petersen Hoier and Esther Anne Boggs, were actors in vaudeville and on Broadway for over 50 years. Chapter I will attempt to cover their fascinating lives. The only grandparent born in the USA was Esther Boggs (1886). Thomas Hoier (1877) was born in Haderslev, Denmark. Both paternal grandparents,

Francis Pinwick McAleese (1875) and Lottie Brown Martha McCabe (1878) were born in Nova Scotia, Canada.

Skipper was blessed with two great loves resulting in marriage. Patsy Lee Shirley was to die at a young age from cancer. Twenty-six years later, the widower would find another keeper, Nancy Dawson George. There are not enough words to express the emotions and pride of loving and being loved by these two extraordinary women.

Skipper and Patsy's children, Paige and Chad would be ages nine and seven, respectfully when Patsy was diagnosed with breast cancer with little chance of surviving. The family's life would be changed forever. Paige and Chad's stories will be theirs to tell, although some of their story will naturally be included herein.

One should note that Skipper was the only imperfect person in the book. Other players imperfections are generally not included. Most imperfections were petty and not worthy of space. The story primarily centers on many events and people that impacted his life or attempts to explain who he was and would become. To prevent boredom, negative behavior of a few are included.

The Preface and Chapters I through IV are presented in the third person and the remainder of the book will be told in the first person. Hopefully this knowledge will help the reader. Chapter V and beyond are mostly in chronological order. The beginning will cover the adventures of Skipper during his first 11 years in New Hampshire, four years in Carlsbad, New Mexico, three high school years in Eunice, New Mexico and four years at Eastern New Mexico University in Portales, New Mexico. The story will then progress to his career starting in Eunice with stops in Boulder, Colorado; Moses Lake, Washington; Little Rock, Arizona; Huntsville, Alabama and finally serving with the United Nations in Iraq as the Chief Weapons Inspector. He will make Huntsville his home starting in 1963 at age 25 and never move elsewhere. He retired at age 57 in 1995 after nearly 33 years with Teledyne Brown Engineering. The book will conclude with his post retirement years.

Chapter I - Maternal Grandparents

On February 18, 1907 following a very brief courtship, Thomas Petersen Hoier married Esther Anne Boggs in Crawfordsville, Indiana. Their daughter Dorothea Elizabeth was born on September 16, 1908 followed by a daughter born Marian Elizabeth on October 17, 1913. Marian would be nicknamed "Tommie" because they desperately wanted a boy to continue the family surname. Thomas and Esther would share a great love of performing on stage for over 50 years. Dorothea bore them a grandson, Skipper and two granddaughters, Bonnie and Nancy. Marian bore them one granddaughter, Carol. They and all their families would survive WWI, the Spanish flu epidemic, the Great Depression, and WWII.

Granddad

Thomas Petersen Hoier was born on June 5, 1877 in Haderslev, Denmark. During his early years his nickname would be "Tommy," but not as an adult. The house in which Tommy was born was built in 1831. It was larger than most and was located on a fjord in Haderslev, Sonderjylland, Denmark. Haderslev was located at the end of a fjord that extended from the Baltic Sea. In the garden was a huge tree house where they served tea every afternoon and, of course, all the delectable cakes and cookies that made Danish housewives famous. *The sweet tooth was genetically passed on.*

His grandson, Skipper, would visit the home in 1984, one hundred years after Thomas and his family left for America. The city had just purchased the historic home and was restoring the house. A workman allowed Skipper and a German friend to tour the four-story mansion. All rooms and grounds were fully explored. *A memorable treat.*

Tommy was named for his grandfather according to Danish custom. His first memory was of a day of sorrow and confusion when his sister died; he was barely three years old. He would have two other siblings, Alex born 1878 in Haderslev and Minnie born 1885 in Chicago. Even as a very small child Tommy loved to read. Long after he was supposed to be asleep, he would read in bed. Denmark shared the sunlit summer nights of the Scandinavian countries. Before he was seven, he had read the Bible from cover to cover in Danish and in German. He had also read parts of the Bible in English and Latin. He would go on to be fluent in seven languages. Tommy had a photographic memory. The King of Denmark, Christian IX, wished to educate him as a prodigy.

The county of Schleswig in the southern part of Denmark was captured by Bismarck in the Seven Weeks War in 1866. The northern zone of Schleswig, which included the city of Haderslev, was restored to Denmark by the Treaty of Versailles after World War I. The southern zone of Schleswig remained in Germany.

Tommy's father, Peter Jacobsen Hoier, even though a wealthy man, was about to be pressed into the German army. Peter decided the family had to immigrate to America. He took his family and fled in the night to Copenhagen in 1884 bound for America. While they were waiting for a ship, the family had a real adventure. Walking in the park with his family, Tommy met the King of Denmark, Christian IX. It's possible this was when the king offered to educate him.

Tommy celebrated his seventh birthday on the ship. As soon as they landed in America they went directly to Chicago where there was a sizable settlement of Danes. Young Tommy went alone to the school to enroll. Since he was very bright, he made such an impression that he was remembered 30 years later. The principal recognized his daughter's (Dorothea Hoier) surname when she was first enrolling herself in the first grade and asked if she was related to Thomas Hoier. When she told the principal he was an actor, she shook her head and said disapprovingly, "My, my, what a waste of good brains!"

Tommy's father, having farms in Denmark as well as a shipping business, decided to take the family to Dodge City, Kansas. Fortunes were being made in the west so his father, Peter, invested all the money he had brought from Denmark in a farm near Dodge City on November 3, 1887. With all their belongings they traveled with high hopes aboard a train to Kansas. The land they found was to be a far cry from the lush country they had left behind in Denmark. They were faced with one problem after another until finally they lost everything. Peter bought a covered wagon and headed back to Chicago in 1889. It was a journey of great hardship. Little Minnie developed scarlet fever. The family ran out of food. At one time, they stopped at a settlement where everyone was celebrating a wedding and they were invited to join the event. Even though they were hungry, Peter wouldn't let his family share in the feast because they could not give the young couple a gift. The Hoiers camped by a stream alone and were within hearing of the fun and music. Another time a prairie fire almost wiped them out but just in time the wind shifted, and they were saved.

Tommy graduated from Lake View High School, Chicago, a real achievement in those days. Through most of his high school days he worked in the Chicago Opera House as an usher. As the head usher he oversaw a group of boys and earned a fair salary. As a bonus he developed a great love of opera and theater, which enriched him all his life. Having money to spend from his salary also affected his life. Following high school, he attended Northwestern University in Chicago to study for a law degree. Thomas was clerking for the law firm of John P. Altgeld (ex-governor of Illinois). He became discontented partly because he earned only a token amount. He would not take a long-range view of his opportunity. Perhaps the romance of the unreal world of opera and theater also influenced him. He ran away and joined the circus.

The circus life was far less glamorous than he thought it would be. Tommy filled all the odd jobs that came up, selling tickets and popcorn, feeding animals, putting up the tent, being general errand boy, and yet he enjoyed it. The circus, however, went broke and he was stranded far from home. He was too proud to ask for help so he trudged home working for meals, sleeping in the fields but making it on his own. He was bitten by the acting fever and never worked in any other occupation other than the entertainment field for the rest of his life. He was well known in the radio and theater community, but not always the star. Thomas was always employed in show business as a comedian and a character actor in road shows, vaudeville, radio, television and on Broadway in legitimate theater. He was highly respected by other members of his profession. He appeared in the original productions of *Merchants of Venus* (1920), *Mr. Peebles and Mr. Hooker* (1946), and *The Survivors* (1948). Thomas was widely known on Broadway for his role, as the father in *Dear Ruth* (1947). His last role was Batista in the original Broadway production of *Kiss me Kate*.

Shows in Carlsbad, New Mexico mentioned in a letter to his daughter, Dorothea, included *Too Much Money* in February 1899 and with the Horace Redpath Chautauqua Co in May 1925. He also did advertisements such as Fleischmann's Gin, which were on billboards and sides of busses all over NY and in newspapers and magazines.

Ironically, he never drank alcohol.

Thomas also wrote several songs that were among the most popular in America. "Don't Bite the Hand That's Feeding You" with music by Jimmie Morgan published in 1915 sold over a million copies. In the 1930s Judy Garland sang the song in a film. The tune was revived by Gene Autry in 1942 at a rodeo in NYC in Madison Square Garden, which caused the royalties to flow again. The song provided enough funds to build a mansion near a beach on Long Island, New York. The song title became a common phrase still used today.

During WWI he wrote the following popular songs; "Four Years More in the White House (Should Be The Nations Gift To You)," "There's A Service Flag Flying At Our House," "The Bravest Battle Of The War Was Fought In A Mother's Heart," and "My Girl Of The Southland" with music by Al W. Brown.

Thomas also performed on many RCA radio programs including several national programs. He was a national news announcer when his daughters still lived at home.

One endeavor was as a Smithsonian guide on a weekly radio program on Sunday mornings in the late 1930s. The program was *The World is Yours* airing at 11:30 am till noon on NBC. Each week he gave a verbal tour of a different room in the Smithsonian, mixing humor with the dialogue. After his grandson, Skipper, was born, Thomas often pretended he was in the tour group. *The World Is Yours* marked its fourth anniversary of continuous weekly broadcasting with its 209th program on June 9, 1940. Produced by NBC in cooperation with the U. S. Office of Education and the Smithsonian Institution, *The World Is Yours* had as its purpose the systematic presentation of the wonders of nature and the work of man as revealed in the scientific investigations and exhibits of the Smithsonian. The program was among the most popular public service programs on the air. Since its inception on June 7, 1936, more than 500,000 letters had been received from listeners. *The World Is Yours* carried by an NBC network of 82 stations, brought the research resources of the Institution to an audience of millions, many of whom never got to Washington to view the Institution's vast collections, or who could make only brief visits there. The central character of the program was Thomas, the "Old Timer," teller of scientific tales, whose behind-the-exhibits stories were the highlights of each broadcast.

On one radio program, *Young Widder Brown*, he played Uncle Josh (weathered and rich in experience as farmer and friend, and a sympathetic guide when Ellen wants to talk over a problem). This program was heard every weekday at 4:45 pm Eastern Standard Time on NBC at least in the year of 1946.

Thomas was a member of New York's prestigious "The Lambs Club." (Americas' oldest theatrical organization). He was about to be honored by the Council of The Living Theater as the only actor in over 200 years of professional theater in America to play one role for 1,000 consecutive performances on Broadway. He played two parts, Henry Trevor and Batista (Kate's father), in *Kiss Me Kate*. The musical won five Tony Awards in 1949 including best musical. Also, Thomas was to be awarded the "keys-to-the-city" of New York by the mayor. He had just signed a contract to perform at the London "Coliseum Theatre" production of the musical. Unfortunately, he died on the table when they were going to remove his gallbladder. The ether killed him before they started the incision on December 20, 1951. (Six months before his grandson, Skipper's father died.)

Grandmud

Esther, at 52, insisted her grandchildren call her Grandmud or Queen Esther, because the "drama queen" was far too young to be a grandmother when her first grandchild, Skipper, was born. *Go figure.*

On November 5, 1886 Esther Anne Boggs was born in Washington, DC. She would have five siblings who reached adulthood: Marian Esther Boggs (1884-1936), Paul Pearson Boggs (1891-1969), Martha Washington Boggs, (1894-1979), Florence Elizabeth Boggs (1896-1949), and Barbara Elsie (1901-1973). All the sisters were gorgeous and would follow Esther into show business. Her brother, Paul, would become sheriff of Nassau County on Long Island, New York. According to a niece, he was a crook who made a fortune as sheriff. Their father, John Willis Boggs II, a very strict Baptist preacher, disowned John III, when he married their mother, Ida Elizabeth Browne, who was a debutante in Washington, DC and grew up in relative wealth. She was also disowned by her family when they married. Ida's father, Honorable Andrew K Brown, Esq, reportedly, was an attorney for President Lincoln.

John was not a heavy drinker, but payday after payday he stopped at the corner saloon and blew most of his earnings. Therefore, their daughter, Esther Anne in 1894 was sent out to work at the of age eight as were the other children at very early ages. Esther and Thomas Hoier were acting in a show called *College Widow* at the time her mother, Ida, had died of pneumonia in 1906. John was murdered (according to family lore) while delivering the payroll to Sing Sing Correctional Facility in upstate New York in 1913. However, the death certificate indicates he died of natural causes.

At a young age according to family tradition, she played the main part in *The Little Matchmaker Girl* a short story, by Han Christian Anderson. Esther performed on Broadway for a couple of years coming home on the horse cars after the show. She played the major part, Topsy, in *Uncle Toms Cabin* and one of the children in *Rip Van Winkle*. Later she went "on the road" with Joseph Jefferson, one of the all-time great actors. The theater company carried tutors for the children.

At age 14 in 1900, she substituted and perform stunts for a German dancer in a musical, *Mr. Bluebeard,* with a flying ballet corps that toured the country. In 1903, she was in the Iroquois Theater fire in Chicago. This caused the greatest loss of life of any American building fire. Dan McAvoy, the star of *Bluebeard*, rescued Esther by carrying her through the rigging above the stage to an adjoining building. This is probably the last time she performed as a dancer, but she taught her sister, Martha, all she knew about dancing. Martha toured both Europe and Australia as a better dancer.

Esther and Thomas Hoier were acting in a show called *College Widow* at the time her mother, Ida, died of pneumonia on November 11, 1906. On February 18, 1907, following a very brief courtship, she married Thomas Petersen Hoier. They had two daughters, Dorothea and Marian.

In 1915 she played the part of Josine Walker in the silent film *Destruction* staring Theda Bada. Theda Bada was the most popular silent film star of the era. She was one of cinema's earliest sex symbols.

During World War I she performed with the USO in Europe for the American service men. She arrived back in New York City on August 23, 1919 on the SS *Printz Friedrich Wilhelm*. The German ship surrendered after the war, then was commissioned by the Americans and made five trips carrying 15,000 US Army personnel home from April into August. The ship sailed the fifth and last crossing from Brest, France on August 14, 1919. Esther sailed on the last ship because she believed the soldiers deserved to arrive home first. The ship manifest lists her as born in Washington, DC with a current address of Baldwin, Long Island, New York and born November 5, 1886. Their mansion in Baldwin was paid for with income from the song written by Thomas "Don't Bite the Hand That's Feeding You."

During a Christmas season, when her grandson, Skipper, was still crawling, Esther knocked the Christmas tree over. She placed

Skipper adjacent to the tree and blamed him for inadvertently upsetting the beautiful tree. No one quite believed her, but it was Christmas. A year or two later she confessed.

After 1951 when her husband, Thomas, died she rarely left their apartment in Manhattan, New York. Then she moved into the Actor's Fund Home, Englewood, Bergen Co, New Jersey in the mid-1960s. Esther's daughters had been encouraging the move for years. The Actor's Fund Home policy was that anyone who had been an actor for more than 50 years was eligible to stay. The only stipulation, that no matter your wealth, you had to donate all your assets to the Actor's Fund Home. Esther had no assets but some of the residents had donated all their millions of dollars. They picked up Esther in a limo, took her to Fifth Ave and purchased a wardrobe including a fur coat. She lived there until her death at age 92 on November 16, 1977, three weeks before grandson Skipper's wife, Patsy, would die on Pearl Harbor Day.

Back row: Uncle Chet, Aunt Marian, Mom, Dad
Front row: Skipper, Grandmud, Cousin Carol, Grandad, Bonnie

Chapter II - Paternal Grandparents

Grandmother

Lottie Brown Martha McCabe was born November 17, 1878 in Diligent River, Nova Scotia, Canada. Her parents, Charles Edmond McCabe (1852-1919) and Martha Elis Victory (1856-1944) owned and operated the only general store in Diligent River. Their home was on the Bay of Fundy, which has the highest tides in the world (45 feet). The beach was very wide at low tide. The McCabe's would rent out one of the bedrooms to boarders such as Francis Pinwick McAleese.

Lottie was a teacher in Nova Scotia living with her parents when she became engaged to Francis (1875-1937). Her life changed dramatically when she was abandoned at the altar in 1905. She then discovered she was pregnant. Her father kicked her out and insisted she leave Canada. In Boston she gave birth to Ernest McCabe in 1906, the father of Skipper.

After her son Ernest was born, she worked in Massachusetts as a housekeeper. She must have been a lovely, cultured woman, because when Dorothea (Hoier) Colin visited in some of the homes where she worked, they still remembered her and spoke highly of her 30 years after Lottie's death.

Two years later, the gorgeous Lottie married Job Colin on June 29, 1908 in South Amherst, Massachusetts. They lived in the small community of Cushman and two years later had a son Everett Colin (1910-1994). Ernest was called a bastard by other children. She and Job would have another son, Marshall Edmond Colin on October 16, 1911 who died as an infant on April 27, 1912. Job died in 1912 when Ernest was six. Both Job and Marshall died of tuberculosis.

A year and a half later, Lottie married a widower, Winifred H. Bangs (1862-1922), on December 20, 1913 in Leverett, Massachusetts. His five children with his late wife, Mary E (1864-?), were out of the nest. Lottie and Winifred would have a daughter, Alice M. Bangs (1915-1979) and a son, Ken, born April 1918.

Lottie died, at age 39, on April 3, 1918 shortly after giving birth to her son, Ken. He was immediately adopted by the McAvoy family. The McAvoy family broke all ties to Lottie's children as did the Bangs family including the jerk Winifred, her husband. Ernest (age 12),

Everett (age 6), and Alice (almost 3) were essentially orphaned. *More later*. She is buried in North Amherst Cemetery in Cushman, Massachusetts alongside Job Colin and their infant son Marshall.

Grandfather

Francis Pinwick McAleese was born in Parrsboro, Nova Scotia, Canada on October 1, 1875. Parrsboro is very near the Diligent River community. He was the eighth of twelve children born to Francis McAleese (1837-1914) who was born in Ballymena, Northern Ireland and Elizabeth Taggart (1844-1911) who was born in Dunminning, Northern Ireland. Francis and Elizabeth were married in Maccan, Nova Scotia on June 22, 1861. Their twelve children were baptized in the St. James Presbyterian church; however, most family members were buried in the Old Methodist Cemetery.

Their son, Francis Pinwick was reportedly a salesman who became engaged to Lottie McCabe while boarding in her parents' home. After he stood her up at the wedding he disappeared for years. About 1945 Lottie's cousin sent a letter to Lottie's son, Ernest, explaining that Francis had knocked on her door in 1936 to inquire about Lottie, who unknown to him had died over 18 years earlier. He was in terrible health, an alcoholic, and died a short time later in Apple River, Nova Scotia on February 20, 1937. Lottie's cousin wrote he was a miserable man.

Step-Grandfather

Job Marcel Colin was born in Springhaven, Nova Scotia on May 24, 1879. Springhaven, near Yarmouth was a small community. They had no stores and one church, Ste Agnes Church, a Catholic church. His parents, Marcel Colin, Jr (1841-1898) born in St. Basile and Rosalie Mius (1845-1884) born in Quinan were married in Eel Brock, Nova Scotia in St. Anne Du Rousseau, a Catholic church, on November 5, 1864 and would have nine children. Job would be the next to last child. Job's father, Marcel was born in St. Basile, New Brunswick, Canada on September 9, 1841. His mother Rosalie was born in Quinan, Nova Scotia, also near Yarmouth, on January 23, 1845. Marcel was known as a member of the Ste Agnes Church choir and a significant supporter.

In 1996 Skipper, the step-grandson of Job, would discover his home in Springhaven, having only a photo taken in 1935. The house looked very different. The current owners explained that they had remodeled the house a few years earlier. Stripping the plaster from the walls and ceilings revealed large beams put together with wooden pegs. The house had been built 125 years earlier, about 1870, by Marcel. They said an earthquake could not bring down the house. Marcel, a ship builder, also built many other homes in the area.

Job was raised as a French Canadian Catholic with his first language being French. He was also fluent in English and could read and write in English. Like his father, Job was a carpenter. He would emigrate to the United States in 1894. Job must have visited Nova Scotia because he reportedly fathered an illegitimate son in 1899, then return to Massachusetts. Later he met and married Lottie in 1908. His stepson, Ernest, would take his surname, Colin. Job would die of tuberculosis in 1912, at age 33.

Lottie and Job Colin with Ernest (Dad)

Chapter III - Fathers

Illegitimate, Ernest McCabe was born in Boston on February 25, 1908, but brought up around Mt. Holyoke, Deerfield, Cushman and Amherst in Massachusetts. His parents' details are found in the previous chapter.

His stepfather Job Colin would provide Ernest with the surname Colin and later Ernest added a middle name Wellwood. It is unknown when or why. His stepfather Job died when Ernest was six years old and his mother, Lottie, died when he was 12 years old. When his mother died, he refused to go to an orphanage and worked on farms or as a clerk for room and board to attend school.

Because Ernest was a good student, his teacher, Ruth, visited a farm where he was working for room and board to find out why he had been absent. She was aware that he had asthma and was concerned. Ruth found him in a barn near death from beatings received from the farmer. The teacher removed him from the farm, placed him in medical care and then found other accommodations for him. According to his half-brother, Everett, Ernest was living on a farm with a Mr. McAvoy, who adopted their infant half-brother Ken. Everett said, "Mr. McAvoy treated Ken like a prince, but treated Ernest like an animal."

According to the employment records compiled by Ernest, he worked on farms around Amherst until December 1923 at which time he traveled to Crescent City, Florida where he was a store clerk until May 1924. He returned to South Amherst as a farm hand until the end of 1924. Ernest went back to Florida where he worked at a variety of jobs: fruit packer, chauffeur, plumber's helper, construction foreman, Macadam Roller operator, and quartermaster on ships. Ernest then returned to the Northeast. He worked in Westfield, Massachusetts, when Everett graduated from Westfield High School in 1928.

Ernest went to work for United Fruit Company in December 1929. He was employed initially as a deck cadet and served through several ranks up to chief mate. He left the company on April 14, 1942. Ernest received a Certificate of Efficiency to Lifeboat Man on April 28, 1927, a Certificate of Efficiency to Able Seaman on May 22, 1930, a Chief Mate License on December 22, 1934, a Master's License on November 19, 1937, a Commission as Ensign in US Naval Reserve on April 17, 1937, and an Honorable Discharge from US Naval Reserve on November 26, 1942. He was promoted to lieutenant commander by the US Maritime Service on June 19, 1943 and was promoted to commander by US Maritime Service, January 6, 1944. He served in the US Maritime Service until June 1, 1945. Ernest was awarded two Atlantic War Zone Bars, a Mediterranean Middle East War Zone Bar, and a Pacific War Zone Bar by the War Shipping Administration. He received a license issued by the US Coast Guard as Master of Steam and Motor Vessels of any gross tons upon any ocean on November 18, 1947. Ernest was the youngest person to pass the Masters Examination or the youngest captain in America according to his brother Everett. *Doubt this is true.*

After reviewing his photo album compiled prior to his marriage, one comes to the obvious conclusion he enjoyed the company of many attractive women in many different lands before marrying an Episcopal nun, Dorothea (Skipper's mother). They would have a son and two daughters.

During the first year of World War II more US Merchant Maritime Service lives were lost than all the military services put together. There were constant pleas on the radio for experienced sea officers to sign-up for the US Merchant Maritime Service. As a result, Ernest returned to sea as the captain of the S.S. *Charles W Eliot*, a ship owned by the War Shipping Administration. The S.S. *Charles W Eliot* was sunk a week after a different captain took command during the Normandy invasion. On June 30, 1944, until June 1, 1945, he served as captain of a new ship, the S.S. *Sun Yat Sun*.

During his years at sea, he sailed to many ports in the Caribbean, South America, North America, Europe, and the Near and Far East.

In the late 1930s Ernest and Dorothea purchased a farm in the township of Rumney, New Hampshire. On February 24, 1947 the farm was sold, and the family moved to West Campton, New Hampshire. They purchased an unfinished house and property. Ernest planted a vegetable garden and finished the house where they lived until November 1948. In West Campton he had started a cabinet shop. His asthma condition became severe and dictated he live in a dry climate free of ragweed. They then set out for New Mexico in late 1948. He lived in Carlsbad, New Mexico until his death in 1952. He worked at the potash mines as a lift operator, a skill he learned in the Merchant Marines. His hobby in New Mexico was hunting for Indian artifacts.

During his time in New Hampshire he taught himself to play the saxophone and the accordion. Both in New Hampshire and New Mexico he would conduct "sing-a-longs" with the family while playing the accordion.

Ernest had a knack for finding and becoming friends with truly unique characters. One was a hermit whom Ernest always invited to Thanksgiving dinner who lived in the White Mountains of New Hampshire in a crude lean-to. Another was a crusty old man who lived in an old school bus (with all kinds of old junk laying around the property) on the desert near Carlsbad, New Mexico. He developed a close friendship with an old Indian Chief (he was a chief prior to New Mexico becoming a state, when there was not always peace with the Anglos). When Ernest died, Indian Chief Sunny Skies was the only man to visit his 14-year-old son, Skipper, to have a man to man discussion.

Thirty years after his death, Dorothea's long-term friend, Sparky, (an intellect) would tell Skipper that Ernest was the smartest man she had ever known. Though she was not a fan due to his behavior.

Ernest's life was like a roller coaster; having lost his father and mother at ages 6 and 12, respectively, then on his own, abused, and becoming an alcoholic. With his faults he also had many redeeming qualities. He was blessed with a brilliant and creative mind, natural ability to lead, sense of humor, unusual charm, spirit of adventure, and enthusiasm for life and love of family.

Chapter IV - Mother

Dorothea Elizabeth Hoier, a beautiful promising baby, was born on September 16, 1908 in Flushing, New York, likely by a midwife. Her parents were actors on Broadway and in vaudeville. At age three or four she taught herself to read. She spent most of her life reading at least three hours per day and likely had total recall. At age five she was observing her father prepare their income tax and told her father he made a mistake. He had. Dorothea had been in all 48 states (some of the 48 states were still territories at the time) prior to starting school, having traveled with her parents on vaudeville tours. She often slept in hotel bureau drawers. She traveled extensively with her parents during many school years. In 1913 at age five, she gained a sister, Marian. Their parents were hoping for a boy. The next best thing was to nick name her Tommie.

Dorothea enrolled in the first grade, by herself, at the same school in Chicago that her father had attended. The principal seeing her unusual surname asked if she was related to Thomas Hoier. She said, "He is my father." The principal then asked what her father was doing. She responded that he was an actor. The principal said, "What a waste of a great brain." She traveled extensively with parents during school years. For the rest of her life Dorothea would say her father was 1,000 times smarter than her. Her son, Skipper would say often she was 1,000 times smarter than himself.

Dorothea was a serious classic piano student. In fact, when a child, she and Hellen Hayes (famous actress) performed together in a recital in NYC. Dorothea was the star of the event. They were both presented bunches of roses at the conclusion of the recital.

Her father built a mansion on Long Island. This afforded an opportunity to stay in one school, providing more stability. Dorothea's Aunt Marian (Boggs) Gad lived in the home and raised her daughter Betty, as well as Dorothea and Tommie when Dorothea's parents traveled. Decades later Betty would say that Dorothea was the most like Betty's mother. Betty said of all the many cousins of their generation Dorothea was the pioneer.

During her teens some years were spent in an Episcopal convent (Convent of St. Anne in Arlington Heights, Massachusetts). Dorothea, Tommie, and cousin, Betty attended high school years while living in the convent. While Tommie and Betty enjoyed cutting up with others, Dorothea would be reading or studying. During high school Dorothea took four years of English, French, Latin, history, math and science as well as other courses. They were exposed to many of the best cultural events Boston had to offer. They each had exceptional intelligence that served them well.

Dorothea wanted to be an English teacher and received a full scholarship from a prestigious college in Massachusetts. However, her mother did not allow her to accept the opportunity being skeptical of the college's intention. Her mother thought nothing was free so there must be a sinister reason for the offer. Always wanting to help others, Dorothea enrolled in Nassau Hospital School of Nursing (NY) affiliated with Columbia University, with no scholarship. She made the highest possible marks in school at all levels including college. She graduated in 1929. According to the 1930 census she was a nurse at Bellevue Hospital on April 10, 1930.

About one year after graduating she became a Novice with the Order of Saint Anne of the Episcopal Church. Her name was Sister Ingrid. She served mostly at Saint Anne Convent for retarded girls and a guest house for elderly women in Kingston, NY. During the 1930s the country was in the deep depression. Because nuns took a "vow-of-poverty" and lived in a convent, their daily lives were materially unaffected. After nearly five years she was required to take her final vows to become a nun for life, which symbolized their marriage to God. In 1935 to forsake their final vows meant they would be excommunicated from the Church. Dorothea, a beautiful brilliant young Episcopal nun was faced with a major life decision. She did not understand why priests could be married and have a family while nuns could not be married but were biologically able to have children. In the future she wanted to have a family. After much prayer she approached the Mother Superior to announce her intent not to take the final vows. The Mother Superior, being a wise woman, suggested she spend a couple of months at her parents', knowing Dorothea's mother, the "drama queen," would likely drive her up the wall.

Sure enough, after being around her mother for two months, Dorothea decided to return to the convent (the Order of St. Anne headquarters was in Arlington, MA) in Kingston, NY and take her final vows. Her mother, Esther, passionately did not like the idea of her daughter being a nun. Esther suggested that Dorothea travel to St.

Thomas for two months. If her daughter still wanted to take her final vows, she would reluctantly accept the outcome. Dorothea agreed to make the journey.

She boarded a ship in New York City bound for St. Thomas and met the ship's second officer, Ernest, on a Wednesday. The following Sunday, Ernest, a charming, handsome, bright man two years older asked her to marry him. Dorothea, the nun, agreed on Monday to marry the sailor in about six months. When the ship dropped her on St. Thomas, Dorothea informed Ernest that if someone asked her to dinner she would accept, and she did.

The ship hit a sandbar which was scheduled to pick her up for the return trip to New York City. Therefore, Dorothea was now going to be delayed about a month returning to her parents. She wanted to tell her parents in person that marriage was planned and not final vows. Now Ernest would be knocking on the door before she returned. *Oops!* Dorothea wrote a letter to her parents explaining why Ernest would be knocking on their door. (The cute unknown letter was discovered by her son after her death, decades later.) It should be noted that Esther did not like the idea that her daughter was to marry a damn sailor any better.

For a couple of years Dorothea lived in Manhattan as a nurse while Ernest sailed. She served as the scrub nurse for the country's top neurosurgeon. At the time, the scrub nurse would normally oversee the pre-surgery preparation of an operating room. However, because the operations took 16 hours she walked in with the surgeon and out at the same time. After about two years she needed lower back surgery. The recovery at that time required a year of bed rest, much of the time in the hospital. In 1937 they moved to a cottage near Mill Brock river in the White Mountains of New Hampshire. In 1938, she gave birth to their first child. Four months before, Ernest received his master's license for large vessels, thereby certifying him to hold the position of a ship captain. This automatically earned him the rank of ensign in the US Navy Reserves.

Dorothea gave birth to their son at a hospital in Hempstead, NY on Long Island. The delivery doctor was the husband of her best friend, Sparky, since nursing school. Sparky was an intellectual as was Dorothea and certainly a character. At the time of delivery, Ernest was on a ship just clearing the NYC harbor heading to Ft. Lauderdale when he received the news. After a few weeks, Dorothea returned to

Manhattan and her parents. Her father, Thomas, greeted her and the infant son at the door and he said, "Ah, the little Skipper." Thank goodness the nickname stuck otherwise being a Junior, he might have been called Ernie or worse.

Mom had Skipper baptized on May 22, 1938 at age two months at the Episcopal Church of St. Mary the Virgin near Times Square in NYC. More than seventy years later Skipper would visit the church when the Episcopal Church of the Nativity choir of Huntsville, Alabama performed. It was special to see the font used for his baptism. The choir never sounded better.

Chapter IV - New Hampshire

In 1937, while living in a cottage near the Mill Brook river in the White Mountains of New Hampshire, my future dad and a friend captured a bear which they hung from a tree by its rear ankles. My dad thought it would be great to have my future mom take a close-up photo of the bear before it was released. *Not one of her favorite moments. That was typical of his humor.*

Unwittingly at Wellington Beach, New Hampshire, while playing in the dirt, I posed at 15 months for the book cover. My sister, Bonnie, was more modest therefore was hiding inside Mom.

In 1939 my folks and I moved from the cottage near Mill Brock river to a farm purchased near Rumney Village, New Hampshire in the White Mountains. Rumney is home to the "Polar Caves" which are well known for their geological sights and glowing rock formations. The family car was a 1938 Desoto convertible. *Were my parents crazy in this climate?* My parents purchased the 50-acre farm in January 1940 about the time my sister, Bonnie, was born. Dad continued to sail at times to provide additional income. To say life on the farm was very different then the cultured life Mom grew up in would be an understatement. She was a classic pianist. Because Mom missed having a piano, Dad purchased a piano in NYC to be delivered to New Hampshire. Tough as it must have been to adjust to farm life she never complained. Mom was an optimist beyond belief, never met a stranger, and always observed the good in people. About two years after my birth, Mom gave birth on the farm in January 1940 to a daughter, with assistance of her friend, Sparky. The daughter was named after her grandmothers: Charlotte Esther. The "drama queen," Mom's mother, was very upset that her granddaughter did not have her name first. One day, Mom held the baby up while bathing her and said, "My Bonnie." Mom knew this meant beautiful in Scottish. Her best friend Sparky's family was from Scotland. "Bonnie" would be known forever by her nickname.

While Mom's only sibling, Aunt Marian, visited from New York, I was placed in a play pen on the screen porch by myself. They heard me fearfully screaming, which was not normal. They could not determine what was the problem. Later my dad discovered bear prints outside the porch. To this day, I have never felt comfortable in the presence of bears.

Dad elected to transform the farm into an egg farm by building a three-story hen house. He did nearly all the work himself. Mom exited the house one time to see me at about three years old on the unfinished roof of the just framed three story hen house. Dad was not aware the climber was on the roof. They never determined how the feat was accomplished.

The hen house basement contained incubators necessary for the egg farm and an area for Dad's cabinet shop. The other floors contained several rooms for the laying hens. For a time one room housed 50 rabbits to sell for their meat and fur. This venture ended one night when a large pet dog was inadvertently locked in with the rabbits. No rabbits survived the night. The next day, because our favorite dog was now a killer, he made a trip to dog heaven.

The winters on the farm were brutal. From December through most of March the ground was not seen. The only form of heat was a wood cook stove in the kitchen and a potbelly stove in the center of the living room. The bedrooms were on the second floor. The windows in the bedrooms were completely covered on the inside with 3/4" of frost. Needless to say, we scurried down to the potbelly stove to dress in the mornings. We were fortunate to have a water well on a hill above the house so that gravity provided us with indoor facilities including a bathtub. Many people in the area had to rely on out-houses. Dad had installed a heat exchanger on the kitchen wood stove thereby providing hot water plumbed to the bathtub.

The farmhouse had a large wooden telephone box on the wall too high for children, but just right for adults to speak into the microphone, which could not be removed. The separate hearing piece that hung on the side, had to be removed and placed at a person's ear. A crank was mounted on the side of the wooden box. Turning the crank at different speeds a short or long ring could be created or any combination of the rings. All nearby phones were on a party line and each had a specific ring code, such as two shorts or a short and long, etc. So, when you called someone all the phones on the party line would hear the code, the idea being that only the party being called would answer the phone. *Right*! During World War II when overseas Dad made a very expensive call to Mom from Europe. She was telling him of some event when the operator (located in the general store in Rumney Village) interrupted to expand on the story.

All food eaten was harvested on the farm from the ground, trees, bushes or on the hoof with the exception of flour, sugar, coffee and cocoa. Food was gathered from the garden and canned or stored in the cellar under the house. We had milk cows, donkeys, goats, pigs, many dogs, ducks, etc. The pigs were slaughtered and smoked for preservation. I did not enjoy having to catch elusive little pigs that escaped from the muddy pig pen. Bonnie and I had specific chores to do before and after school. Before school I was to clean out the stalls and provide feed/hay for the livestock in the barn. Believe it or not, most of the time I enjoyed these chores. The one task that was never liked, which was probably started at a young age, was keeping the two wood boxes full. Another thing I did not like was having to stir a glass of milk to keep the cream from rising to the top. One of the many benefits of living on the farm was the berries, fruit trees, and mint growing by the creek, which allowed me to partake of many treats.

Rumney Village was one of a few villages in the township of Rumney founded in 1767. It had only one store, still the only store. The Rumney Village Store, founded in 1865, sold such items as flour, sugar, coffee, clothing such as coveralls, animal feed, and gas for vehicles. Mom made many of our clothes from the feed, grain, and flour sacks. These sacks were made from cloth with many patterns. Feed sacks were selected based on the desired pattern when purchased. The store also housed the US Post Office (there was no home delivery) and the telephone operator switchboard. In the store center was a potbelly stove surrounded by seats for visiting. The gasoline pump was the type that required cranking the gas from an underground tank to a transparent tank above the crank station which also contained a hose for the car. You cranked the amount you wanted in your vehicle or can into the transparent tank. You then placed the nozzle in your vehicle and allowed gravity to empty the amount in the transparent tank to the vehicle.

Across from the general store was the town hall. The bottom

floor housed the town fire engine. The second floor consisted of one meeting room. All matters concerning the township were voted on by all adults of Rumney, a true local democracy. The township also contained a church, a small library, an icehouse, and an elementary school. The icehouse contained ice cut in blocks from a nearby lake during the winter and stored in an old abandoned mill on the river. The stored ice was covered in sawdust and delivered to homes during the summer to be placed in their ice box. I remember a man stopping by to place ice in our ice box whether we were around or not. The egg farm also had a deep abandoned water well near the house, which was also used to preserve food, being cold at the bottom. The school had two rooms with two old maid teachers who were sisters. One teacher taught grades 1-4 and the other taught grades 5-8. Students in grades 9-12 had to catch a train from the village of West Rumney to Plymouth.

A young lad on a farm had many opportunities to learn his limits and that parents possessed a lot of wisdom. Dad was someone to listen to and obey. The woodshed had more than one purpose. My sister, Bonnie, and I were very close and found much to do. We could explore the woods, swim in a clear creek, build snowmen, etc. Mom, a classic pianist, was a joy to listen to when playing. Dad played his saxophone and accordion. Music was part of our lives. We gathered at the radio on Sunday evenings and listened to Amos & Andy and others.

On the farm we had many animals. We had a billy goat and nanny goat as well as their two kids. Billy loved to chase Mom, especially when she was hanging cloths on the clothesline. Nanny was never a problem, although the two kids were hard to catch.

There was a small pen

which housed chickens near the woods. One early morning Dad was awakened by a loud commotion from the pen. He saw a red fox trying to get in the pen. His very long rifle in the bedroom was handy. He quietly opened the bedroom window and killed the fox. He had the fox converted to a stole including head and tail in NYC. Mom was delighted with the surprise present as evident in the photo.

As we aged, Bonnie's and my chores increased and changed according to the season. In the spring we trudged through mud often with the melting snow. We helped plant the garden and spread manure on the hay fields. In the summers we helped with haying, which consisted of cutting the hay using a mower and raking it into rows. Both of these steps used a team of horses. The hay was then loaded loosely on an old flatbed truck and unloaded into haystacks. Haystacks were structures with posts supporting a roof and diagonal boards to keep the structure from leaning and the hay in place. We gathered strawberries, blackberries, blueberries and more, to eat fresh, with most being canned for winter. Also, plums, apples, pears and many different vegetables were also harvested and preserved. Rhubarb and mint grew wild near our little creek which ran close to the house. Mom made fantastic strawberry rhubarb pies and rabbit stews, which are rarely prepared decades later.

Life was good, then Japan bombed Pearl Harbor. The routines on the farm changed. Dad was torn between staying on the farm or answering the call for experienced officers to join the United States Maritime Service (USMS). The USMS lost more men in the first year of World War II than all the other services put together.

Dad answered the call and was initially commissioned as a Lt. commander and was promoted to commander a year before the end of the war. He served as a captain of several Liberty ships during the war. Dad did not talk of the war and died when I was 14 before I learned of his war experiences. While visiting decades later with Dad's brother, Uncle Everett, he informed me that Dad was instrumental in two Navy policies being changed. The first occurred when Dad had items on the ship desperately needed by our troops. The seas were very high, and the Navy escorts refused to sail. He sailed. When returning Dad told the authorities that if the Navy escorts did not have enough "brass ones" to protect them, then he was returning to the farm and did. A week later Dad was contacted and told that if the captain of the Liberty ships wanted to sail the Navy escort had no choice but to sail. The second policy change came when the Navy placed guns on the Liberty ships with gunners but not under the command of the ship captain. Dad, and I suspect others, said there could be only be one commander on a ship. If they did not place the gunners under his command, he was returning to the farm. He did. About a week later Dad was contacted and told the gunners would be under the command of the ship captain. He returned to war. Uncle Everett told me during the visit that my dad as the captain had orders to rendezvous with a tanker at midnight. When barely in sight of the tanker he had a sense that something was wrong and gave orders that the ship would avoid the tanker. His officers pleaded with him to proceed to the tanker or he would be in a heap of trouble. Dad could not explain why he felt they should not proceed. Later they found out the Germans had taken over the tanker and were waiting for them. Dad never lost a ship or a man during the war. One ship he turned over to another captain was sunk a week later at Normandy.

Mom now had the task of keeping the farm going. This cultured city ex-Episcopal nun was up to the challenge. Being a nurse, she worked in a hospital during the war's early years.

While she worked in the hospital, Bonnie and I were housed in the hospital. Bonnie was an infant and not a problem but being a toddler, I got into things. For a time, the hospital was having many electrical problems. They discovered I was crawling around putting woman's hair bobby pins in electrical outlets. *This discovery solved the electrical problem.*

Back on the farm Mom was faced with many problems such as the pipes in the cellar under the bathroom tending to freeze when the temperature got down to minus 40 or lower degrees. She was always proud of the solution she discovered. By placing a string of lights under the pipes, they did not freeze.

Limitations on the transportation of goods due to a shortage of rubber tires, and a diversion of agricultural harvests to soldiers overseas all contributed to the U.S. government's decision to ration certain essential items. Typewriters, gasoline, bicycles, footwear, silk, nylon, fuel oil, stoves, meat, lard, shortening and oils, cheese, butter, margarine, processed foods (canned, bottled, and frozen), dried fruits, canned milk, firewood and coal, jams, jellies and fruit butter were rationed by November 1943. Ration books contained removable stamps good for certain rationed items, like sugar, meat, cooking oil, and canned goods. A person could not buy a rationed item without also giving the grocer the right stamp. Mom would make butter and other things. She would barter with these when she did not have a necessary stamp or items were not available.

The custom at the time was for the family to cut a Christmas tree in the woods. After children went to bed on Christmas Eve the tree would be decorated. During the war Mom invited a couple over to help her decorate the tree followed by a hot toddy.

During the month of March, the maple trees produced an abundance of sap. Doris Avery, a neighbor, would loan us a couple of oxen along with a sled with large runners. The sled containing several milk cans was pulled by the oxen through the snow in the woods with Mom at the reins. Bonnie and I would retrieve the buckets hanging from spigots driven into the maple tree and pour what we did not drink into the milk cans. An exceptional tree, after a really cold night followed by a very warm day, could produce 30 gallons of sap. These trees were rare. A large tree would have several buckets. I remember, after the war when Dad was home, Bonnie and I doing our homework in the small sugar shack in the woods. The sap was boiled in a large half-spherical vat with a wood fire underneath. Our folks played scrabble, while Dad occasionally skimmed stuff from the liquid. Thirty gallons of sap were required for one gallon of maple syrup. Some was further boiled to achieve a delicious maple sugar.

After completing our chores, we walked about a third of a mile to the school bus stop on the main highway where a bridge crossed the Baker River. The river flowed through the center of town. The school was close to the center of town. One of the blessings during winter was using our sleds to go down the road about a third of a mile to the school bus stop. Our road was a dead end with only one dairy farm (Doris and Howard Avery) beyond us allowing us a clear shot down to the school bus stop. On the Mr. Avery's return from delivering his full milk cans to the dairy, he would pick up our sleds we left in a snowbank and drop them at our farm. This saved us the task of pulling them uphill to our farm. During the first and second grades I would teach Bonnie much of what I learned at school. After completing the first grade Bonnie was promoted to the third grade.

Our family was new to the area while all other families had been there for generations and typically had not been out of the area. Our folks were extraverts, charming and bright with a sense of humor. Neither ever met a stranger. Mom was the only medical person in the township and Dad, respected as a ship captain, were accepted. Children in the 1940s tended not to accept outsiders. No children close to our age lived nearby, therefore Bonnie and I did not have many opportunities to develop friends before school age. Being shy, unsure of myself, always the smallest kid in the class until partway through the 10th grade, and an outsider, the task of making friends at school was always a challenge. One of the benefits of being shy was observing, and thereby learning from the mistakes and successes of others rather than learning the hard way. The downside was feeling inadequate. However, having Mom and Dad as parents, having grandparents preforming on Broadway and an uncle that served as an Army Officer in the Battle of the Bulge made us feel special and lucky. I naively felt special because Dad had a small dock with the only motorboat on the sizable Stinson Lake. Even this bonus did not likely expand my very small circle of friends.

In the summer our milk cows were let out of the barn daily to roam in the fields and forest. The area was surrounded by an electric fence that Dad insisted I test each morning to make sure it was working. The first time tested, I felt a very unpleasant shock. It did not take long to discover how to test the fence without being shocked. Not sure his approach was based on his humor or teaching me to think for myself, be resourceful, and find solutions. It was likely a little of each. The cows had cowbells hanging from their necks which made it easier to round them up at the end of the day; one of my chores. Without the cowbells, they were not always easy to find.

Dad had purchased a small bicycle for me in Belgium. Small bicycles were not common in the USA, nor did others in Rumney have a bicycle. A week before the end of the first grade, just after the Germans' surrender, I was riding the bicycle before school started. As I was riding around the back corner of the school, a six grader turned the corner at the same time. He was carrying a hand carved wooden dagger and stabbed me in the right eye. The dagger penetrated about two inches and touched my brain. *Explains a lot.* As I was walking around the front corner of the school the two teachers, old maid sisters, came out to ring the bell for school to start. They saw me pull out the dagger. One fainted, the other took off running. A girl in the eighth grade ran a quarter mile down the road to the nearest phone and called my mom, the nurse. My dad had just returned from the war that morning after I went to school. They picked me up at school about the time I passed out. With Mom and me in the back seat of the 1938 Plymouth, my Dad sped to the nearest hospital two villages and a town away. The doctor operated including removing many splinters. The doctor did not believe survival was likely because of potential infections. Due to Mom's medical connections in NYC, penicillin was obtained. At the time, the limited supply of penicillin was generally reserved for the military. Being informed that my sight would not return did not faze me. Receiving bowls of a rare treat, ice cream, in the hospital, certainly helped. After two weeks in the hospital, my left eye started seeing a green sickening seaweed color. They said sight would return in that eye, but not the other. Two weeks later the right eye started seeing the same sickening color. Sight returned to 20-20 in both eyes. I did not miss the farm chores and enjoyed being treated like royalty by the hospital staff. About a year later, dagger boy dropped out of school and while working in a sawmill cut off two fingers. Mom the only medical person in the area treated him. I asked why she could treat him after what he had done to me. Mom explained it was her duty. *Learned a lot from her.*

Life on the farm returned to normal. Dad purchased two new surplus army trucks for $100. One was a dump truck. He converted one to a tractor and the other to a snowplow. The tractor had many uses including cutting the firewood for the stoves. A wide belt that circled the tractor's rear tire was attached to a drum mounted to a shaft driving the circular saw blade. Winters required a lot of firewood. Dad modified the other truck by removing the dump-bed, reoriented the dump hydraulics to raise and lower a snowplow that he mounted on the front of the truck. Dad had to keep the area cleared near the hen house for large trucks that picked up the eggs during all seasons. He also plowed snow from county roads to increase revenue.

Life was not all work and trauma. One summer I attended a 4H camp for a week. The camp had wonderful facilities including a nice beach on a lake. Being away on my own for the first time, I was very homesick. Early on I begged to go home; that did not work. Ended up having a good time. *Lesson there somewhere.*

The family attended the New Hampshire State Fair which was almost a wonderful experience. The fair was large containing many exhibits and contests including the judging of home baked goods, vegetables, farm animals, etc. There were also sulky horse races, oxen pulls, horse pulls, and lumberjack contests. A sulky is a lightweight two-wheeled, single-seat cart that was hooked to a harness just behind the horse. The wheels looked like large skinny bicycle wheels. The jockey sat low between the wheels. The ox and horse pulls consisted of a team of either pulling a sled loaded with a large weight. The team pulling the most weight the farthest was the winner. All events were exciting. To top it off, a friend of mine and I found cases of warm sodas behind a concession stand. Never having had a soda, we hid there and drank until we became very sick. On the way home I was questioned about not feeling well. Knowing the correct answer would be the wrong answer,

I was mum. The photo is an early picture of Bonnie and me.

One morning before school Dad impatiently tried to hurry me through breakfast to get me started on my chores of cleaning stalls and feeding the stock. When I arrived in the barn, I discovered two donkeys, Jack and Jenny. The night before Dad had arrived home after Bonnie and I had gone to bed. To Mom's horror, he had brought them home in the back seat of our Plymouth. Not a pretty sight. Before school Dad taught me a few lessons such as do's and don'ts. Learning the hard way, one learns not to walk behind a donkey as they are inclined to kick. The following weekend, Dad and I drove to an abandoned pony farm in Canada. He had permission to obtain a set of harnesses that fit the donkeys. This allowed them to be harnessed as a team. During the winter Dad and friends would fell trees in our forest. After removing limbs, they used horses to drag the logs to the sawmill or to the house for firewood. I would tag along and latch the donkey team to a small log and then try to coerce them to pull the log. This was a real challenge as they were stubborn, but once they started to pull it was difficult to stop them.

A friend visited and wanted to ride a donkey. Knowing Jack was a challenge to ride, I suggest he take Jack. I mounted Jenny, an easy ride. Jack took off with my friend across a field and through an empty open haystack. Of course, one of the cross boards between two posts knocked the *no longer* friend off of Jack. This was Jack's favorite way to remove a rider.

Living on a farm created many opportunities for families to bond, learn and be creative. Dad played the saxophone, then purchased a used accordion and taught himself to play. The family would sit outside in Adirondack lawn chairs and sing together. Toys were not purchased, they were made. There was not a *Toys "R" Us* in Rumney,

NH. We could not afford purchased toys in any case. I fondly remember at a young age building a sailboat by sawing a V on the front of a board. Using a hand-crank drill I bored a hole for a mast. I used a dowel for a mast and made a sail from cloth to slip over the mast. Never sailed well, but was fun to play with in the cold, clear creek.

Off and on Mom's mother, Grandmud, and Mom's friend, Sparky and husband would visit. Granddad could not always join them because of commitments on stage. They all loved skiing during the winter months and the pleasant summer weather. The townspeople treated our lovable entertaining grandparents, both being actors on Broadway, as celebrities. They remembered them fondly decades later.

One day, Mom drove us slipping and sliding through a blizzard to White River Junction, NH. Mom was not a world class driver. We mounted a train there to visit her folks in NYC. Mom took Bonnie and me to see *The Yearling*. It was the only film I would see until age 11. There was an orchestra in a pit playing before the film started, a custom in NYC theaters at the time. When younger, Granddad took me to Radio City Music Hall to attend a live radio show. I remember they held up signs when we were to be silent, applause, laugh, etc. Granddad was an actor and radio personality and introduced me to several friends including famous actors. Being young the significance of this went over my head.

On one visit to Manhattan at age eight I persistently asked if I could take Bonnie and visit Uncle Everett in Brooklyn by way of the subway. Mom explained the three subway changes and bus ride required. Bonnie, age six, and I had a grand time on the round-trip adventure. Our parents did not underestimate our abilities. This gave us confidence and the ability to solve problems which served us well throughout our lives.

At a young age Bonnie and I were riding in the backseat of a car with Aunt Marian sitting in the passenger seat while riding through Harlem in NYC. I had seen few black people before and I said, "Look at all those niggers." I did not know that was a bad word. The normally very pleasant Aunt Marian turned around and verbally blistered me as though hell was just around the corner. To this day I feel uncomfortable hearing an ethnic slur or joke. Often, I have asked people not to tell ethnic jokes in my presence. *Thank you, Aunt Marian.*

Nancy, our sister, was born in 1946, nine months after Dad returned from the war. *Hi Nancy.* While at sea Dad had no health issues but had asthma in New Hampshire. In February 1947 the farm was sold, and we moved to West Campton, New Hampshire, still in the White Mountains. I do not know why we moved from the farm. Looking back, I suspect it may have had to do with his behavior while on an alcohol binge. Mom and Dad bought an unfinished house on the main road with the rear facing the large Pemigewasset River. The house also included adjacent property along the road. We moved into the unfinished house without plumbing or electricity. Dad finished the house. He installed drywall, plumbing and electricity, and made cabinets, etc. Dad offered to pay me $20 to fill in the six-foot-deep sewer ditch running down a sloped incline. The task had to be completed before school started. *Worst bargain I ever made.* The highway we lived on was the main road to tourist attractions and was a two mile walk to school. This occasionally made for a profitable combination as empty soda and beer bottles were worth two cents and quart size bottles five cents when collected and turned in to the grocer.

Dad moved his cabinet shop from the farm to a building owned by the new neighbor. They formed a partnership to build cabinets. Dad planned to build small cottages on their adjacent property for tourist. Mom visited NYC to earn wages as a nurse for a few months. During this time, I received my last and deserved spanking. I only remember receiving three. While not brutal, they tended to be sufficient to last a few years.

The one room schoolhouse covered grades 1-8 with one teacher. The one room had a potbelly stove for heat in the center. The

back deck had two side-by-side out-houses, girls and boys. I started the fourth grade in the fall with only one classmate. He was a jerk who constantly made fun of the teacher's son who attended school in a different town where the teacher lived. Consequently, the teacher did her best to avoid our grade. My education took a nosedive. Might explain a lot. As always, Bonnie did well in school. She had four classmates. One grade had no students. The photo was taken decades later, obviously closed as a school.

One of the benefits of living in West Campton was a pond near the house allowing us to ice-skate. There was a nice lake with a beach in the neighboring town, Campton. Bonnie and I took swimming lessons. To pass the final test, you were taken to a deep part of the lake in a rowboat and tossed in the water. This was the first time we were in over our heads in more ways than one. After a brief moment of panic, I started dog paddling.

While Mom worked as a nurse for several months, Dad's

asthma continued to worsen. After losing weight his doctor indicated he might not survive another year in New Hampshire. The doctor recommended moving to the southwest. The neighbor that Dad had formed a partnership with had provided the building as his part of the arrangement. The "partner" kept all Dad's woodworking tools/equipment, ignoring their partnership, which caused Dad to lose his investment. This left the family with few resources.

Mom and Dad made arrangements for me to stay with the dairyman and his wife, the Avery's, who lived next door to the farm we had owned in Rumney. This meant changing schools during November in the 5th grade. They arranged for Bonnie and Nancy to stay in the Convent of St. Anne in Kingston, NY where Mom had been a nun for five years. Mom and Dad then set off for the Southwest.

Life was very different living on the dairy with Doris and Howard Avery. Their very small home was not finished inside. No drywall, just exposed studs. They were nice but were not used to a child being around all the time. They were very strict, except when it came to their Chihuahua dogs. I was assigned many chores on the dairy farm. School was difficult due to the lack of instruction in West Campton, being shy, and not being embraced by other students. The schoolteacher for grades 5-8 made us draw names from a hat. You were then expected to give the person whose name you drew a present. I asked the Avery's for a dime to buy a present. They said no because they did not believe in giving presents at Christmas. I wrapped a used #2 pencil with teeth marks and gave it to the correct student. The student complained. I was chewed out by the teacher in front of the class. The only presents I received were two books (Robinson Crusoe and a Zane Gray western) sent by mail from my parents. Made my Christmas. *Not sure either were read.*

In February 1949, I was placed on a train to NYC. Mom and Dad had retrieved my sisters from the convent and met me at Grand Central Station. Bonnie remembers that when I spotted them, I ran past our parents and gave her a long hug. We headed for Carlsbad, New Mexico. They had also seriously considered Yuma, Arizona. Thank goodness Yuma had ragweed, my Dad's worst allergen.

On leaving New Hampshire, perhaps it is a good time to reflect on who I was at nearly age 11. Having lived through the tail end of the depression, Dad being deployed during World War II, the war rationing, and living on a farm with many chores and responsibilities prepared me for numerous joys and tragedies to come. Sacrifices by all were the norm during those times. Significantly woven into the above conditions were my parents' and maternal grandparents' influence. Mom was a nurse, hopelessly optimistic, an intellectual, full of God's spirit, an adventurist, creative, never met a stranger and up for all challenges with a sense humor. Dad, who had a miserable childhood and was a binge alcoholic, had an exceptional and creative mind, sense of humor, a strong sense of duty, and like Mom, a strong work ethic. Neither ever underestimated the ability of their children. We were expected to meet our responsibilities. I left New Hampshire on the adventure to New Mexico innocent, never a victim. I took a strong sense of duty, loyalty, joy, optimism, and pride in contributing to family needs.

Chapter VI - Carlsbad, New Mexico

Our tired 1938 Plymouth carried Mom, Dad, Bonnie, Nancy and me on our journey from New Hampshire to New Mexico that required several days. We always slept in the car. Needless to say, there was little room for much more than us and a few necessities. All household items had been sold including Mom's prize possession, her piano, a significant sacrifice. My most vivid memory was traveling on a narrow, eerie road through Louisiana with swamps on both sides including tall skinny trees that seem to provide a roof over the road. *Ichabod Crane came to mind.*

We arrived late one day in Carlsbad, New Mexico to our adobe home purchased on Ash St. by my parents. The walls were about 16 inches thick. The house had a large front porch, a small rear porch, a small living room, kitchen, two bedrooms, and one bath. Our first morning was March 1, 1949. My 11th birthday would be three weeks later. Dad would soon enclose the rear porch to become my bedroom. The room would hold only a single bed with no room on either side. The kitchen door barely had room to open into the room. Dad had installed an outside door opposite the kitchen door. I was thrilled to have my first bedroom. Ash St. was not far from the Eddy County Courthouse and like many streets at the time, not paved. The powder-like caliche surface was a wonderful source of house dust when the wind blew, which was always. Taping windows and more did little to keep the sand out. Paint on license plates was gone after a good sandstorm.

To say going from the worst winter in the White Mountains of New Hampshire to the worst spring and summer in Carlsbad was a cultural and weather shock, would be an understatement. This was nothing like a romanticized story I had read before the trip. The tale was of a young Mexican boy wearing a large sombrero and poncho in Mexico with a donkey on a beautiful arid mountain.

One pleasant new experience was milk being delivered in glass bottles to the door and the milkman picking up the empties. It may have been my first taste of homogenized milk. On the farm we had only raw milk not pasteurized. The homogenized milk was a real bonus for me as I had not like the cream rising to the top of the glass.

I enrolled in Eddy Elementary School located less than two blocks away. The fifth-grade class had many students with no other grades in the room as in the New Hampshire's one room schoolhouse. Being shy, the smallest student, and a "Yankee," and far behind the other students did not help me assimilate. Next door to our home was a boy, Johnny, in the fifth grade. He was also considered a "Yankee," being from Michigan. His father seemed mean and to be avoided. Johnny, a couple of years later when we attended Eisenhower Junior High, was caught vandalizing the school. I had already distanced myself from him. This taught me a valuable lesson concerning who one should associate with. The teacher met with Mom at the end of the school year to inform her I was not ready for the sixth grade. Not a big surprise considering how poor the schools were in New Hampshire compared to New Mexico schools. At Mom's request the teacher passed me and agreed to tutor me during the summer to prepare me. For two weeks, I visited the teacher's home for tutoring. Then the sandy beach on the Pecos River in Carlsbad became very attractive. *So much for tutoring.* Also, the neighborhood children would gather mostly in the middle of our street to play games during the summer. I was proud to be the Monopoly King. We never received an allowance or pay for chores. Late in the summer I walked to a farm on the other side of the

Pecos River to pick cotton. This entrepreneurial spirit only lasted a few days as the money earned did not match the long walk, effort and hot sun.

Dad first worked as a painter. Later he was employed by a potash mine as a lift operator that transported people a thousand feet or so into the mine. His skills obtained as a seaman qualified him for the personnel lift. This job provided good pay with benefits.

The first summer Dad built a separate single car garage of concrete blocks with a framed roof. He negotiated with me to install the wood shake shingles on the garage. *My negotiation skills were not yet developed.* Dad had a special hatchet he trained me to use in the art of splitting the shingles and nailing them to the narrow strips, without damaging the shingles.

In 1949, Mom developed TB in one kidney, which was removed in Lubbock, TX. She apparently died on the operating table. She remembered seeing a bright light and looking down on the operating room before joining us again. She was to stay in bed for a year and advised not to work again. It was no surprise to us that she returned to nursing for many years.

During our time in Carlsbad, we attended Grace Episcopal Church. Mom daily attended morning mass. Except for Dad, the family was involved in all available activities. I sang in the youth choir, served as an acolyte, attended Sunday school classes and joined the parish's Boy Scout Troop. This was the first time we lived where there was an Episcopal church.

The sixth grades were in portables behind Eisenhower Junior High for the first time. There were two specialized teachers in the class, one in the morning and a different teacher in the afternoon. I was still catching up with the others. The male teacher required us to put our real name at the top of our papers rather than nicknames. This being a first, I was not sure how to spell Ernest, as sometimes I spelled it correctly and sometimes spelled it Earnest. The teacher in front of the class asked in a gruff voice how I ever reached the sixth grade without being able to spell my name. Being shy and embarrassed, I crawled into a shell for the rest of the year.

During the following summer, I discovered movies. Near the courthouse was a movie theater that showed double features, a serial, news and cartoons for ten cents. I did odd jobs to earn the dime, then landed a paper route that included our home. The daily evening and

Sunday morning route had been neglected by the previous paperboy. I had to pay the newspaper company for the papers regardless of collections. Weekly you were encouraged to knock on the door and collect the paper fee. I quickly increased the route by 25 percent. I first walked the route until Grandmud sent me a 3-speed bicycle with skinny tires from New York. Not sure there was another multi-speed thin tire bicycle in New Mexico at the time. The thin tires were useless with all the sharp stickers in New Mexico. I partially filled the tires with a substance that would fill-in the sticker holes. Not real effective. When I had saved enough money, Firestone sold me a nice bicycle that was a great improvement. During the spring peddling into the wind was impossible but going with the wind was a white knuckler.

Bonnie and Nancy took dancing lessons. The studio owner had known our grandparents decades earlier from her dancing days in vaudeville and Broadway. *It's a small world.* Granddad's shows in Carlsbad, New Mexico had included *Too Much Money* in February 1899 and with the Horace Redpath Chautauqua Co in May 1925. New Mexico did not become a state until 1912.

Before starting the seventh grade, I expressed a desire to learn to play Dad's "C" saxophone manufactured in 1920 and since discontinued. The saxophone was small like me. He agreed, but with the understanding that if I started, stopping was not in the cards. *Big mistake on my part.* Practicing was not fun. Because there was no "C" saxophone sheet music, the band instructor recommended using oboe sheet music. One of the tasks highly encouraged by the junior high school band was selling magazines subscriptions door to door. Being the smallest in my class, along with my humble ways allowed me to sell a lot more subscriptions than anyone else. *Did I mention also being adorable and persistent?*

The seventh grade at Eisenhower Junior High helped me catch up but not all the way. We had different teachers for each subject. The math teacher told Mom that I was the best math student she had in her 30 years of teaching. The next year she was in a mental institution.

During the 1950 Christmas season, the family except for Dad, headed for NYC to visit family and Mom's friends. The four-day train ride was an adventure of going from one end of the train to the other and watching the many changing scenes. I enjoyed chatting with other passengers, especially the oldest. They were interesting with their many tales sprinkled with healthy doses of wisdom for this 12-year-old. We had a layover of a few hours in Chicago. Mom thought we should experience the "EL" while there. My sisters and I were reluctant to get on another train during the break. Mom's enthusiasm won us over as always. She did enjoy life.

We stayed with Mom's sister, Aunt Marian, Uncle Chet and their daughter, Carol, in Ramsey, New Jersey most of the time. Uncle Chet had attended the top math high school in America, graduating fourth in his class. His parents came from Russia. His father was a Rabbi, and later Uncle Chet became an active Episcopalian. Uncle Chet served during the Battle of the Bulge as an officer. He received a medical discharge for MS as a captain shortly after the war and became head of the math department in a New Jersey high school. Looking back, he was the best male role model I had growing up and beyond. We viewed our first television at their home. Cartoons were our favorites.

We visited Mom's family, including my grandparents from nearby Manhattan, during Christmas for the first time in my memory. The best surprise was a Lionel Train Set, the only Christmas present I ever remember receiving from Grandmud and Grandad. Back in Carlsbad, I was able to exercise my imagination by designing and building a little town using balsa wood and colored cellophane.

We also spent a few days with Mom's best friend, "Aunt" Sparky and her family. They lived on Long Island in a large two-story home with quarters for their servants. The property included a whole block ringed with trees. Reportedly the house had been occupied by General Howe, leader of the British forces during the Revolutionary War. Even though Sparky, her husband Art Wenderoth, and their children Cathie, Janie and Walter were not related, they were considered family. They were addressed as "Aunt" Sparky and "Uncle" Art.

On New Year's Eve the producer of the *Rosemary Clooney TV* show visited Sparky and Art to wish them a happy new year. After we were introduced, he asked Mom if Nancy and I would be available to perform on the *Rosemary Clooney TV* show. My mother reluctantly agreed. Her childhood experiences, having parents in show business, caused her to not want her children near show business. The show was live, and my part was in a Staten Island Ferry scene following a commercial. I was shining Tony Bennett's shoes while he sang. I then stood up and put my hand out for the fee. He gave me a silver dollar and I departed the scene while he finished the song. I was thrilled to have the silver dollar souvenir. The union scale fee was going towards the train ride back to New Mexico. Good ole Mr. Bennett tracked me down and insisted on getting his silver dollar back. I like his music, but *him* not so much. Nancy, a week later, was in a live Mohawk Rug commercial, the show sponsor. Nancy was lying on a carpet coloring with a smile. We returned via train to Carlsbad.

One morning Dad insisted on giving me a ride to school, a first. When going through the high school zone a few blocks from my school he bumped into a car. I heard a student say, "Look at that drunk." Embarrassed, I slithered from the car and stealthily walked to my school, hopefully not seen. There were many reasons I was proud of Dad, but there were occasions when a few dents were put in a son's pride in his father.

Following the seventh grade, I attended the large Boy Scout Camp Dale Resler near Weed and Cloudcroft, New Mexico. The BSC was in the Lincoln National Forest in large timber country at an elevation of 7,000 feet. One night our scout troop had bivouacked a good distance from the main camp. The next morning three of us were assigned to clean up the camp site then catch up to the others who were headed to the main camp. The two fellow Boy Scouts, Paul & Peter (not actual names), and I became lost for the entire day. We would go up and down hills and creeks through the forest. We came too close to a bear for my taste. Speaking of taste, we had not eaten all day until we found a long-ago abandoned spider infested shack that contained a very small (2" tall) box of raisins. This was before food expiration dates were marked on containers. We shared the box of delicious raisins. Late in the afternoon we discovered an unused single lane road. We decided to follow the rutted grass road downhill. Finally, the grass road dead-ended into a well-used single lane rutted road. After walking along the newer road, an old pickup stopped and gave us a ride to the main Boy Scout Camp. It was about 5 pm when we arrived. We had left the overnight camp site at 7:30 am. They had not missed us. This would be the only time I was associated with Paul or Peter.

A few months later Paul was found hanging from a door, in the nude with his hands tied behind him. The rope was tied to the knob on the opposite side of the door. That day reportedly, Paul had been in a fight with some young Mexicans. The next-door neighbors had heard foreign sounding voices that had stopped abruptly just before Paul's parents returned home from the movies. The sheriff ruled the death a suicide. This story is included to illustrate the times. I had heard that "rumbles" occurred between whites and Mexicans. Being an unconscious sort, this went over my head. I have never knowingly been a racist concerning any group. Thanks again Aunt Marian and of course, Mom.

A new school, Alta Vista Junior High, was completed and would be occupied by many Mexicans. This would be my first experience of being around a different ethnic group. Our home was in the district. The C-sax and I started the eighth grade and reluctantly joined the band.

I became good friends with another paperboy, Ken, who lived across the Pecos River. We had similar aptitudes and interests. We swam daily two miles up the middle of the Pecos River from the beach, then swam back. He had a new Cushman Eagle motor scooter. During the eighth grade, I purchased a well-used Cushman motor-scooter for $25. At age 14 one could get a driver's license. I immediately did. After getting a perfect score on the written, the policeman escorted me downstairs to take my riding test. I did not know how to drive a car, not being able to see over the steering wheel. They had to test you on the vehicle you brought to the station. He saw my motor scooter, said, "Damn," turned around, walked back inside and told me I passed.

Ken and I built model airplanes from scratch using balsa wood and cloth. We then bought little gas motors with propellers. We also built crystal radios from scratch using copper wire wrapped around empty toilet rolls, broken hacksaw blades, a crystal, etc. I purchased a Hallicrafters S-38C short wave radio that theoretically could receive stations all over the world. *It did not cooperate.*

Grandad was about to be honored by the Council of The Living Theater as the only actor in 200 years of professional theater in America to play one role for 1000 consecutive performances on Broadway. Also, he was to be awarded the "keys-to-the-city" of New York by the mayor. Grandad was playing the role of Batista in *Kiss me Kate*. He had just signed a contract to perform on London stages. Unfortunately, he died on the table when they were going to remove his gallbladder. The ether killed him before they started to cut on December 20, 1951. We were blessed to spend his last Christmas with him. Grandad was fluent in seven languages and lived a fascinating life of more than 50 years on the stage, as a radio personality, and song writer. His unexpected death was a huge loss to the family and the theatrical world.

Dad occasionally took me with him to hunt for Indian artifacts, his favorite hobby. On one outing we discovered items in a cave on a high cliff that were over 2000 years old, according to experts. We had to repel down from the top to reach the small cave opening. I was encouraged to go in the small opening because Dad would not fit. The cave was large inside, which consisted of several feet of sand the size of fine powder. Later Dad returned to build a wood frame with screen and sift the sand over the cliff to collect the Indian artifacts. He built a display for the items that would reside for years in the lobby of the Eunice High School that I would later attend.

I reached my 14th birthday in March of the eighth grade. Near the end of the school year, for the first and only time, Dad said he loved me. Of course, I knew that; Mom had explained that Dad growing up had no father or role model and did not know how to be the father he wanted to be. Two weeks later, early in June, a week after school was out, Dad went hunting for Indian artifacts in our 1950 Plymouth. I sensed something was wrong and asked to join him, but he said, "not this time." He did not return. This was six months after Granddad died. Planes searched for Dad without success. Mom had to make mortgage and car payments, provide food, pay for utilities, etc. My paper route and Bonnie's babysitting helped the cause. We had no car, so she walked to the hospital where she worked as a nurse. I remember walking to a grocery store with her to buy a loaf of bread. Mom had forgotten about the tax and did not have the penny sales tax. The clerk would not sell her the bread she needed to feed us that night. When we were outside, she cried. The only time I would ever see her cry.

In September, a week after school started, a Ranger found Dad in a desert canyon near Sitting Bull Falls, about 45 miles as the crow flies southwest of Carlsbad. There was not much left considering three months of summer heat and wildlife. The car had not done much better and was considered totaled. I was instructed at school to go home on my way to pick up my newspapers. Mom gave me the news and did a fantastic job, as always, explaining everything. Mom explained that she had asked Dad for a divorce because her conscience could no longer expose their children to his behavior when drinking. Mom told him she loved him and that when the children were out of the nest, he could return to her. I knew this was a very difficult decision and did not fit with her deeply held religious belief that one married for life. I went on to the paper office to retrieve my newspapers and sat there on the sidewalk with the other paperboys and rolled papers for delivery. My Dad was on the front page with speculation of how he died. One of the paperboys much older and bigger, a bully, said my dad was a coward. Before remembering that he was more than twice my size, I immediately tore into him. He never bothered me again. Soon after that he lost his paper route. The first thing I did when returning to school after the funeral was to drop band and sign up for the shop class.

Dad did not leave a will which caused numerous problems for Mom. She was forced to hire an attorney for my sisters and me to ensure we were not cheated. Her attorney was good, but the judge was not. Dad's life insurance with the potash company was paid after an inquest to establish that he died from a self-inflicted gunshot within two weeks of his last day at work. He had been automatically terminated after being a "no show" for two weeks. The family car was considered totaled. The Plymouth dealer, member of our church, provided Mom with a new 1952 Plymouth until the company life insurance was paid. Mom continued to work at the hospital and take care of us, difficult as that must have been. The judge seemed to be dragging his feet at every turn while I was in the ninth grade. I continued to do odd jobs in addition to my paper route to help, until Mom received Dad's life insurance.

A summary of Dad's life: His mother, Lottie McCabe, was a teacher in Nova Scotia living with her parents and had been stood up at the altar, then discovered she was pregnant. Her father kicked her out and insisted she leave Canada. In Boston, she gave birth to Dad in February 1906. Two years later she married Job Colin. They lived in a small Massachusetts community and two years later had a son Everett. Dad was called a bastard by other children. Job died from tuberculosis when Dad was six and his mother when he was twelve as a result of childbirth. As an orphan, Dad worked on farms for room and board and attended school. Because he was a good student and had been absent for a week his teacher, Ruth, visited the farm to find him in a barn near death after being severely beaten or more by the farmer. Ruth got Dad medical care and other accommodations which were not much better. Dad worked many miserable jobs to survive then went to sea at a young age as a cabin boy. He would work his way up to be a captain of large vessels, reportedly the youngest in America. Dad came back from World War II with the rank of commander after serving as captain of several ships along with shouldering several additional responsibilities. He had become a binge alcoholic and suffered from asthma. He would be sober for two to three months then go on a two to three-day binge. Seven years after WWII this would claim his life. Sparky, Mom's friend, an intellect and knowing many brilliant people, decades later told me Dad was the smartest man she ever knew. *What a waste and tragedy.*

After Dad died, partly because I was so little, adults would just pat me on the head and move on. A couple of weeks after Dad was found, one of his best friends, Chief Sunny Skies (1900-1972) visited me. Dad always had a knack for making friends with unusual people. Chief Sunny Skies was the last Chief and Medicine Man of the Acoma Pueblo southwest of Albuquerque. The Acoma Pueblo is the oldest continuously inhabited community in North America dating back possibly to the 4th century. The Acoma tribe is reportedly 2,000 years old. He owned the Hitching Post on Canal Street in Carlsbad and was widely known as an exceptional artist for his silver and turquoise jewelry. Chief Sunny Skies explained to me my responsibilities as I was the only male in the family and now a Brave. It was my duty and responsibility as a Brave to make sure my mother and sisters were cared for and protected. He presented me with a Brave's drum he made especially for me. It was 12 to 15 inches in diameter and about five to six inches deep. The chief handmade it from deer skin he personally tanned and painted with natural dyes. The paintings included several symbols that he explained. He was the only person to talk to me as an adult. I give Chief Sunny Skies a lot of credit for my behavior and attitude during the process of becoming a man. *A remarkable gift.* Years later after college, Mom lost my most prized procession when she moved. *Mom was a saint, except for this transgression.*

It would be more than two decades before I truly would

understand what Mom endured while hiding her pain and struggle during this period. She did her best to protect her children from her grieving so that we might heal with less to be concerned about. She had to endure the unknown of Dad's mysterious disappearance, provide financial needs during desperate times, and mourn the loss of her mate.

Dad's death would be a relief because it removed the uncertainty of his status since his disappearance and it eliminated the experiences his drinking would have created. That does not mean I did not miss him and long for a living father. Later I would have realistic dreams of seeing Dad, perhaps on some level because of a closed casket and wanting to know him as an adult.

Being an unconscious sort, it would not occur to me for many years the many qualities Dad had planted in me. These qualities were provided on purpose and some unwittingly. The characteristics included a strong work ethic, engineering aptitude, live life to the fullest, do your best, good manners are important, passion, loyalty, duty, sense of adventure, a can-do attitude, be self-sufficient, learn from experiences, do not stray from lines drawn by parents or authorities, and not to be an enabler of bad behavior. He would leave me with many of these qualities, but also the fear of looking like a fool, fear of becoming an alcoholic, shyness, and being unaware of myself. The unconscious side of me likely shielded me from perceived unpleasant events.

Another of Dad's character friends he had introduced me to lived in an old gutted school bus on the south side of Carlsbad. The bus was parked in a rocky field amongst a dense field of short cactus. Also scattered around the field were lots of unique items you could only classify as junk. From time to time after Dad's death I would visit him and listen to his crazy tales filled with humor, his laughter and wisdom. I suppose unconsciously part of the reason for the visits was searching for a father figure and because males of my father's generation were not in my life at the time.

During ninth grade at Alta Vista Junior High School I joined the radio club, took algebra, English, history, science, shop, drivers' education, etc. Most of the other ninth grade boys signed up for general math. Because that class had too many, some were forced to transfer to the algebra class. The algebra teacher was the best teacher I ever had. The transferred boys hated math. She would lecture, then break us up into pairs, one good math student with one not so good. This made both students better because the good student learned by teaching and the poorer student understood when the material was explained one on one by someone his age. At the end of the year the transferred students wanted to take more math.

Years later Mom told me the school principal, asked her to drop by. She assumed that Bonnie was the reason because she was acting out. They said they were not worried about her because that was normal. The concern was because I was withdrawn and too good. At some point later during the year I received a paddling, a rite of passage by peers. *I was fine.* I borrowed the new Plymouth and taught myself to drive on new paved streets laid out for a new development near our home. I did not want to start driver's ed with no skills. One benefit of taking drivers ed was for the first time hearing a girl tell a racy joke. I still remember it even though I remember few jokes. I was a very late bloomer and girls were not yet fully on my radar.

Early in the ninth grade I purchased a new Sears Allstate scooter which was really a Vespa 125 made in Italy. After four months the Sears Vespa engine and transmission died just before the warranty expired. Sears provided me with a new Cushman motor-scooter until mine was fixed. It did not cost me a cent. Four months later and four days before my Vespa was fixed, the loaner engine and transmission expired. Just before summer, I had saved enough money from the paper route to purchase a new Harley Davidson 165. Ken and I joined the local American Motorcyclist Association (AMA). We entered the Carlsbad AMA Chapter cross-country races on Friday evenings. The trails were different each week (after dark at times). The race season started in May and ended in October. Trails typically crossed the Pecos River, sand dunes, ravines, fields of cactus, mesquite, etc. Hill climbs were also included. In May, I started the racing season against men typically in their 20s and 30s with bigger motorcycles. At age 15, I was the points champion at season end.

After Dad's death the Mother Superior, Audrey of the convent in NY left her duties to visit. Also, "Aunt" Betty, really a cousin, and her husband George Ruffe also visited. They lived in Coral Gables, Florida. Mom, her sister, Aunt Marian, and "Aunt" Betty had lived under the same roof much of their youth. "Uncle" George did not like the idea of my wanting to buy a motorcycle. When we were alone, he tried to persuade me to buy a Willys Jeepster, a convertible, instead of the Harley that I was focused on. He explained the Willys had excellent gas mileage, was safer, and a used one was about the same cost as the Harley and was a good choice for my paper route. I was not to be persuaded. Mom did not weigh in on the discussion. Later in life, as a parent, I suspect Mom may have asked Uncle George to persuade me to buy a car.

Near the end of the summer Mom was hired as the school nurse in Eunice about 70 miles due east of Carlsbad and six miles from Texas. Eunice was in the heart of the Permian Basin (oil country) with a population of less than 3,500. The school system had oil wells pumping on the school property, therefore had millions in the bank. The state salary cap teachers could be paid was based on experience and education. In order to hire a certain teacher they wanted, within cap limits, the school would build a beautiful brick home with an attached garage that was nicely landscaped and lease it to them for $11 per month including utilities. Upon retiring the home became the teacher's. The students they taught tended to get top state honors in academics, sports, science, music, etc. Nationally 20% went on to college, 80% of my class would go on to college. The facilities were some of the best in the region. Mom had the same vacation and holidays as we did. Her salary was on the same level as teachers which was far more than nurses were paid in hospitals.

The judge seemed to be dragging his feet at every turn while I was in the ninth grade. He took his time approving the sale of the house, so Mom signed a contract with the buyers to pay rent until the judge approved the sale. This would allow us to move to Eunice, New Mexico. Six months later the judge approved the sale. Meanwhile the renters painted rooms black, trashed the place and generally ruined the house before skipping out. Mom had to give up the equity and additional funds to get rid of the house.

Chapter VII - Eunice, New Mexico

In 1953, a year after Dad's death, this 15-year-old, 5-foot, 100-pound, shy, anointed "Brave" (by Chief Sunny Skies) was to start his sophomore year. A week before school we started a new adventure in a special place, Eunice, New Mexico providing us with many joyful experiences. The four-year high school had 250 students. Driving through the small oil field town most might question that it was a special place. You had to peel the onion to see the beauty and character. Mom rented a small house for several months while a small three-bedroom home was constructed with my first real bedroom. Bonnie and Nancy shared a room.

The sophomores were to meet in the high school auditorium to sit in alphabetically assigned seats. Next to me was an aisle seat marked Cobb. I had not met anyone in Eunice. Before we were to take our seats, the other classmates were all standing and chatting about the summer, etc. The prettiest and bubbliest girl was holding court. She was obviously very popular. Being shy and not knowing anyone, I was the only one sitting. Before all were told to take their seats, the girl came over and sat on my lap, put her arm around my neck and said, "He's cute, I'm going to keep him." Being a very late bloomer and not having any social skills concerning girls, I was very embarrassed and at a loss for words. Yvonne Cobb was dating Ronnie Patterson (handsome personable jock and later class president). They married after high school and enjoyed many happy years.

I did not fit into any of the cliques and being the smallest person in the class with no experience in sports did not help. Buddy Burnett, another newcomer, the only other person in town with a motorcycle (a Cushman Eagle) and I became good friends. During much of the fall, each Friday, after school, I rode my small "Harley" to Carlsbad (70 miles west) to complete the race season. I finished as the AMA points champion for cross country racing against bigger machines driven by much older drivers. One day Mom came home finding the kitchen floor covered with newspaper, motorcycle engine and transmission parts. Curiosity forced me to disassemble the nearly new engine, etc. to the smallest part. When I reassembled it with no left-over parts it still operated like new. *Never a doubt.*

Since age 12, I provided for every financial need other than room and board. Needing money, I soon found a job in the Five & Dime store as the stock boy. Having had a paper route in Carlsbad, this was my first experience having a boss. Stumbled at first and learned a lot about the difference between "self-employment" and being supervised.

I missed school most of February with a severe case of the mumps. I did go out for tennis in the spring, but never played in a meet. By May I had grown nine inches in nine months. I would reach six feet by the end of my junior year. To this day I still think of myself as short.

Mom was required to take nine semester hours each year per school policy. During the summer following my sophomore year Mom, Bonnie and Nancy spent the summer at the University of Colorado in Boulder. Mom always trusted my judgement and that I was capable of taking care of myself. This nurtured a can-do attitude. I stayed home by myself during summers and provided for most of my own food and other needs. Having spent my early years on a farm, then supporting myself outside of room and board, it never occurred to me this was a burden, only a natural contribution to the family. That summer I also worked in a small cafe with no air-conditioning washing dishes part time earning 40 cents an hour and meals. Working over boiling water in more than 100-degree temperatures in New Mexico was not my favorite job. I was the only employee. The owner was a character resembling the stereotype of an old sailor on a dock smoking a pipe with a beard. The mayor, school superintendent, principals, council members, fire chief, police chief and judge all attended the First Baptist Church and considered dancing a sin. Hence, it was against the law to dance in the city limits. The cafe owner did not attend any church but was a very good man blessed with life stories that were good for teens to hear. He allowed the teens to dance in a small room in the cafe with a jukebox. He was keeping the teens off the street, not drinking and staying out of trouble. Truly a public service. He was visited by town fathers and told he must stop the teens from dancing, or he would be escorted to the Eunice city limits and not to return. He did not stop the teens from dancing. One day he was never seen again, and the cafe was closed.

That summer, Vern Campbell, also in a fatherless home, and I built from the ground up a 1942 Ford coupe for $25 with junk yard parts from Ford, Mercury and Lincoln vehicles. The result was not pretty but ran. Vern soon drove the car into a wet curve too fast, hydroplaned, rolled and totaled the car. Near the end of the summer,

Vern, his mother, his sisters and I crowded into an un-air-conditioned car. My first real vacation. We visited the Grand Canyon, Las Vegas including a Hoover Dam tour, and more on the way to San Diego to visit some of their family. I remember an attractive cousin of Vern's trying to get me in bed and wanted to do something I knew not to do. My shyness intervened along with the possibility of being caught and having no way home. *Later regretted passing up such an opportunity, girls were certainly on my radar by that age.* We then visited several attractions traveling along the coast to Washington to visit more family. I remember going scuba diving in a clear and very cold creek in Washington. Another day, I was the first to jump in a swimming pool. I came out faster. Then I spotted some ice near the corner of the pool. We then headed back to Eunice via San Diego. Vern had purchased a car there on our first visit and we drove it home. California was light years different then the Eunice culture, values and attitudes. *Not necessarily a good thing for California.*

My high school years were good years in many ways. During high school I took four years each of math, English, history and science along with electives. At home, there was never sibling rivalry, only support for each other. Bonnie was more outgoing, popular, a cheerleader and later the football homecoming queen. Bonnie arranged for me to ride in the only seat available on the girl only pep squad bus including cheerleaders to a football game in Ft. Sumner, New Mexico over 225 miles from Eunice. On a slow bus, to be the only male was pure heaven. My junior year, Bonnie, after much prodding convinced me that another cheerleader, Marie Edwards (*did I mention a very pretty blonde*), would go out with me if asked. Although scared of being rejected, I finally had my first date. It was to a basketball game, not a low-profile date I hoped for. I entered the gym with Marie, feeling a strange mixture of pride and embarrassment. At the door of her home we kissed, my first. I could get use to that and tried. She quit school to marry. *What a loss.*

In Algebra II Coach Shotten had written a complex problem on the blackboard. He picked out a good math student to go to the board and work the problem. When the student was unable to, Coach tried and failed. He asked if anyone else wanted to try. No hands went up. When he was about to erase the problem, I asked to try. The real accomplishment was not my successfully solving the problem, but for the first-time volunteering to go to the front of a class. Although brief as it was, the enemy, fear of looking like a fool, had been knocked off my shoulder for a moment. This fear would never be completely conquered. Beating the enemy once was a small, but important, step. Later in life I would stand on a stage, brief for four days, and field a multitude of questions on many subjects in the front of a room filled with customers, PhDs, engineers, a company vice president, and more. Not only was I comfortable in this setting but actually enjoyed it. The enemy still raises its head in some settings, such as an adult Sunday school class.

That year Mom drove me to Lubbock, Texas to a hospital where they discovered I had a growth in a canal located in my neck. They recommended a few radiation treatments. On one of the dates Mom had a schedule conflict and needed the car. With her reluctant approval, I rode my "Harley" the 150 miles to Lubbock. A long 300 miles averaging about 50 mph in strong winds.

My junior year, another outcast Yankee and good math student, Mike McClannahan, who had lived in Eunice a few years became a good friend. The prior year he attended the NM Military Institute in Roswell and succeeded in getting expelled. His wish had been granted. To say Mike was a character is an understatement. Other than intentionally getting kicked out of NMMI, he was a good guy and state track star. After high school he attended NM School of Mines in Socorro as an engineering student. Later he attended ENMU.

One spring Sunday afternoon our junior year, Mike and I went rabbit hunting in Mom's car. We parked in a gully several miles from Eunice and set out on foot looking for rabbits. Of course, we never fired our .22 rifles. Upon returning to the car, a rough mean looking man with a shot gun was sitting on the hood of Mom's car with all the tires flat. He said, "You have to go to the police to get the car." He claimed his land was posted (it was not from the north, the way we arrived). He was a scary dude. We hoofed it to town. Not far from my home the mayor stopped and asked us if we needed a ride. We did. He dropped us at my home. After leaving our rifles in the house, we could not figure out how to get Mom's car without going to the police. We dropped by the very small one room police station. NM State Trooper Rainey said, "Wondered when you boys would show up, been waiting for you." We explained the situation. After getting into his vehicle, he stopped by a service station to pick up a spark-plug pump to air up the tires. He informed us that if the old man had done any more damage to Mom's car, "He would show us how the sheep herder kicked the shit out of his dog." The man was still sitting on the hood. After installing the spark plug pump, I tried to start the car. It would not start. I looked in the glove box and it was empty. It had been full. The man said the stuff was in his car under the seat. He finally admitted he had also removed the distributor rotor so we could not start the car. He insisted we open the trunk because we had illegal items there. The trunk only had the spare and jack. With the rotor installed we were able to inflate the tires. The man said we had run beef off his cattle and killed two horses and wanted us jailed. The state trooper asked Mike and me when we could be at the judge's office the next day. We said after track practice. The trooper then told the man to be there at that time. The man was angry because he was not asked when he was available.

After track Mike and I went to Judge Bowden's office. The scary hermit and the NM Trooper, Rainey, were there. The judge asked Mike and me to go over to the pool hall across the street and await further instructions. Shortly, the trooper came in the pool hall and said everything was settled, we were free to go. The judge had told the man that if he proceeded Mom could sue him for damage to the tires, etc. Judge Bowden had a knack for dealing with issues. If a teenager was in his court, he would make certain the parents did not pay the fine. His typical technique was to require them to prepare a ten-page paper on a subject he chose, then requiring it to be graded by "Lila T." the tough high school English teacher. Teens did not intend to be in his court.

The summer following the junior year found me working in a garage for the owner Dub Dunnam. He was considered the best mechanic in that part of the world. Dub was a character and great teacher with an exceptional sense of humor. He was the role model this teen needed. He was the father of three girls and a son, all very bright, attractive and well-liked by all including adults. Billie was in my class, Bethene a year older, Jerry was in Bonnie's class, then Jennette (my infatuation). When a brave young man arrived to pick up one of his daughters, Dub, for fun, sat in their living room always stroking his shotgun and asking where they were going and when they would be home. *There was no way I would date one of Dub's daughters.*

Again, I was on my own during the summer, following my junior year, while Mom went off to college with Bonnie and Nancy. During the summer, I would find time to play poker. A friend had keys to a service station where he worked. We played in a back room, sometimes we played penny-ante all night. We considered the backroom important to avoid the police. My current guess is that the police likely knew. Fortunately, I always walked off with more money than I had at the start. No one lost more than 50 cents. Few of us earned 50 cents/hour working.

I spent the summer working for Dub. Working for him was a learning experience in the garage and about life. In front of his garage were gas pumps. Customers expected full service that included having windshields cleaned, oil checked, car floors swept, tire pressure checked, and gas pumped. Each time a car pulled up to the pumps a bell would ring in the garage. The attendant (that would be me) would then ask the driver, with a smile, how much gas they wanted. Dub had a very old small tank truck that he drove to the refinery to acquire his gasoline. All the name brand service station large tankers got their gas from the same refinery tanks. However, they claimed their gas was superior to less expensive independent station gas. Gas prices were about 20 cents a gallon.

In the oil fields most teens and some others got "drip" gas from a variety of sources. Preferred drip was clear, like water, raw unrefined gas that was acquired, typically, late at night. Reportedly, clear drip needed a little oil added to protect engines. When the clear drip was not available, and one was desperate, open earth tanks containing black unrefined petroleum were sources. Unavailable meant the clear drip tanks were being watched. The petroleum companies tended to turn their heads, but the problem was sneaky "Feds." They did not like untaxed gas. We each had favorite drip sources, not revealed, but shared stories of nearly being caught.

Towards the end of the summer prior to my senior year, I decided to go out for football. I was now six feet weighing 145 pounds. The coach suggested I play the halfback position. He had seen me and a few others goofing around with a football during the summer. Being unsure of myself, not feeling comfortable in a high-profile position, but wanting to handle the football, I requested to try out for center. He was okay with that. In those days you played both defense and offense. Centers generally played middle linebacker. When leading in the fourth quarter of the first game, coach sent me in as center and middle linebacker. No one had face masks except for a few offensive backs (they only had a simple bar). On the first play, after hiking the ball our back was running down the field. I was still pumping my forearm in the player's face across from me. Big mistake, unknown to me, he was an All-State player. When I bent over to hike the ball on the next down, his face was bloody. He said, "I will get you for this" and did for the rest of the game. I would start only one game. I loved playing middle linebacker.

Vern Campbell did not like football and wanted out but did not want to be tagged as a quitter, in my opinion. The coach had a zero tolerance for fighting. The penalty was to be kicked off the team. The day we received our senior rings, Vern punched me during one scrimmage play when I hiked the ball. At the time, it seemed only to numb my face. He wanted to fight, my response was that I would and wanted to meet him after practice. After showering he was long gone and never returned to football. It turns out he had blackened both eyes, broke my nose and broke a middle front tooth off at the gum thanks to the new class ring. The nerve was hanging, but not too painful as long as air did not touch the nerve, otherwise very sharp pain. I was closed mouthed. There was no dentist in Eunice. The next morning before school, I drove myself to a dentist 40 miles east to Kermit, Texas. He cut the nerve off at the root end and packed it. I returned a week later to receive a temporary cap. He recommended waiting until the end of football season to install a permanent cap. He suggested a gold cap because it would be more durable during my active years. After football season, I visited the dentist returning home with the gold cap which extended to the gum line. *To say Mom was upset with the dentist is a huge understatement.*

During our senior year, class of 1956, the small movie theater closed. It had 2 or 3 seats on each side of the aisle and had seen better days. The classic 1971 movie *The Last Picture Show* and its declining 1951 north Texas town could have been Eunice. Bonnie would be depressed after seeing the movie because it was too realistic. A drive-in-movie opened allowing all sorts of opportunities.

After football season, feeling pressure from Coach Shotten, who had been our Algebra II teacher our junior year, Irvin Smith and I attended a NM National Guard meeting. We both joined that November (me because of the extra money). We attended monthly meetings until going to a two-week summer camp as an anti-aircraft unit at Ft. Bliss (near El Paso, Texas). I failed to send a change of address when attending college. As a result, unknown to me, about 2-3 years later they gave me an Honorable Discharge. I discovered after college that I was eligible for the draft and not a member of the NMNG. Irvin (also later an engineer) became a life-long close friend. His family accepted me as one of them. He had two brothers and sister. For decades, on annual visits to Eunice, his parents were my first stop. His mother lived to be over 100 and still a joy to visit to hear her stories and feel her spirit and love. Her stories about life at a young age before and after New Mexico became a state were fascinating.

During the senior year my circle of friends would broaden, although the shyness and being unsure of myself would remain unchecked. Charlie Kyle, the nephew of Judge Bowden, moved to Eunice from Arkansas for his senior year and we became close friends. He was an All-State player in basketball his junior year in Arkansas. Coach Stringer believed stalling the ball from the start would win games. It did win many games, but in a boring way. Adding both teams points rarely exceeded 20 together. There were no rules to prevent stalling. Charlie was accustomed to fast paced basketball in Arkansas. Coach Stringer would not allow players any fancy moves. In the first game Charlie instinctively passed the ball behind his back allowing a teammate to make an easy basket. Coach sent him to the bench for much of the season. Hobbs, New Mexico, the next and much larger town played a different style of high school basketball. They hosted the Sunshine Tournament during the Christmas holidays. They invited the top teams in Texas, Oklahoma and New Mexico. It would be 25 years of the tournament before Hobbs High School lost a game, a championship game. They scored over 100 points every game. The last tournament I watched they averaged 114 points a game. Their coach was voted the "National High School Coach of the Year" twice.

Although Charlie was benched, he held his head high and longed to be a member of the Hobbs HS team. He would have been in his element. When we graduated, he left Eunice reportedly never to return. I would learn decades later Charlie settled in Artesia, New Mexico, not far away. We had shared many good times. Charlie was also a good math student. Not many would sign up for math during our senior year, although the quiet Mr. Richard Brown was a great teacher. I was not a great student in some other classes.

My senior year we visited Mom's sister and family in New Jersey, Grandmud in NYC, and her best friend Sparky on Long Island during the Christmas holidays. This was the first time we had visited since I was twelve. Uncle Chet would take me to a local high school football game and spoke to me as an adult and equal. *What a treat.* We stayed with "Aunt" Sparky, "Uncle" Art and children a few days at their large home. Uncle Chet, "Uncle" Art and I gathered in his barroom and I listened to their WW II experiences. All the women and children gathered in the kitchen at the other end of the house. I made the near fatal mistake of trying to keep up with their drinking. This would be my first time to drink. After a bit I slipped away. Being sick is not fun. Going up the stairs, the handrail was my best friend. I then hurried to the bathroom.

During March the basketball team went to the state championship tournament in Albuquerque. Four of us decided to drive up for the games. Lila T. Brown, the English teacher, informed us we would receive an "F" for the semester if we missed school for the games regardless of how we performed in class. We went anyway and had a great time. On the next report card, I received an "F" even though my papers and tests reflected at least a "C+". It was not my favorite class or teacher. I visited the principal, Mr. Caton, thinking he could solve the problem. After all, his son was the center on the team and my Mom was the school nurse. He told me he was helpless and that at times during life we simply should separate ourselves from someone when a problem could not be resolved. He recommended I drop English to avoid the "F" on my transcript. I did.

Once again, during track I continued to lose meets when I ran the mile race. I realized too late sprints were more my strength. Still not wanting to be rejected and choosy, dates were rare. Bonnie continued to be my spy to ensure when I asked a girl out a rejection was not in the cards.

There were fund raisers during the school year for a senior class trip. A previous class trip had been to Chihuahua, Mexico. The students were escorted to the city limits and informed no subsequent EHS classes would be allowed to visit their city. The Eunice school superintendent, Mr. Conway, then set a new policy forbidding senior class trips to be more than 500 miles from Eunice and only in the USA. Mr. Conway approved our choice of a week in Colorado Springs, Colorado a little over 550 miles from Eunice. It may have not hurt that his daughter, Claire, was in our class. The fund raisers had produced enough money to give us each $50 for our individual expenses as well as fund all other expenses. Two Greyhound style school busses transported us to Manitou Springs to our motel. The class sponsors (teachers), Mr. Brown and Mr. Davis accompanied us on the trip. Both were quiet and passive. As respected as they were by all, they may not have been good choices to keep 18-year-olds in check. In Colorado at 18 years of age a person could be served 3.2 beer. This caused some problems for others. Being fearful of becoming an alcoholic like my father, I was reluctant to drink. We had many adventures such as visiting local attractions, horseback riding, ice skating at the Broadmoor Hotel and more. At the Broadmoor ice rink, we rented skates and were told to wait until the U.S. Olympic Team finished practice. I was the only one who had ice skated before, although it had been many years since I had in New Hampshire. Eager to impress the class for the first time, I mounted the ice only to discover the Olympic Team had not finished and found myself sprawled on the ice. *Not my finest hour.*

When the busses were pulling out early in the morning to head for home Yvonne Cobb asked if Ronnie Paterson was on the other bus. Normally he would sit with her. They soon discovered a few of us missing. They finally found us in a motel room still in a poker game that started the night before. We had been told if the busses left without us, we would be on our own. On the way home, we stopped for a tour at the Colorado State Prison at Cannon, Colorado. A few of the popular classmates had taken up the sport of "shoplifting" to see what they could get by with. They bragged about the items taken from the prison gift shop. The items had been made by the prisoners and typically their only source of income for basic necessities. Later on, at a stop to get fuel for the busses the same students entered a curio shop. Sometime after the Eunice superintendent received a bill for $200 which he quietly paid himself. He set a policy of no more class trips. Because the junior and sophomore classes had started raising funds for their trip, he reluctantly did not cancel their class trip, but added restrictions.

Soon after returning home from our class trip I bravely got a flattop haircut. This was against Mom's instructions. Two years previously she had told me if I got a flattop "my bags would be packed." She said, "The shape of my head was a problem." While believing that was not a literal threat, I never wanted to upset Mom as she had enough on her plate. When Mom saw the new cut she said, "That looks good, you should have done that sooner." *Go figure.* Decades later in 1979, to be her last Christmas, she gave me a throw pillow with the words "God made just so many perfect heads the rest He covered with hair." *The pillow is still proudly displayed.*

The 1956 EHS class numbered 65, the largest before or since. At the time, the national average number of students that attended college was twenty percent. Eighty percent of our class attended college. Our class produced an ambassador, two federal judges, engineers, school administrators, teachers, coaches, successful entrepreneurs, civil servants, a career military man, and a cowboy.

Before HS graduation, I was filling out the Eastern NM University application at the kitchen table. When reaching the line titled Major, I asked Mom, "What does that mean?" She replied, "That is your main course of study." Mom suggested engineering because I was good at math. Not even really knowing what an engineer did, in a heartbeat, I entered that. In hindsight, for my aptitude it was the best decision I could have made. Eunice HS was one of the best in NM. Therefore, any student with a "C" or better was accepted by any state university and exempt from admission tests and remedial courses. ENMU in Portales was the closest (130 miles) and least expensive state college. Each semester required about $450 which covered tuition, fees, room and board, and books. I also needed to budget $20/month to cover gas, toiletries, haircuts, clothing, entertainment, laundry, Sunday evening meals, etc. Part of the money needed was earned working at college.

With no expected help to fund college, I started working as a roustabout for a local pipeline company for 50 cents/hour. Watching weathered old men earning the same on the pipeline reinforced, for me, why I was going to college. Workers showed up at 6:00 am with a lunch bucket. The foreman would pick out who he wanted that day, the rest went home. I was not going to earn enough for college, even though I was always selected.

Four of us decided to try our luck in the far opposite corner of New Mexico. We piled into a car pulling an early 1930s camper and headed to Farmington which was booming. The moldy gutted camper had only one light bulb in the center dangling by its wire. Farmington had no places available for rent. Even families were sleeping in the city park (tents, campers, etc. were not allowed). The main street was torn-up, rutted and muddy. It reminded me of the old western boom towns. We were fortunate in finding a doorless barn that the farmer allowed us to park our camper beside. He had a cold-water shower head in one of the stalls and ran an extension cord to our trailer. The camper was so smelly we only stored our belongings inside when we worked. We slept on the ground in our bedrolls. Only during bad weather did the farmer let us sleep in the leaky smelly barn. We worked for a company making 90 cents/hour and all the overtime we could stand. Overtime paid $1.35/hour. We were building a pipeline across the Navaho Reservation. The heat conditions were extreme and the work backbreaking. I averaged at least 14 hours/day seven days a week. We ate breakfast in a local cafe and bought two box lunches they had prepared. At the end of the long days we were not sure a cafe would still be open.

A week before college we were to stay for the first time in an isolated mountain lodge about 60 miles from Farmington. I was the helper on a truck. I was dirty after a long hard 17-hour day and entered the lodge about 10:30 pm looking forward to the first real bed since Eunice. In the lobby sat two company executives at a table. They motioned me over and told me that was my last day. I was immediately taken to town and told my pay would be available in a few days at the office. They had decided the next three employees to walk through the door would be laid-off. They acknowledged I was one of their best workers, seeing me hard at work loading timbers on the truck at a sawmill that day. I needed that last week to have enough for college. They were not to be swayed. The decision was final.

I arranged to sell my precious "Harley" if I could bring it to Farmington. I had no transportation, so the other Eunice dudes dropped me on the highway to Cuba, New Mexico the next day before 6:00 am. I planned to hitch hike to Albuquerque, hop a freight to Clovis, then hitch hike to Eunice. My truck driver, the first to stop, offered to give me a ride to a point 45 miles out where he had to leave the Cuba highway. The 100-mile road across the Navaho Reservation was desolate uninhabited with very little vegetation. After he dropped me off, when no cars came along, I began to think my plan was a bad idea. A family with young children stopped and asked where I was headed. I told them Clovis. So, the children squeezed together to make room. It was a pleasant journey with a nice family who dropped me, out of their way, on the highway towards Portales. Mom was attending ENMU for summer school, living in the University Apartments. This was Friday and she would be going Eunice after classes. After walking miles and no one offering me a ride, a gentleman picked me up then dropped me at Mom's apartment, out of his way. She was getting in her car headed for Eunice. *Luck is a wonderful thing.*

I had purchased a 1949 Ford sedan early in the summer from Ronnie Patterson when a deal was too good to pass up. In order to have enough funds to start college, I needed the money the Harley would bring. I removed the wheels and other Harley components and removed the Ford backseat for the Harley. I then loaded a 40-gallon barrel and Jerry Army cans in the trunk to hold drip gas. Bonnie joined me for the nearly 600-mile one-way ride to Farmington. I delivered the Harley, picked up my belongings in the trailer, then the work check. On the way home, Bonnie remembers her fear when a tire blew out at 100 plus miles/hour although the car never swayed going down a long hill in northern NM. She was impressed with my driving skills. At the time retread tires were all I could afford. For a few dollars, tires with little remaining tread could be recapped. *Luck is significantly underrated.*

My tenure at Eunice High School was a godsend. This great school gave me the education greatly needed and a feeling that things could be better. I had arrived likely grieving, shy, unsure of myself, no knowledge of girls other than sisters. I would make lifelong friends, learn that kissing was great, claim a sense of adventure, but still be naive, shy and unsure of myself. I would go off to college with a strange mixture of excitement, mystery, and uncertainty.

Chapter VIII - Eastern New Mexico University

"Freshman orientation week" at Eastern New Mexico University occurred before upperclassmen arrived on campus and classes began. My assigned counselor was Robert C. Pendergraft, an engineering instructor, who would have to approve my class choices every semester. The best advice he gave me that week was to plan my four-year curriculum and make sure prerequisites were taken as early as possible. With few engineering students, not all courses were available every semester or year. To ignore this advice could mean going to college an extra year. Financially that was out of the question. I was able to find a much-needed job on campus working in the cafeteria for Ruth Blake, affectionately called "Ma Blake." This also helped pay for the surprise expense of a necessary slide rule and required drafting instruments.

While ten Eunice classmates would start at ENMU, I did not arrive with a buddy. In subsequent years close Eunice classmates Mike McClanahan and Irvin Smith would transfer to ENMU. Jim Stephenson from Fort Sumner, New Mexico was assigned by ENMU to be my roommate in the freshman dormitory, Roosevelt Hall. Mom had bought two twin bedspreads, with my blessing, for our room. They were a hit with Jim. He was a great roommate who also liked the room tidy. Not having classes or a major in common, we generally ran with different friends. Freshmen were required to wear, until homecoming, a small green beanie with our names hand printed in white on the bill. Skipper would not fit so Skip would have to do. Hence, everyone from college still know me as Skip. Few people had spoken to me in the past likely due to my limited response because of shyness. I was surprised when meeting people on the sidewalk or hallways and they would say, "Hi Skip." Being an unconscious sort, I thought they were remembering me. This and many other events throughout college helped build my confidence and shed the shyness. I had a roommate in Chaves Hall, Paul Helvey, my sophomore year tell me I was the most unconscious person he ever knew. To further make the point, when I was 75 years old while looking in a high school yearbook, a girl, Micky Lee, had written about my hazel eyes. I had always "known" they were brown.

My driver's license, passport, and all documents including Top Secret applications during my life agreed they were brown. I checked the mirror and saw hazel eyes staring back. In some areas my wife, Nancy, can confirm my being unconscious about myself.

An acquaintance allowed me to store my drip barrel and cans in a dilapidated barn near Portales. I would go home every other weekend with laundry and to collect more drip for the first couple of months. In hindsight this did little to help me assimilate into campus life. Two students from Chicago went home with me one weekend. They reluctantly went dripping with me to fill the car, Army Jerry cans and a 40-gallon barrel. My favorite drip was about 150 yards north of my home. Located in a relatively new subdivision, our street turned into a dirt road beyond the subdivision. You could see the drip source from home. Late that night, we had just finished getting the drip, loading up the adapter and hose, when I spotted a car with its lights out slowly coming our way from the north. I told the Yankees to start running south to my home, and that the fine was $100 for each person caught. The sneaky car turned on his lights to give chase. I had jumped into my car and headed south with lights off going through a large deep mud puddle then turned into a side street in the subdivision and circled around to my home. The "Fed" had hit the mud puddle and was stuck. We watched, from my house, as the frustrated "Fed" called on his radio for a wrecker while remaining in his car. The Yankees had nearly suffered a heart attack and still shaking said they would never visit Eunice again. At the end of the semester, they went back to Chicago and did not return. *Evidently, they were not up to living in "Billy the Kid" territory.*

Before the drip adventure, I was at a friend's house off campus listening to a clone of Johnny Cash. The two Chicago dudes and others were at the jam session. At some point the Yankees asked if we wanted to eat pizza. We had not heard of pizza. They discovered a restaurant in Clovis that prepared them. Off to Clovis we went to partake of this wonder food according to our Chicago friends. Anchovies, also unknown to me, were on the pizza. I did not like the pizza. I tried pizza again at age 25 at Terry's Pizza, the only pizza in Huntsville, Alabama. *Good food.*

Our math instructor, Lucile Buchanan, told her classes if we successfully worked all the extra credit problems on homework assignments and tests you would receive an "A" for the course. John

Guthals and I got every problem correct. We had two math courses our first semester. She gave us each a "B" in each class. Going together for moral support, we asked, "Why only a B?" She said we were two of the best four students she ever had, but we had not participated enough in class. She had not mentioned this was important or part of the grade. I had rationalized that to raise my hand was depriving other students of an opportunity to get points and that Ms. Buchanan already knew of my knowledge. She destroyed my goal of only getting an "A" in math classes. *Not the best way to motivate students.*

Mr. Pendergraft would not approve my curriculum for the first semester unless it included a speech class. I dreaded speech class every day, worried that I might have go to the front of the class and speak. *No argument that it was beneficial.* My only difficult course was chemistry, a four-semester hour course each semester. The students having chemistry in high school typically did well. Those who struggled had not taken chemistry in high school. That would be me. I always focused 110% in any class. There would be only two tests: one at mid-term and the final. They would be averaged for the final grade. The chem labs only provided a required check mark. I realized during the midterm test that chemistry was more of a memory course. I was not known for my study habits. That needed to change. With concentrated studying in chemistry the rest of the semester, I pulled out a passing grade. *Whew, close call.*

At the beginning of Engineering Drawing, Mr. Pendergraft informed the class that his engineers would not graduate ignorant about the world. He said on each test, in addition to the course material, there would be a geography question. He expected us to be prepared to draw the USA with all 48 states and capitals on the first test. Alaska and Hawaii were territories and not yet states. Each subsequent test would be devoted to a continent. We would have to draw each country and capital. *Years later this was appreciated.*

Each spring the university celebrated and survived Rodeo Week. During Rodeo Week we were expected to dress as a cowboy or cowgirl or suffer the consequences, generally a trip to a water tank. My calves were larger than anyone's, even those on the Greyhound football team. I did not have cowboy boots. A cowboy friend gave me an old pair of his that I slit up the sides so that I could get them on. The university had the oldest rodeo in college land. That it is a tough sport is an understatement. Many freshmen typically signed up to attempt to ride a bull, bareback bronc or saddled bronc. I was told the stock would come from Mexico and be easy to ride. This particular year, 96 of us with limited intelligence signed up. My choice was bull and bareback bronc events. The stock company delivered *professional* rodeo stock. The Brahma bulls and bronc were mean and scary. The stock owner decreed that he would not allow his animals to be ridden by so many riders because it would ruin his stock. A few voluntarily gave up their ride. Those remaining would be allowed to ride, determined by a lottery. These would not be seen as cowardly, just stupid. I relied on the drawing. The good news was not having the opportunity to ride. Did I mention some survived Rodeo Week sober? *Fun week.*

During the summer following the freshman year, I worked in the oil fields as a roustabout. That included working on a pulling-rig. It was not fun. Each day my clothes, including boots, were covered with black oil. The pulling-rig was old and dangerous. I would also unload bags of cement from boxcars. Returning to college in the fall was a blessing.

A few weeks after freshman year, my grades arrived in the mail with a "C" in engineering classes that I had aced and should have received an "A." When returning to ENMU in the fall, my first stop was to confront Mr. Pendergraft for an explanation. He told me my scores were the highest in the classes. However, I would only get a "C" in his classes until my lifestyle changed. He further stated engineering students were expected to study until 2:00 am. Spending every night dancing at the Student Union Building (SUB) was out of the question. He did continue to give me only a "C" in his classes. In a small engineering college, the option of avoiding his classes was not possible. I would learn much in his classes and liked his teaching style. Even when a choice of teachers was available, I would select his classes because I learned more. My lifestyle did not change but at some point, he started giving me "B's."

Chaves Hall would be my home during my sophomore year and first semester of my junior year. My first roommates were forgettable as I will explain later. All activities on campus were covered by the fees paid at the beginning of each semester. The Greyhound football team would have an undefeated season. It was great to watch the Greyhound basketball team, theater, movies, go to dances and more. Portales offered little to do.

On Halloween six of us idiots decided to go out of the city into the countryside to drink, thereby avoiding the risk of being caught. I drove and parked the car under a large cottonwood tree at the corner of a dirt crossroad. Because I was driving, I was only sipping on one beer. I was standing by the rear fender on the driver's side talking with Jay Turnbow. I noticed two of our party, who had started drinking earlier, were dragging a board with several mailboxes. I immediately told them that was a federal crime and to return them to the posts they had taken them from. They were too drunk to replace them. About that time a farmer drove up and said he was going to report us. We reinstalled the mailboxes then headed to town and hoped the farmer would not follow through. He did. *Not the fun filled Halloween we expected.*

We, like fools, decided to drive back to the country to check. Even though no one was near the spot of the crime, we were pulled over by County Deputies and taken to the Sheriff's office in the courthouse. They interviewed us individually. I went to the bathroom with two others and told them to be sure and pass on to the others that we had picked up John Guthals after we had gone to town. I knew John was on "Social Probation" at ENMU and would be expelled. He was released. The rest of us would spend the night and until 5:00 pm the next day on the top floor of the courthouse in the jail. Because we had been in my car, the Sheriff decided I was the leader. He could not have been more wrong. I was placed in a solitary confinement cell with no glass in the barred window, a bed with an old stained mattress, sink with rusty water and a curbed latrine. It was cold that night without heat and an open window. This inspired a desire to never be stupid again. Not sure the goal was achieved. The next morning at about five o'clock, by standing on the bed, I could see the bank clock on the square through the high window. I checked for the time again after what seemed like an hour. It was only five minutes later. So went the day. Outside my steel door with a small window, I could hear parents say to their wayward son that they had always taken him to church. How could this happen? That was when I first thought of our parents being contacted. Late in the afternoon, Mom was escorted into my cell. No other parents were put in the cell with their son. Mom was grinning and asked how I was doing. She was always a champ. Mom in her wisdom knew I was having a learning experience and did not need her to weigh in. I knew she was there for support but not to solve my problem, that was my responsibility. This was typical of my parents' contribution to building character in their children. I will always be thankful for their wisdom.

She had talked with a dean she had known when attending summer school. He told her we would not be expelled but would be on "Social Probation" for the duration of college with the understanding that ENMU would not be available if in trouble again.

At about 5:00 pm we were collectively brought before the judge. The others one by one were presented and fined $10. The judge asked me who tore off the mailboxes, I said I did not know. He said I must have been too drunk to drive. He then charged me with drunk driving. I had no idea what the fine would be but assumed about $25. Knowing I was innocent but believing hiring an attorney would cost more, I pleaded guilty. He fined me $100 and suspended my driver's license for a year. I told him I wanted to change my plea. He said no to the request. Big lesson never plead guilty when innocent. Two years later I would watch him allow someone else to change their plea to not guilty.

Not the end of the story. The FBI would visit the campus a few weeks later and interview each of us separately. I was the last interviewed and explained that I had been standing near the rear fender talking with Jay Turnbow and had not seen who removed the mailboxes. The agent said, "That's funny, that's what all the others said about themselves." Nice friends to steal my honest testimony. The FBI told us there would be a review and if they decided to prosecute the US Marshall would take us into custody. Never heard from them again.

At this time, the university did not allow students to pledge fraternities or sororities until their sophomore year, nor were national Greek organizations on campus or Greek houses allowed. Regular meetings would occur in classrooms. Tau Kappa Tau (TKT) was considered the top fraternity, although the other fraternity (ASO) had some great members. The first roommates in Chaves Hall wanted to join TKT. We all attended the "Smokers" to check out the fraternities and to be checked out. I remember being approached by Maurice Hodges, a football star, and being asked about myself. I was flattered "Mo" would be interested in me. It went over my head that the interest was to help in deciding on how he should vote. The roommates would only receive an invitation to join ASO or nothing. On the other hand, I only received an invitation from TKT. I would learn years later that I was at first blacked-balled. Dale Tayler had addressed the members and persuaded them to take another vote and that I would make a good TKT member. Joining TKT was extremely important in helping me escape from my shell. The members were exceptional individuals that helped me grow and would provide friendships that continued throughout my life.

Hell Week for the Greek's was designed to be bad news for the pledges. Each pledge of TKT had to dress up as a girl and acquire the signature of each member on their TKT paddle. The signature allowed a member to have the pledge bend over for a paddling.

Back to my roommates who were very upset at not receiving an invitation to TKT and that I had. One night they returned to the room with others about 2:00 am. Barely able to stand they invited me outside to beat the hell out of me because I was joining TKT. Being on "Social Probation," I knew no good would come of joining them and that they were only directing their disappointment at me. I shortly started rooming with Jay Turnbow, then Paul Helvey, Red Conner and Jim Cain. Room 323 in Chaves Hall gave us the advantage in water balloon fights. *Thank you, gravity.*

I did enjoy my technical courses in math, engineering, physics and geology. During the sophomore spring semester students were required to take a Sophomore Comprehensive Test. If you were weak in a subject, ENMU required a student take a class in that subject before graduation. I was going to be required to take a literature and history course. Putting it off until my senior second semester, I signed up for Literature of the Southwest and History of the Southwest. Both courses were fantastic. I would wonder why I had not taken more of these types of courses while in college.

During the spring semester, another engineering student and I visited Texas Tech with the idea of transferring to a better-known engineering college. A visit convinced both of us that staying at ENMU was the correct choice. This was partly because of the size of TT and the size of classes. Also, we were received as though we were just a number. At TT we were told that the thermodynamics course would have two hundred in one classroom. At ENMU we would have seven students. My study habits would likely have resulted in a "C" at TT. My thermodynamics professor, Dr. John Penick, delighted in embarrassing students at every opportunity. Therefore, I was prepared every day and earned one of the two A's in the class of seven.

Paul Helvey and Zetia George, after several attempts, persuaded me to ask Rhea Ellinger for a date. We double dated several times. I must thank them for collectively reducing my fear of rejection and putting a dent in my shyness armor. While most might think this was trivial, it was a turning point for me. This was the time Paul said, "You are the most unconscious person I have ever met."

Another adventure would be "Leaders Retreat." Leaders Retreat was a week organized and managed by the student government. The event was held at the Cloudcroft Lodge in big timber country (Lincoln National Forrest) at about 9,000 feet and over 200 miles from campus. The leader of each student organization was invited. The legitimate organizations included were academic, athletic, religious, and social groups. There were 44 delegates and nine administration and faculty advisors in attendance. There would be several committees that would meet for four days to develop resolutions. Each committee would include an advisor, who was not to speak unless asked a question. On Friday, we met in a general assembly to vote on each committee's resolutions. Representing the Engineer's Club, I was assigned to the Facilities Committee. Because Dr. Floyd Golden, the University President, was privy to the university and the state government plans in Santa Fe, he was assigned to our committee. He also knew what structures could not be removed, including trees. While we addressed several topics, the one that I remember most was the desire to add a natatorium to the campus. We had to decide its capability, location and funding source. We decided to remove old buildings near the gym and decided the best way to fund the natatorium was by adding a $10 fee that each student would pay each semester. Our resolution passed the General Assembly and a natatorium was dedicated about 18 months later at the 1959 Homecoming. There were even committees that decided if a college instructor needed to be replaced. If the General Assembly approved the resolution, the university followed through with the recommendations. The legislative body passed 64 resolutions to improve campus life. We worked hard during the day and of course played hard at night.

One weekend I was to ride to Eunice with a friend rather than drive my 1949 Ford. Paul Helvey asked if he could use the car during the weekend. The Ford did not have antifreeze. I told him he could, if he promised to drain the radiator each night and refill it to prevent the block from busting. Sure enough he did not, and the engine block busted. An acquaintance across town had a small single car garage and said that I could work on it there. The Ford was inside with a lot of shelves at the garage end. I had the hood up and had removed the heads and more to discover a busted block. My plan was to find a used block in a junk yard. Meanwhile the house occupants brewed some beer, capped in quart bottles, and placed on the shelves in the garage near my opened hood. Of course, they had prematurely capped the beer bottles. The result was sticky glass all under the hood and in the engine. My first car went to car heaven, a junk yard.

A friend, Don Chaney, from my class in Eunice and an ENMU student, and Jay Turnbow, my roommate, started a rock and roll band, "Ivy Jives." It included a drummer, Charles Gaddy and his wife, Darlene, on the piano and a musician on electric base. Don was the lead singer and Jay the electric guitar player. Jay was a Chuck Berry type player. He would go on to have a fantastic career in music and reportedly even played with Bruce Springsteen. Later in life he would teach guitar at San Juan College in Farmington, New Mexico and still maintains a studio in Alto, New Mexico. I can remember being awakened by Jay at 2:30 am with his amplifier turned down singing "Peggy Sue" which was a song he took the lead on in the band. The Ivy Jives were very good and would produce an album.

I noted in my sophomore yearbook in preparation for my story, the ENMU University President, Dr. Floyd D. Golden, wrote a note; *"Skip, you are known the campus over as one of the hardest working young men in school. There are many students, but the good ones are few and far between. I know you will keep up the hard work and uphold your fine record. Best Wishes, Floyd."* Small colleges are great. It was a good school year.

During the summer weekends after our sophomore year, I would ride with Don Chaney to the places (Eunice, Hobbs, Carlsbad, Artesia, etc.) that the Ivy Jives played at dances for high school and college students. I would help them set up their equipment before they went to work. I would have the task of dancing with a lot of new friends. *Tough duty.*

At the beginning of the summer six of us college fellows were dragging main in Hobbs as were six college girls in another car. One of our guys knew some of them. Three of the girls traded places with three of us. An attractive girl, Lynn Madera, was sitting by me and different from anyone I had known. Lynn had been attending a finishing school in Fort Worth, Texas and graduated from Hobbs High School in 1958. When we drove past the public swimming pool on the east side of Hobbs, she stated she had not lowered herself to ever swim there. When we passed the Hobbs Country Club on the west side of Hobbs, she let me know with her nose clearly elevated that was where she swam. The new gang of twelve decided to have a pool party the next night at a motel, owned by one of the girl's parents. No way I could see to gracefully ditch the snob. During that evening, four of us were standing together when my *"buddy"* suggested the four of us double date to go to a dance at the Women Civic Center on Friday night. Not to be a party pooper, I agreed. Lynn decided she wanted to leave the dance at 8:30 pm. She was spending the night at her friend's home. After pulling into the drive, she continued with snobbish comments. To this day I can't believe my next move. In the back seat, I turned her over my knee and produced a few mild slaps on her bun and informed her she was a spoiled brat. Obviously, I did not know her father, Rufus, was broad shouldered, muscular, and 6'5". Her sister, Sharron, also attractive but down to earth, said her sister was consumed with rage for weeks. At the end of the summer Sharron told me Lynn wanted to go out with me. That would not happen for about two years.

Employment that summer consisted of working for the telephone company in the main office building on the frame and not in the hot desert. Mike McClannahan was working as a lineman for them and got me the job. The frame was several feet long and consisted of several shelves. Each shelf had many rows of small thin posts that would have small wires soldered to them. A pair of wires would be connected to a pair of posts for each telephone in Hobbs. There were two of us assigned to the frame, the other fellow being a permanent employee. Many Hobbs telephone customers were complaining about static or no service when I started. I noticed the frame buddy was creating sloppy solder joints and was lazy. When not implementing a specific work order, I would spend my time re-soldering many suspect solder joints. By the end of the summer, customer complaints were rare. They tried to convince me that a career with the phone company would be great for me. To their dismay, I returned to college. *Great choice.*

I was in Chavez Hall room 323 with Paul Helvey, Jim Cain, and Jay Turnbow during the first semester of my junior year. I realized that taking an additional six semester hours of math, beyond what was required for engineering, would give me a second major, mathematics. This was a no brainer, so I did. Engineering and related classes continued to be challenging but not enough to deter me from continuing to spend time at my favorite place, the SUB dance floor.

TKT members would continue to influence me in positive ways. There were also good times, such as beer busts at the sand-dunes. I would be infamously known for my swan dives from the top of them. I was on the TKT intramural six-man football team playing center and middle linebacker. The center was eligible for a pass. We were fully suited out which was not common on college campuses for intramural football. We played tackle, not flag football. Paul Helvey was the quarterback and Jim Cain the coach. I was to catch my first touchdown pass. Playing center in high school, I was not eligible to receive a pass and as middle linebacker, I never managed an interception. The TKT team was made up of college or All State players except for me.

Soon after college started my junior year, one of Mom's friends wanted $50 to get rid of a large 1952 Buick Special four door sedan with a straight eight engine that leaked and burned oil. It was not a typical college car, but it had a great heater and radio. Cars had bench seats at the time and the back seat had lots of leg room. Great car for double dating. It was good to have wheels again.

At the start of the second semester, money had gotten tighter even though I worked in the cafeteria. I moved off campus and shared a house, adjacent to the campus, with Jim Manes, Harlan Averitt and his younger brother Deryll. We were all members of TKT. We had many good times in the house, and some should not be documented to protect the innocent. For some events such as Rodeo Week, our house was a gathering spot.

This year my "Shipwreck" costume would be remembered. At the last minute, after a few beers, I decided to wear only a red and white striped (about 3-inch-wide stripes) towel like a diaper. I placed a thin (1/4-inch-wide, in style at the time) belt to hold it up and turn the towel ends over the belt. I had a date with Nedra Cundy. *Her mistake.* She was a very clean cut, strait-laced young lady. Some might say she was a prude. Needless to say, during a band break, we went to the cafe/soda fountain room to get her a soda. By this time, I was feeling no pain and likely unwittingly wanted to be a clown. Having no pockets but reaching inside my towel discovered I had no money. From then on, each time I spotted her on a sidewalk or in a hallway, I would turn around and disappear.

Class officers were elected each spring for the following year. R. E. Peterson, a good friend, who was the current student body president, corralled me a few minutes before registration for class officers was to be closed. He persuaded me to register to run for vice president of the senior class. He assured me no one else had registered for that position. I would be elected automatically. So, I did. He told the same thing to another good friend of mine, Bobby Dyess. As friends, neither of us liked running against one another.

We had to make posters to place around campus. One of mine said "Vote for the man with the golden tooth." Still had that big gold front tooth. We had to give a speech to the whole student body, my worst nightmare. Jim Manes helped me polish my speech. I had memorized the speech and placed it on a 3x5 card. Sitting near the front of the room waiting my turn, I went over the speech in my head several times. Each time I could not remember a word in the middle. I reached into my pocket to realize the card was not with me. When I stood in the front of everyone giving the speech, the evasive word was still nowhere to be found. When I got to the word it just popped out. *Life can be good.* I lost the election by nine votes. However, it was a great experience that I am thankful for. Jim, trying to make me feel better said, "You lost the election at the Shipwreck dance when you were at the counter fumbling. Bobby was sitting in the room wearing a tie. Several studious students were also sitting at several of the tables."

Early in the summer before my senior year at ENMU, Martin Miller, Jerry "Rabbit" Golson and I were going to one of their homes in the Amerada Petroleum Camp in Monument, New Mexico. Both of their parents lived in the company owned homes. This would be my only visit to the camp for many years. I spotted a very nice-looking girl across the way who was laughing, full of life and with nice legs. She had on short-shorts, popular at the time. I asked who she was. Martin, a rather reserved and spirited individual, said, "Her name is Patsy Shirley and too good for you and she has a feller." Rabbit, an extravert and great dancer, confirmed both points. *So much for that.*

Early in the summer Bill Hicks (who was president of the student government our senior year) and I double dated with sisters a few times until my date became Miss New Mexico. Bill continued dating her sister, however my status was insufficient to be part of that scene.

Alan Sudbrock married my sister Bonnie and he got me a roughnecking job making $1.96/hour on the rig where he worked. The rig was in Texas southwest of Jal, New Mexico. A 45-mile ride on paved roads and 45 miles of rough rutted dirt roads. The trip took nearly two hours. We worked the evening shift (3 pm until 11 pm). We would leave home at 1:00 pm and be back home at 1:00 am. We worked seven days a week and finished drilling a well every 13 days. Each 13 days we had to work double shifts for two days. The wells were one mile deep. During the summer, the only females I saw were my sisters and Mom. I was ready to go back to college.

Alan told me years later that when I drove away from the rig at the end of the summer, it had inspired him to go to college. The second semester Alan, Bonnie and their new baby, Shonna, moved to Portales and lived in the University Apartments, affectionately known as Vetville. He was a goof off in high school. He would hold down three jobs and improve his grades from C's to A's and B's.

Eunice celebrated its 50th anniversary at the end of the summer with an old west festival. Main Street was closed to traffic at night with street dancing and more. Not to be in full western wear was a guaranteed trip to the water tank in the middle of Main Street. *A great week.*

I headed to campus a week early to provide assistance to the incoming freshman ladies. Jim Manes, Paul Helvey, Jerry McFadden and I rented a house near Mac's Driven-In Cafe a few blocks from campus. I had a self-induced policy my senior year never to date the same girl twice in a row to avoid the "Senior Sweats." For some reason during one's senior year if you went with the same person for a period of time, you would end up married. I knew financially and emotionally marriage was not possible. My goal was to be at least 25 years old and financially independent before marriage.

Jim and I bet the other would be the first not to have a date every night of the week. Walking someone to her dorm as the SUB was closing would count as a date. Jim would start dating only Mardy Yarbrough. He lost the bet when Mardy went on a band trip. I decided to keep up the idea, which I did until March. I had a date with Doris Scott for Saturday night. A few of us were sitting around that afternoon and decided to go to Clovis. So much for my string of dates. Some students of the fairer sex would use the excuse that they had to wash their hair when they did not want to accept a date. Doris was mostly a good friend and had recently broken up with a steady boyfriend. Therefore, I told her over the phone that I needed to wash my hair and could not make it. I had a flat top haircut. *Big mistake, I was black balled in her dorm.*

All of us roommates were elected by our class as the four candidates for the Senior Beau. Paul would be elected by the total student body as the Senior Yucca Beau.

A few weeks after school started, Jim and I decided to rent a very small apartment over a small single car garage. The "penthouse" cost us $35/month including utilities. We received one free meal by working in the ENMU cafeteria. We could get sandwiches at the SUB cafe at noon from the student coeds that only wanted a milkshake. If you had a meal ticket you could eat in the cafeteria or in the SUB and get a sandwich, chips and a milk shake. The ladies did not want the sandwich, so we feasted. To say money was tight was an understatement.

During the Christmas holidays, I returned to the roughnecking job. This time on the day shift. We left for the rig at 5 am and returned at 5 pm. The winter weather was fierce. You could not touch metal without gloves because your hands would stick. Sometimes the rain with winds would come down at 45 degrees. Not fun to be on the derrick.

Irvin Smith and I would head for Hobbs in the evening to attend a different party each night. Sometimes we returned just in time for me to go to work. We had met two girls at one of the early parties and continued to see them at subsequent parties. One of the parties was hosted by Lynn and Sharron Madera. At some point of the evening, the girl that I had been seeing at each party was sitting on a sofa on my left and Lynn on my right. Both thought I was supposed to be their date for the evening. To escape the awkward dilemma, I started to get the family Chihuahua drunk. *Not my best idea.* I was chasing the dog on my hands and knees until bumping into two legs. The dog had run between the legs of Lynn's father, a 6-foot 5-inch muscular man who had just returned from the movies with her mother. *More awkward.* He picked up the dog and said, "I think you need to go outside." Soon after, because Irvin and I were in poor shape, Lynn and Irvin's "date" helped us to his car with the intention of driving us to Eunice but went back in the house for coats. They returned to discover the car had escaped. Irvin had "come to" and slid behind the steering wheel. He told me the next day that he straddled the white line of the two-lane road for the 20-mile trip to Eunice with his foot in the carburetor.

On the last day of work, I had a very severe pain in my lower abdomen. I found myself in one room of the six bed Eunice hospital.

The doctor said it was an appendix attack and he should remove it immediately. I pleaded with him to allow me to return to college until finals were over in three weeks or I would lose the whole semester. He agreed if I would not walk anywhere. I discovered that dancing caused no stress, but walking did. I maintained my conditioning on the SUB dance floor. I arranged for all my tests to be on Monday and Tuesday of test week. After the last final test on Tuesday I drove, fast as always, the 130 miles straight to the Eunice hospital. They immediately operated at 5 pm with Mom, a nurse, in the operating room. Mom had insisted on an anesthesiologist from Texas. Turned out to be a great idea, as I crashed on the table. A pathologist in Dallas, after examining my appendix, confirmed the doctor's opinion that it would have ruptured within 24 hours. The following Saturday two coeds drove to Eunice to visit me in the hospital. The doctor turned them away. He did not want me exposed to anything. I was not happy with his decision until coughing and feeling the pain. *Good doctor.*

The Natatorium had been dedicated during homecoming as planned. I felt some pride that ENMU had taken our committee recommendation from Leaders Retreat. Swimming was my sport. During an intramural meet swimming the 200-yard free style for TKT, I was about a pool length ahead of everyone. On the last leg, I took in some water and survived by hanging on the side of the pool gagging. *Again, not one of my finest moments.*

The Kappa Delta Alpha sorority sponsored the "White Rose" formal ball each year for all Greek organizations. At some point in the evening, they would form two columns with members facing one another in their white gowns. Holding long stem white roses, they formed a tunnel-like approach to a throne for the "Most Eligible Bachelor." My senior year the sorority selected me and announced my name at the ball. It was an unexpected surprise and emotion filled walk through the tunnel to sit on the throne. *Life is good.*

The student Press club sponsored a nightclub atmosphere event each year off campus at a place with a stage and a different theme. It was one of my favorite events. Men wore a coat and tie and dates were dressed in evening attire. The tables had red and white checkered tablecloths with a candle in a booze bottle as a center piece. The entertainment consisted of several performances on the stage. Our senior year the theme was a South Pacific club called the "Bamboo Club." My date that night was a coed that I failed to tell how much she meant to me when pressed two weeks earlier. To give her an answer seemed to be a commitment that I was not in a position to follow through on. Before going in the club, she informed me this would be our last date. She was one of the performers on stage, but her planned performance was a secret. She sang, "I'm Gonna Wash That Man Right Outa My Hair" from South Pacific. *Stop laughing, it was not funny!* No amount of groveling would change her mind. She had given up on this idiot. The good news is that she married a friend of mine. They were Camelot reincarnated and were fortunate to find each other.

(Left to right) Kathy Murphy, Hobbs, "Best Pledge," Ernest Colin, Eunice, "Most Eligible Bachelor," and Doris Scott, Causey, "Most Outstanding Member."

I was elected Vice-President of TKT. In the spring the Greek organizations received the Board of Regents approval to petition national Greek organizations for affiliation on campus. As a result, we four TKT officers drove to Texas Tech and visited several of their fraternities. One fraternity stood out as the right fit for TKT. We recommended TKT petition that fraternity the next fall. Many TKT members graduated, leaving a different makeup of members. They chose a different fraternity that appeared to me as being more interested in just having a good time.

Near the end of the senior year, Irvin Smith had purchased a

1959 Ford convertible at an auction in Lubbock, Texas at a very good price. A week later he spotted a 1959 Buick convertible he wanted. He called to see if I wanted the Ford. I did and arranged a loan with payments to start a month after graduation with nothing down.

Robert Pendergraft, my engineering counselor who had to sign my curriculum each semester, insisted I take Elements of Meteorology, taught by James Rowan, against my objections. Having heard that he could be talked into giving a higher grade, it was the only class I ever cut or that did not receive my normal 110% focus. Two days before graduation, I requested to meet him in his office. I inquired about my grade. He said I would receive an F. I informed him this would prevent my graduation. He proceeded to tell me that he had talked to other teachers about me and did not understand why I did so poorly in his class. He then started lecturing me that if I had to do things like roughnecking and other hard labor maybe I would appreciate the opportunity before me. I did not reveal I had done those things to get through college. He then asked me what I needed to walk across the stage. I said a D, but a C would be nice. He said flip a coin for a C or D. I did and it rolled around behind the lounge chair he was sitting in. Mr. Rowan asked what came up. I was faced with a dilemma; would he get up and look if I said a C. Wisely, I was honest and said a D. He dismissed me saying, "I will think on it." I got a D. Five years later, when taking flying lessons, I would regret not studying to get an A. *Stupid once again.*

By some miracle, I walked across the stage with a BS in Engineering and in Math as well as a minor in Physics. I received letters from family with congratulations. Reading Mom's letter still brings tears to these eyes. She could not have given me a better present, for that one still lives.

It seems like a good idea to attempt to express what the last four years did for me. They would be my best four years. I arrived on campus alone, very shy and unsure of myself. Looking back, while the academics were important, what the students gave me wittingly or unwittingly was critical to any success during my career and beyond. Lifelong female and male friendships were made with students that were leaders and standouts in their own right. A classier group of students who each excelled in their chosen field could not be found. Reading notes in the ENMU yearbooks jogged my memory and confirmed how many outstanding individuals became good friends. *I am the luckiest person to walk through life.*

Chapter IX - 1960–1963

I had considered joining the Navy to become a pilot just before graduating. I was willing to sign up for three years to get a commission, but not four years to be a pilot. Although not known at the time, I would likely have found myself in Vietnam before the four years was completed. If I had joined the Navy, my journey through life would have been totally different. These thoughts never occurred to me at this juncture of my life.

The reality of making a living was staring me in the face. I discovered that graduating from an unaccredited engineering college made finding an engineering job a challenge. Companies wanting engineers visited campuses such as Texas Tech. The other reality was that petroleum companies near Eunice had no openings. With a car payment due in a month and being broke, I started roughnecking again on the same rig as before. After six weeks with a little money, I visited Houston, Texas to look for a job. I was offered two engineering opportunities at a large petroleum company. One was in the USA with a monthly salary of $300 with no overtime pay and I would be required to work at least 80 hours per week. The other was in Saudi Arabia with a salary of $400 with no overtime pay working at least 100 hours per week. Both jobs required me to serve for two years as a roughneck and roustabout. It did not matter to them that I had already done that work. I did not like Houston. Out of money, I returned to Eunice.

Before Houston, while roughnecking, I arranged for someone on a different shift to also work my shift for two days on the Fourth of July. I returned the favor so he could have two days off. Jim Manes, who had accepted a teaching position in the Alamogordo school system, and I headed to Ruidoso, New Mexico to celebrate in my Ford convertible with the top down. We were cool dudes. No motel rooms were available anywhere near Ruidoso. We drove to Alamogordo, still no luck. We decided to sleep in a city park in the car. Forgetting the back seat was not very wide because it was a convertible I said, "Dibs on the backseat." This dummy did not get much sleep.

After returning from Houston I applied for a job at a bank in Hobbs. They required all candidates to take an all-day test. We would hear who was to be selected within a few days. At that time, they told me I had the highest score and was too intelligent to be considered.

Have to wonder about banks.

I then applied for an assistant project engineering job at a construction company that was tripling the size of a Skelly Oil gas plant just south of Eunice. I would become the project engineer before the job was completed the following May. My mechanical engineering, drafting, and surveying classes would be put to use.

During that summer, I dated Lynn, "the snob" that I met about two years earlier. She was a student at the University of Arizona and home for the summer. She had matured significantly and was certainly not a snob anymore. I had met her parents under better conditions than at the past Christmas party at her house. Having dropped by her home one day, I visited with her mother, a real lady, while Lynn was practicing the piano and discovered she was a great pianist. She had not told me she played the piano. I already knew she was a straight A student and had a sense of humor. At the end of the summer Lynn asked if she should return to college. I had begun to care a lot for her but was not willing to make the commitment her question implied. In spite of my fondness and the family millions, I suggested she would be wise to finish her education. I returned to the ENMU homecoming and took a student, Patsy Shirley, to the game and dance.

In the fall, I would mostly date Kay George from Hobbs. She had been a cheerleader at ENMU but was laying-out the fall semester. Zetia George, who I thought hung the moon at ENMU, was her sister. The Eunice HS wanted to use my gorgeous convertible to carry the Homecoming Queen to the middle of the football field before the game started. I had a date with Kay that night and we arrived at the stadium a little late to find the troops were close to panic. Nevertheless, everything went well. Kay and I went to the VFW hall after the game. She had to drive us to her home on the west side of Hobbs. She headed my car towards the highway going into town, slid me behind the wheel, put the transmission in drive and said, "Go home." She would tell me later that I kept changing shoulders on the road going into Hobbs. The next morning Mom made the comment, "You must have had a good time last night." How did she know? Then I saw my car parked in the middle of the front yard. Never had parked there before.

I received notice in October from the "draft board" to be at the county courthouse in Lovington to go to Ft. Bliss by El Paso for a physical. Nine of us boarded a Greyhound Bus to El Paso where we were to stay in the YMCA. I met an engineering graduate of Texas Tech and we headed to Juárez to party. Feeling no pain, we did not have the two cents required to cross over into the USA. The gate on the pedestrian side of the bridge going into Mexico was locked. We looked across the road to the pedestrian side of the bridge going into the USA. The guard had his feet up and was catching some z's. We climbed over the locked gate on the Mexico entrance to get into El Paso. We made it to the YMCA in time for our fellow draft board travelers to throw us in cold showers before making the bus trip out to Ft. Bliss at 6 am. After going through the physical, we were required to take a written test. By this time, I was sobering up and had a hangover. I laid my head on the desk during the instructions and fell asleep. I woke to see the others taking the test. I sped through the test not reading several of the multiple-choice questions. Before boarding the bus, they told us whether or not we had passed the physical. I had expected to fail the physical portion and be declared 4-F, thereby not eligible for the draft. I was told I made the highest score on the written test. *I should not have read all test questions on tests in college.* I had told my bus-mates that I expected to fail on the way out to Ft. Bliss. The last to get on the bus, I was asked if I passed. They all laughed when I gave them the bad news. I sat next to Joe Gill, a star football halfback from ENMU, who had also been in TKT. Joe said, "I was also surprised when being declared 4-F."

When the Lea County bunch arrived back in Lovington, we notified the draft board lady that we had all passed. She said, "You would be drafted into the US Army in about two months. If you want to do something different, you needed to act." To be drafted meant spending two years in the Army, two years of active reserves and two years inactive reserves. The Army Reserves had a six months program that consisted of serving six months of active duty in the Army and 5-1/2 years of active reserves.

I went by the US Army Reserve unit in Hobbs with the intention of joining the six-month program they offered. The retired warrant officer there tried to find a record of my New Mexico National Guard service. While looking, he called the draft board lady and told her of my intention to join the reserves. He asked her to lose my file until my records were found. Five months later, they had no luck finding my record in Santa Fe or anywhere else. He suggested I sign up for the full six-month program. I did. This would force them to make a decision. They stated I would not have to serve the six-months of active Army duty because of prior service and to resubmit the application with six years in active reserves without the active Army duty portion. I did. They rejected that submittal stating I had only sign up for three years increments of service in the National Guard, so I only needed to sign up for that amount. I did. They accepted this application in June which was a year after college that included seven months of trying to escape the draft. I was headed to Colorado to look for a job when Mom got the news. The retired warrant officer told her, "If he makes it back to go to the two-week camp at Ft. Bliss with them, he was in. Otherwise Skipper will be drafted." The unit would caravan from Hobbs to Ft. Bliss in very slow Army vehicles. I returned and asked the captain of the unit if I could arrive at Ft. Bliss a day late because I was scheduled to be best man in a wedding. He agreed. I was determined not to miss being best man in Jim Manes' marriage to Mardy Yarbrough. It was to be one of the greatest honors I have experienced. Both are outstanding as individuals and as a couple.

The evening I arrived only one soldier, Tom (not real name), was in the barracks. The rest had gone to Juárez, Mexico. Having a car, Tom and I headed for Juárez. The first bar we went in was all but empty. We decided to go to the bar next door after only a few swallows of beer. Taking the bottles with us we were confronted by two policemen. They asked us to give them the beer. Tom did, I asked, "Why?" *Wrong response.* They put me in a police car, took me to the police station and put me in jail. Fearing the US Army MPs would find my name among the incarcerated, I made up an alias. The jail cell faced an open courtyard with corrugated tin strapped to the door to keep the courtyard light out of the cell. The cell walls were very high with no roof. There were 27 Mexicans in the cell leaving no place to stand much less sit or squat. The curb-like latrine with a drain was occupied by inmates curled up and asleep. Three inmates immediately threw me in the back and said to stay there. I assumed that it was a good idea to follow their instructions. I had, over a period of time, managed to squat against the back wall. Soon I decided the Army stockade was a better idea. I advanced to the door with the corrugated tin and pounded on it, requesting to make a phone call. My three new friends tossed me to the back of the cell again and said to be quiet and stay there or I would never leave the cell. I believed them. After about two hours the cell door was opened and a guard hollered, "Cloleum." Hoping this was close enough to my name, I darted out of the cell. He escorted me to the station main lobby and said I was free to go. Others in our reserve unit had paid my fine of $15. The authorities had told them I was charged with having open beer on the street, hitting an officer, and resisting arrest. Only one was accurate. The friends were able to describe me by my gold tooth. *Thank you, Mr. Dentist.* They had bumped into Tom, who I had just met that day, in a bar and asked where I was. He told them and continued partying.

Mom and my sister, Nancy, had gone to New Jersey for the summer, a year after my graduation. At the same time, I ventured to Denver, Colorado looking for an engineering job. I arrived there with $20 and a car payment due at the end of the month. In my car were all my belongings. After sleeping in the car the first night and shaving in a ratty service station bathroom, I called Dick Billeisen, a fraternity buddy from college, who lived in the area. His mother answered the phone and told me to come right over. They had a large home and she insisted I stay with them until a job was found. *Lovely lady.*

I had heard that Patsy Shirley went to work for Beech Aircraft in Boulder. Not having her contact information, I called Beech and asked for her. She took the call and I asked if she knew of any openings and gave her Dick's telephone number. Shortly, Patsy called to say she had set up an interview for me the next day, Wednesday. During the interview, they made me an offer paying $3/hour for an engineering position that would start on Monday at the Beech Aircraft Research and Development facility in the same group where Patsy was employed. Later I learned she told them we were cousins. She was so well liked I was offered the engineering job. When discovering we were not cousins, they would tease her about having a kissing cousin. *She did know how to kiss!*

Patsy was living with family friends, Chuck and Wanda Garman, from New Mexico. Her parents were close life-time friends with Wanda's parents. By September, she would get her own apartment a few blocks from the University of Colorado campus. Several years later the Garmans would move to Huntsville, Alabama and Chuck would continue to work for Beech Aircraft.

On Thursday, I looked all over Boulder for a $1/day bed. The only bed available was a canvas army cot under a sewer pipe located about two feet above the cot. Adjacent to the University of Colorado campus, I spotted a sign "room for rent" in a new building. I knocked on the door to find out the room was taken. However, he said the two guys in the other duplex apartment were looking for a roommate. They were only there for summer school and later would drop their courses before finals. After telling them my financial situation and that I would not get paid for three weeks, they said, "No problem. We can split the rent the following month. We have a charge account at a Mom & Pop grocery nearby and we will clear the balance. Then we can split the bill three ways at the end of each month." They wanted to have a celebration party because I was moving in the next day, Friday. They asked if I knew anyone to ask to the party. I said, "Not really." No problem, they volunteered, that they were in with five sororities and would have me a date. The dates I had during this time were all attractive, filthy rich with lousy personalities. I had been spoiled at ENMU. These guys partied every night until after I went to work in the morning. After six weeks, we were evicted by the landlady. They headed to Las Vegas to celebrate. I found a new roommate from work.

The first project that my boss, Travis Durr, assigned me was to test the pitch and yaw actuators for the Atlas missile. They had been failing for two months and they could not determine why. They were using an arm with the correct moment of inertia to simulate the rocket engines. I decided to design a disk with the same moment of inertia and had it made in the manufacturing division. The actuators started passing. They thought I must be a genius. I never have figured out why it worked.

Irvin Smith visited from New Mexico. We entered the Sink (student beer hangout, you only had to be 18 years old to drink 3.2 beer). Just before us, four boys were allowed in that were likely 15 years old. We were asked for our ID to verify our age. Go figure, we were 23 years old. I never carried a wallet, so I could not enter. I had been intent on showing Irvin what the big time was like. *Kind of embarrassing.*

I had restricted my dating to one real New Mexico young lady, Patsy. A wise change and adventure. We enjoyed live folk music popular in Boulder and dancing to the great tunes from the 1950s, especially Chuck Berry. We joined the Beech mixed bowling league. While I carried a higher average, I remember one-night Patsy bowled 214 while I sweated trying to break a hundred. I never bowled 200. We both waterskied every day after work on a private lake with a gentleman from work who had a hydroplane. Snow fed the lake, therefore we quickly learned to ski without getting wet. The lake had a slalom course setup which was challenging. Patsy's parents, Ebb and Lucille, visited in the fall and we drove through Estes Park and Two-Mile Highway to Rocky Mountain National Park. Great parents, Patsy drew the best of the best at birth. We occasionally attended St. John's Episcopal Church in Boulder. Patsy was raised in a small Baptist Church in Monument, New Mexico. Not having attended an Episcopal Church before, she asked if I would take her. *This would be a first for me escorting a date to a church.*

I returned to ENMU for Homecoming. Jim Manes remembers me introducing the "Twist" dance to the campus. I was introduced to a member of the national fraternity that TKT chose as their replacement. He said, "Oh you're that guy, you're a legend." My towel costume at shipwreck evidently became a legend. Several of us were riding around and I kept talking about how great Boulder was. Finally, Irvin said firmly, "We have heard enough." That's what good friends do when one steps out of line. I will never forget <u>why</u> he chastised me. *Great friend.*

I drove to Eunice for Thanksgiving. Irvin Smith and I drove to Juárez, Mexico to get inexpensive booze. Before leaving work at Beech Aircraft, several people requested I pick up gallon containers of booze they wanted. Irvin and I smuggled 30 gallons and loaded them in my Ford's trunk. It took working all night; we were tired. The booze barely fit in the trunk and the back bumper was nearly dragging. On the way out of El Paso, we picked up a hitchhiking solider and asked if he minded driving. About halfway to Carlsbad, there was a roadblock where the Border Patrol was checking for illegal immigrants. The solider stopped, Irvin and I pretended to be asleep. The Border Patrol asked the solider to open the trunk, he said, "This is not my car." The officer looked at the sleeping beauties and said, "Go on." We dodged a bullet as the booze had no US tax stamps. *Isn't luck wonderful?*

I dropped Irvin in Eunice and headed to Boulder. About 11 pm, just south of Colorado Springs, the car turned into the median of the four-lane highway hitting a tree head-on just inside the driver headlights. The large tree did not shed a leaf even though the car was going about sixty. I broke my second toe on the left foot when stomping on the brake as I hit the tree. The bolt on the brake petal nailed my toe. Otherwise, I was fine but very sore for a week. The driver's door was jammed, so I quickly went out the passenger door to check on the cargo. Nary a drop was lost. I hid the booze across the highway in a field of high grass. There had been no traffic. The first cars would not stop to help. Finally, one stopped, and I asked him to call the police at the first possibility. Two hours later, a slow driving State Patrolman stopped and told me to get in his car. He took some notes. He never asked me if I was okay or any other questions. After finishing his note taking, he said a wrecker was on the way and for me to get out. He drove off. I caught a ride with the wrecker to a little town three miles up the road. I told the driver the name of the *nice* patrolman and the judge listed on the two tickets the patrolman had asked me to sign. He said, "The patrolman and the judge were the worst in the state." He volunteered that nothing was open in the town. He said the laundromat used to be open at night, but because of teens, they now locked it up. He pulled into the junk yard, lowered the car and went home. There was a telephone booth a few feet from my car. I called Patsy to ask her to pick me up. Being very cold, I retrieved two army blankets from my car and curled up in the phone booth. It was about 90 miles to Boulder. She arrived in her VW Bug. The front-end trunk of the VW held three gallons, we loaded most in the back seat to the ceiling to be covered with blankets and the remainder at my feet and on my lap. We arrived in Boulder in time to go to work. Fellow workers immediately took their booze. *A memorable Thanksgiving.* The insurance adjuster's brother-in-law owned a body shop, so the car was not totaled. The repair work took months and never was right.

Beech closed the facility for the Christmas Holidays, so Patsy and I went to New Mexico. When we returned to work, the whole department (60 people) was immediately laid off, including Patsy, except for me. She returned to Monument, New Mexico to work for Amerada Petroleum where her father, Ebb, worked. I would not see her again until March.

During the winter I would learn to snow ski. One day Dick Billeisen and I would ski in blizzard conditions with the high temperature of minus 20 degrees. We had to peel the snow off our faces at the bottom of a run before getting back on the ski lift. We nursed wine skins riding up the chair lift, which did little for the cold. There was almost no one skiing that day. *Great day.*

I was starving at Beech and received an offer that would be a huge boost to the pocketbook. The job was in Moses Lake, Washington on the Titan I missile sites. After returning home to visit family and Patsy, I headed to Washington. I stopped in Los Alamos, New Mexico to visit Harlan and Jan Averitt and other ENMU friends. They had a great welcoming party. On the way to Moses Lake, there was a massive winter storm starting in New Mexico and continuing to Moses Lake. I would push snow with the bumper all the way for three days. I had to report to work on a Monday. I was crossing over Deadman Pass just south of Pendleton, Oregon and ruined a tire on top of the pass and had no spare. Do you know how long a convertible stays warm? After getting the tire off the car, I waited for a vehicle to come by. A few hours later a 1938 Plymouth, with cardboard in the passenger window, stopped. The young couple said they had closed Deadman pass some time ago. They had persuaded the police to let them cross because the young preacher had to conduct a service somewhere. The tire and I rode down the mountain in the back seat to Pendleton. They dropped me at a truck stop. The owner said the new Sears tire was ruined, but there was a small Sears store that might stock the fully warranted tire. I had told him I had less than $2 dollars that I had been saving for gas to make sure I could get to Moses Lake. We went by a used tire place which did not have the right size but one that would fit on the rim. He paid $3 for the tire. Back at his truck stop, he mounted the tire on the rim. Meanwhile they had opened the pass. An 18-wheeler picked me and the tire up and dropped us at my car. I had to remove a wheel from the front to put it on the back and mount the wrong size tire on the front to prevent the rear-end from being damaged. Doing that with a bumper jack on a slope in the snow is a challenge. I stopped at the truck stop to pick up my tire and settle up. He would not take a check but told me to mail what it was worth. He did not trust checks, but people never failed to send money. Then he gave me $2 and said, "Stop at a grocery store, buy a quart of milk and a package of donuts." He knew I had not eaten since the previous day. Of course, I followed his suggestion. Late on Saturday night, I arrived in Moses Lake and stopped at the first motel with a vacancy sign on. I was allowed to stay without paying money.

They knew I would receive an advance per diem check on Monday.

On the new job, it was mandatory to work a minimum of 12 hours/day seven days a week. The job would be demanding, which I liked. I was assigned to one of the missile sites and later would become the Silo Captain for one missile launch site.

The Titan I was the United States' first nuclear, multistage, intercontinental ballistic missile (ICBM). The propellant was the very volatile liquid oxygen and kerosene. The silos were nine stories deep below ground covered with massive doors to withstand a nuclear attack. There were retractable work platforms on every level to conduct maintenance and load fuel. The missile had to be fueled, then raised above ground to be launched. After the installation was completed, my task was to supervise union personnel to activate and test the hydraulic control work platforms, hydraulic doors, logic controls and to ensure the launch system would raise the missile. Seems simple enough but was not. There were many sensors, hydraulic cylinders, control valves and pumps that had to work in series and in sync. A control room (about 10' by 12') housed hundreds of relays to operate the system. Today the control room would be a chip less than the size of my small fingernail. As a Silo Captain, I supervised other engineers. The work could be dangerous. One day I was walking across a 10-inch-wide beam in the center of the silo, as I had many times, and panicked. Straight down nine stories was a concrete ridge. This time, in the middle of the stroll, I couldn't move. It seemed like an eternity before I was able to squat down and wrap my arms around the beam and slither to the beam end and safety. I was not afraid of heights and have no idea why I panicked. Some were killed or maimed before we "turn-keyed" the system to the Air Force.

I had been in Moses Lake about six weeks when a light came on in this unconscious brain. At this point of my life, I was finally able to support a wife financially and emotionally. Patsy was more than I deserved, and, to my amazement, I finally realized I loved her. Sometimes I am a slow learner. She was beautiful through and through, highly intelligent (she had not yet figured that out, but I had), athletic, humorous, full of life, passionate, a truly good person in every respect, and to top it off, a great dancer.

Even though only 24 years old and never discussing marriage with Patsy or myself, I called and asked her to marry me. She said yes, to my surprise. I then asked when she could join me. She said, "Two weeks' notice was required at work." Before she arrived, I had picked out engagement and wedding rings and rented a fully furnished two-bedroom cottage on the lake with a dock and ski-boat. Patsy loved to water ski. I asked my boss if I could take a few days off for my honeymoon. He said, "No, the work schedule was mandatory." He made it clear calling in sick for three days, but no more, was not a problem and offered congratulations.

I picked Patsy up at the Seattle Airport the day before Good Friday. Her weight was perfect when last seeing her in early March. She was now scary skinny to my surprise, which worried me. She recovered. Not yet married, the two bedrooms came in handy. We were married on the Monday following Holy Week, April 23, 1962 at St. Martins Episcopal Church.

The only attendants at our wedding were our witnesses, Ben and Beverly Snodgrass, who we knew in Boulder, and the priest. Ben was also working in Moses Lake. Due to nerves, we both shook during the service until we were announced as Mr. and Mrs. Ernest Wellwood Colin, Jr. We were ready to share a wonderful journey.

We headed on a happy, joyful ride 300 miles to Vancouver, Canada for two nights in a honeymoon suite on the 17th floor of a grand hotel. The room had a dining room, living room, kitchen and bedroom. It was decorated with new Early American furniture, very popular at the time.

We arrived just in time for the last seating in a fine restaurant on the top floor. The formally attired waiter with white gloves asked us for identification when I ordered a bottle of champagne. I was flattered, but Patsy was two weeks short of being 21. He refused to serve her. I asked if he would bring me two glasses, he smiled and agreed. After finishing a great meal with toasts to our future, we returned to the room.

The next day we visited the gardens in Stanley Park, rode a ferry to Victoria Island and back. The following day we left early to return to Moses Lake via the World's Fair in Seattle. Because the Fair had just opened and tourist season had not started, we were able to visit every exhibit except the Space Needle (there was a line). It was a fantastic and magical honeymoon.

We would water ski often and host fish-fries. Sometimes we would invite several people over without having fish to cook. One could catch more than enough brim and crappie in 30 minutes from our dock to feed an army. We joined another recently married couple, who grew up in Washington, on a camping trip to Lake Wenatchee. We also spent a weekend where they grew up in the tri-city area of Richmond. *Great times in Washington.*

The job on the Titan I was drawing to a close about five months after arriving. I interviewed with Lockheed in Palo Alto, California and with Paul Hardeman, Inc on the Titan II missile sites. Lockheed was stingy and Hardeman was not.

Near the end of our stay in Moses Lake, I sold the 1959 Ford convertible (should have been totaled) for what I had paid Irvin Smith for it two years earlier. I purchased a demo 1962 Corvair with the Ford money. We loaded all our belongings in the car and headed for New Mexico with $3,000 in the bank. The government needed wheelbarrows to pay those who worked on the sites. The USA desperately needed the ICBM's in order to be operational to have a strong position when dealing with the Soviet Union.

I dropped Patsy at her parents' home in Monument, New Mexico, and I headed to Davis-Monthan Air Force Base near Tucson, Arizona for two weeks of training on the Titan II propellant transfer system.

The Titan II missile ICBM was the successor to the Titan I with double the payload. Titan II carried the largest single warhead of any American ICBM. Unlike the Titan I, it used hydrazine-based hypergolic (when two propellants come in contact with each other they will ignite without help) propellant which was storable and reliably ignited. This reduced time to launch and permitted it to be launched from inside the silo. The missile was always loaded with fuel and ready to launch from its silo by simply opening the doors. Their hypergolic nature made them dangerous to handle; a leak could (and did) lead to explosions, and the fuel was highly toxic. The training at Davis-Monthan Air-force Base prepared us to handle the toxic propellants and familiarized us with the system. Our task was to take over the transfer system after construction crews had finished installation. We were to clean the piping system including pumping stations located at the bottom of the nine-story deep silo, dry-test, and wet-test the complete propellant system. The wet test included loading the actual propellants from headers above ground that were connected to tanker-trucks into the simulated missile tanks in the silo. Running one hundred yards in 120-degree temperatures near Tucson in a Self-Contained Atmospheric Protective Ensemble (SCAPE) suit within a specific time was miserable. Because the suits were heavy and I could not breathe, it seemed like I sweated a quart in the 100 yards.

Meanwhile, back in Monument, Patsy totaled the VW bug she had sold her Dad when we married. Seat belts were unheard of at the time. In a wet 90 degree curve the VW rolled, the driver's door opened and stuck in the ground, pivoting the car over her as she was dumped in a mud puddle. She did not call me in Tucson because she did not want to interrupt the training with me rushing to New Mexico. It seemed she was most upset because the bruising had faded before I returned.

We headed to Little Rock Air Force Base in Arkansas for a new adventure. Because the missile 18 site construction housing was not available in Jacksonville, Arkansas or Little Rock, we finally found an unfurnished rundown duplex in Jacksonville. We had to scrub everything and paint walls, ceilings and all cabinets. We bought furniture including appliances.

Not long after getting settled, Patsy's mother, Lucille, encouraged her to divorce me on the grounds I would turn out like my Dad. Mom, unwittingly thinking we were all family now, told Lucille that my Dad had died an alcoholic and more. Big mistake. Lucille kept insisting. Patsy assured Lucille that would never happen to me. She further added that she had made her bed and she was going to enjoy sleeping in it. Patsy did have a sense of humor. The subject of divorce never came up again.

The company believed two teams would be required to conduct all 18 sites. There were two other test engineers heading up dry-test teams. One had been assigned to test the first missile site that was ready. The second missile site was assigned to the other engineer. They were expected to finish a site within two weeks. To my surprise, I was supposed to be a backup, if needed. My future employment did not look good. The first two teams had not completed their assigned sites after about six weeks when a third site was ready. On a Friday, I was told to purchase new tools for a new crew and have special tooling fabricated by Monday because I would be heading up a new team. I arrived with equipment at the site along with several union members. None of the crew had been on a missile site before or had any training. My first task was to appoint a foreman from the union guys. I picked the tallest, largest, meanest looking man with a large scar on his face to be my foreman. Figured the others would follow him. I outlined our objectives and how we would get the site ready, including performing a dry-test in preparation for a wet-test. We finished the site in two weeks. The other teams still had not finished their sites. After they finally finished their sites, those teams were laid-off. I was on my fourth site. The company decided my team under, my leadership, could easily do all sites on schedule. At some point, the foreman decided to move on to another job. By this time, I knew the crew well enough to pick a new foreman. I later had to fire him for laying out drunk for three days.

Patsy and I joined a mixed bowling group from the company. We also explored the Ozark's, fished and more. Occasionally we attended Trinity Episcopal Cathedral in Little Rock. The lady next door in our duplex unit had crawled for 48 hours across the East-West German border to freedom. She said it was so terrifying that she would not do it again. She worked in a PX, met and married a member of the US Air Force. He was currently assigned to a base in Newfoundland. She taught Patsy German and furthered her education in cooking. Her 12-year-old son and I would toss a football many days. His mother found a condom in his dresser. She asked Patsy if I would ask him about her finding it because his father was deployed. I awkwardly asked why he had the condom. A teacher had passed them out for some science project. He did not know the main use and had wondered why some of the classmates had giggled.

Near the end of the project I fired a union steward for poor performance (actually he was also sabotaging our work per instruction from the union boss to slow down the project). There was a no-strike-clause in the contract. However, the union boss asked all his stewards to resign over the weekend. Monday morning all sites were shut down as well as a dam project in northern Arkansas. The union members would be fined $100/day if working without a steward. I called in Monday when no one would enter the gate. The union boss, company head, and an Air Force General and Colonel showed up at noon to try and resolve the problem. The union boss, at one point, was about to physically attack me when the company head stepped in the way. *Good executive.* While the officers were just there to observe, the General finally asked if I would accept the union member back but not as a steward. I said, "I could not in good conscience, but if the company said to, I would live with the decision." We started back to work, and I transferred him in two weeks to a construction team. They laid him off. The subject never came up again.

In June, my talents were no longer needed on the missile sites. Paul Hartman offered me a lucrative job in Australia, however I did not want to be hopping around so was terminated. A friend, Bill Buckles, had moved to Huntsville, Alabama with his family after he was terminated in January. He was employed by Brown Engineering and working on the NASA project to go to the moon. Patsy and I planned on returning to Colorado to live. We decided to visit them in Huntsville. Bill set up an interview with Brown Engineering. I told them it would be at least three weeks before I would accept their job offer. We returned to New Mexico, Patsy stayed at her parents and I headed to Denver and Boulder with high hopes. No one was hiring. I called Huntsville to accept the job offer and started on July 23, 1963. Little did I know I would remain with them until retiring nearly 33 years later.

We could not find a motel room within 50 miles of Huntsville. We discovered from a friend, Chuck Garman, working for Beech Aircraft that Beech rented an apartment for their employees when visiting Huntsville on business trips. Chuck said we were welcome to stay there, but there was only a single bed available. No problem, after over a year, we still considered ourselves newlyweds. After a few days, we found a room at a low-level motel, the Barclay Motel. A month later we moved into Huntsville's best motel, the King's Inn on the Parkway. We would be there until they finished building one of the apartments at the University Apartments. We started attending the Episcopal Church of The Nativity.

A couple of months after moving to Huntsville, Patsy decided to go to work. She got a good secretarial job with Boeing Aircraft Company. We would now need two vehicles because our job sites were in opposite directions. I purchased a new 1964 Chevrolet pickup for hunting and fishing. Mostly I used it to help others move on weekends. Pickups were not common modes of transportation at the time. It would be decades later before I purchased a new vehicle.

I worked at Marshal Space flight Center (MSFC) on Redstone Arsenal in one of the NASA buildings (Building 4610). I shared a cubicle with Harry Butcher, Russell Booth and John Reeves. Sadly, they have died. This NASA branch of advanced technology was not yet fully staffed. My first of several assigned tasks involved zero leakage tests of hydrogen, helium, oxygen, and nitrogen. I was also asked to prepare a NASA Internal Note (widely distributed) on a thermal test conducted on the instrument section between two stages of the Saturn

V rocket. I kept asking the NASA Branch Manager for more assignments. In December, I received my first formal review receiving high marks in all categories. The Brown Engineering supervisor said, "You were not given a raise because you hired in too high." I had refused their first offer. *Later, I discovered the Personnel Department had made an error with my engineering classification. When I was processed in, they had not given me the correct engineering title. It was corrected after my transfer.* He further stated, "You are upsetting the customer by requesting more work, thereby frustrating the customer who is trying to build an empire and that does not help." I asked for a transfer.

Patsy and I traveled to New Mexico for a great Christmas. The biggest honor for me was walking my sister, Nancy, down the aisle when she married Gaylon Taylor. Bonnie was her maid of honor.

On New Year's Eve in 1963 snow started to fall about noon. Travis and Lynell Durr were to host a New Year's Eve party at their home for the Colorado crowd from the Beech Aircraft department. I had found all of them jobs that fit their engineering skills in Huntsville, except Travis. He founded TMC, a company that specialized in cleaning missile, aircraft, and space craft items. By 2 pm Travis had called all of us to come straight from work to their home or we might not make it that day. We did not go to our apartment until 5 am after 17 inches of snow had fallen. *Memorable party with good friends.*

Chapter X - 1964–1967

Before my transfer request, one task I had been assigned required a lot of time conducting research as well as extensive experiments. Not sure why I was the one getting that task unless they wanted to keep me occupied. The project was to develop empirical equations to calculate pressure drop in corrugated hose and bellows in straight and curved sections. I searched the free world archives and known Soviet information. The only article I found was by a highly respected engineer published in "Product Engineering." I disagreed with his empirical equations on several points.

The NASA Branch Manager had set up a program for two of his 30 engineers to give a presentation each Friday morning to the whole branch. This required the engineer to give a twenty-minute presentation followed by ten minutes of questions. The NASA Branch manager and others would critique the presenter's technical content, charts, grammar, vocabulary and how they fielded questions. Each week two engineers would be covered in blood. I was scheduled to give a presentation a week before my transfer. They said I could opt-out because of my leaving the branch. Although dreading my turn in the barrel, I agreed to go ahead. The presentation materials consisted of preparing 2'x3' charts to be mounted on a tripod. I hardly slept before the presentation. I scrubbed my presentation of pronouns and adverbs that were two of the biggest criticisms in the past. During the presentation, while shooting down the famous engineer, the NASA manager kept asking a new hire, a past thermodynamics professor, if I was correct when I referred to a law of physics to make a point. The professor always agreed with the point. The norm was to make the engineer bleed because of grammar, technical points, presentation material, etc. after the question answer period. The NASA manager praised me in all categories. *A first.* The effort was worth the experience, as painful as it was to prepare and dreading the moment. Then NASA delayed my transfer. I was frustrated because in 30 minutes they changed their mind about me when they had eight months to discover my potential and did not. Two months later they let me transfer after replacing me with Dale, an engineer with a master's degree working at Pratt and Whitney in West Palm Beach, Florida.

Dale had a catamaran sailboat that he raced in West Palm Beach against sailors competing in the Olympics. He had won a race against the top dog. He would race at the Lake Guntersville Yacht Club near Huntsville, with me serving as first mate. Dale's wife, Mary Jo, would become a good friend of Patsy.

I transferred into the Brown Engineering Test Laboratory in Research Park. I was able to shine there almost immediately because the engineers there did not have the right experience. The experience at Beech Aircraft fit well. The Test Laboratory purpose was to conduct reliability, vibration, shock, acoustic, high and low temperature, humidity, vacuum, hydraulic, high pressure pneumatic, cryogenic, electronic, EMF, etc. tests on components, subsystems, and systems. In the beginning, these were primarily for the Saturn I, Saturn V, Apollo, and support systems. Over time, military, aircraft, satellite, Space Lab, Shuttle, and automobile systems would be tested. I loved the variety of engineering skills that were required. I did not like the idea of focusing on a narrow engineering field.

After we moved to Huntsville, many of our colleagues from Beech Aircraft had moved to the Rocket City. They would be the center of our social circle. They all had a great sense of humor and enjoyed life. Travis Durr was a truly compassionate, charismatic, extrovert character. He knew us well in Huntsville and had been our boss at Beech. Riding with him one day and unlike him, out of the blue he said, "I have never seen anyone love someone as much as Patsy loves you." *Love is blind.*

Patsy enjoyed her job at Boeing Aircraft Company but had other plans in mind. In the spring she stopped me in the middle of the stairs in our apartment. Patsy said, "I think we should consider starting a family." This unconscious young man had never thought of the idea. However, being of sound mind and recognizing her loving, yet firm, tone and approach, I agreed. I suggested we plan on a March baby to avoid her going through a hot summer pregnancy. She liked the thoughtful idea.

Patsy was a bridge player. I was not familiar with the card game. She and Rosalind Duncan, a friend, conspired to be sure I learned. She and Fount, her husband, a retired Col., invited us to dinner. They suggested we play bridge with males against females. The wives were more experienced and serious, but we won, and I was hooked.

Alan Fount, Bonnie's husband, graduated from ENMU on May 28, 1964. They had two daughters, Shonna and Cheryl, who were diagnosed with hemophilia at ages 2-1/2 and 1-1/2, respectively. Generally, it was believed only males could have the condition. They had a severe case in each of four factors which allow blood clotting. Normally only one factor is present in hemophiliac patients. Because of medical bills, Alan would have to drop out of college. Patsy and I sent them $200 per month for several months so he could graduate. They made paying the loan off a top priority. They moved to Huntsville following graduation and stayed with us in our apartment. By October, Alan found a job in Dallas allowing him better opportunities. This also allowed significantly better care in a clinic specializing in hemophilia. Later, during blood drives, Brown Engineering employees donated at least 1,000 units of blood to Bonnie's daughters. *Their generosity was extremely important.*

Work continued to be interesting. The Test Lab was organized into three main groups: engineers, program managers, and laboratory technicians. The engineer group was headed by branch managers who had section chiefs reporting to them. The engineers reported to the section chiefs. There were two program managers. The Test Lab had two major contracts. One was with NASA's Marshall Space Flight Center (MSFC) located in Huntsville and one with Kennedy Flight Center (KFC) at Cape Canaveral. The technicians were to be headed by a foreman. I recommended Mac McCaslin for this position because the technicians were not well supervised. Mac had held an equivalent position at Beech Aircraft Company in Boulder, Colorado. He was the only Colorado friend to work in the Test Lab. He was a quiet, experienced leader who quickly righted the ship. He was also Travis Durr's best friend.

An ENMU engineering professor, Dr. Penick, had on more than one occasion told us, "The definition of an engineer was someone who could do a job for one dollar that would require two dollars to complete by anyone else." My Dad had demanded that you do a task correctly the first time. Having to redo a task was a failure. Correctly also meant a quality result. He was tough on these points. My parents and theirs instilled in their children a strong work ethic. Must be in our DNA because I see it in my children and grandchildren. The above lessons served me well throughout my career and life.

One of the Colorado group's hobbies was hunting. Of course, I joined them hunting dove, quail, ducks and geese. I did not have a shotgun so one of them loaned me one.

Each year we returned to New Mexico for Christmas. Patsy suggested we not exchange gifts in 1964. I agreed with the suggestion. On Christmas morning at her parents' home, I opened a present from her. Santa Claus had not left her a present from me. *Big mistake.* My present was a 12 gauge Browning automatic shotgun with a 30" ribbed barrel and factory recoil pad. *Women lie and men are stupid.* The gang (*no longer my friends*) had helped her pick the ideal shotgun for me knowing of the agreement and not giving me a heads-up. Patsy did not expect anything but was mostly embarrassed in front of her family for not receiving a present from me. Again, women lie. What can one say to correct a *faux pas*?

In 1965 we would outgrow our apartment. We moved into a small, three-bedroom, one bath house in February that we purchased on Kirkland St. across the street from Bill Buckles and his family. He had arranged my interview with Brown Engineering.

I was to learn from another engineer that Mac had tired of hearing engineers complaining that I received the choice assignments. He told them, "Skipper has forgotten more about testing than all the rest of you put together know." He heard no more complaints. Not so sure his statement was accurate. *Loyal friends are a wonderful thing.*

In early February Patsy stopped working at Boeing Aircraft to prepare for a new beginning and become a stay at home mother. Expecting our first child in March, Patsy's mother, Lucille, arrived a month early to help with the newborn. The doctor had predicted an early March baby. On Saturday, April 10, 1965, I was with friends scouting hunting places and had not returned until after 5:00 pm. At 3:00 pm Patsy had gone to Huntsville Hospital in labor. I would sit in a small waiting room with four folding chairs near the labor room. I cannot express the experience of sitting with my mother-in-law until our child arrived at 6:00 am Sunday morning. I must confess Patsy had a more difficult night. I had prayed for a son. Mom's maiden name died with her father and the Colin name would die unless I sired a son. When she presented me with a daughter, Paige Michelle, the tears rolled down my cheeks. I couldn't have been more thrilled. I still get emotional when thinking of that moment. The name Paige we had picked together, and I had selected Michelle as the middle name. The devil in me expressed that Paige's head looked like a Dr. Pepper bottle, Patsy's favorite drink. *Not all humor is appreciated.* Her head was elongated likely because of the difficult labor. The good news was that her head soon recovered, and she became the most beautiful baby ever. *See the photo.*

At work I was assigned the task of qualifying a large liquid-oxygen relief valve to be used at KFC in Florida. Oxygen and nitrogen have many of the same characteristics. They both have the same ability to leak through small pin holes and both liquify at minus 320 degrees. The major difference is that oxygen will explode or burn easily, and nitrogen is inert. Using liquid nitrogen as a substitute would be sufficient to qualify the value for use on ground support equipment. I was visiting with Chuck Garman, a friend from Boulder, who still worked at Beech and now lived in Huntsville. He, a cryogenics engineer, and I talked about the upcoming tests. *Cryogenics is the branch of physics dealing with the production and effects of very cold temperatures.* I discovered Beech Aircraft was going to be conducting tests on a complex nitrogen cryogenic system in Boulder. I knew designing and building an adequate test system at Brown Engineering Test Lab would be costly and require a significant amount of time. I asked if he thought we could piggy-back on their test. He said technically it was possible. I was able to arrange a subcontract to conduct the tests at Beech Aircraft, assuming I would be on site in Boulder during the test phase. The normal per diem when traveling was $16/day but $9/day when traveling more than 30 days. The company could extend the $16/day amount if the manager agreed. I was scheduled to be in Boulder for two months. The customer was fine with this but Don Martin, the Lab manager, was not. He said, "I have no issue with your going to the VP. I wish you luck." I did, which did not help. *Learned an important lesson. Bosses do not overrule their subordinates in the management chain.*

Meanwhile, I started flying lessons in a Cherokee 140. After soloing I would have fun going up each Saturday morning flying over fields doing slips and other fun things. On the way to Colorado, I dropped Paige and Patsy at her parents' house in Monument. I stopped at the ENMU campus to visit Don Smith, Irvin's brother. Don was working for an insurance company. By coincidence, we both had logged 28 hours of flight time. We drove around all afternoon sipping beer and talking about the joys of flying. He had recently married Herma Loy Elliott. She was still a student at ENMU and had been Miss New Mexico the previous year. That night we watched the Miss America pageant. Herma Loy enlightened us on the behind the scene activities and competitive nature of the contestants.

In Boulder, because college had just started, no apartments were available except one complex which only rented to students with no babies allowed. I was persistent with the apartment manager daily, promising that Paige did not cry. She finally relented allowing me to return to New Mexico to bring Patsy and five-month-old Paige to Boulder. On the way through Portales I stopped at Don Smith's home. Herma Loy answered the door and informed me that after he and I had talked about flying, he called his Dad the next morning to borrow $5,000 dollars. Don was now in flight school in Oklahoma for six months to become a commercial pilot. After graduating he would go to work for Eastern Airlines.

The two months scheduled time at Beech ballooned to eight months. Beech was having problems with the test setup. The test was finally successfully completed. Patsy became good friends with the apartment manager. When we were leaving to return to Alabama, she told Patsy that Paige was quieter and less of a problem than the students. While in Boulder we were able to snow ski regularly, a sport we both loved. During that winter the temperature reached minus 14 degrees in Huntsville but never dropped that low in Boulder.

Back in Huntsville we enjoyed being home. Apartment living was limiting, especially in winter. I had been promised a promotion to section chief as soon as an opening became available before we had gone to Boulder. I had expressed my concern about "That being out of sight being, out of mind." They said that would not happen. It did. The saying is true. However, soon an opening became available and I was promoted.

We made the usual trip to New Mexico for Christmas in 1966. Patsy and I left Paige with grandparents and headed for Ski Apache near Ruidoso. We stayed in Ruidoso at a log cabin with a fireplace. The crowds from the holidays were gone, meaning no lines at restaurants,

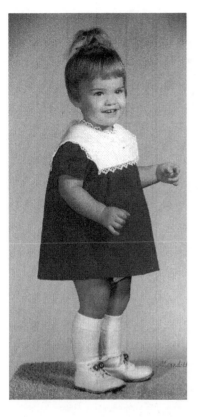

ski rental shops, ski lifts, etc. The snow condition was near perfect. On the first run at the top, Patsy started down first and after getting up to speed she did a summersault lost a ski and a contact. I saw her ski headed towards a lone pine. She was okay so I looked for the ski so she could continue skiing. Meanwhile the ski patrol arrived within a few of minutes and loaded Patsy in a basket and headed down to the lodge. I skied as fast as I could down the mountain. They beat me to the lodge. She decided to enjoy the lodge for the day. I returned to skiing and looked for her ski. That night we stopped by the rental shop in Ruidoso to explained how we lost a ski that likely went over a 1,000-foot cliff, therefore we needed to pay for it and rent another pair. The owner and his son said not to worry about the cost of the ski because it would likely show up in the spring after the thaw. If it did not, he would send us a bill. The next morning the owner and his adult son voluntarily drove the 45-minute distance to help find the ski. They found the ski in short order. Only a foot of the back of the ski was visible in deep snow and only the edge could be seen. New Mexico people are fantastic. We skied two more days and headed to Monument and children. *Life is rough.*

Patsy and I had decided that two children were the right number for us and that two years apart was best. On May 7, 1967 we were blessed with a son, Chad Wellwood. The family history suggested having a son was not likely, so when Patsy presented me with a son to carry on the family name, I was deeply moved and unexpectedly tears flowed. Prior to the birth, I would tell Patsy's mother, Lucille, that if a son was to be born then it would be named Ernest Wellwood Colin III. She was less than amused, but I let her believe this for months. *Sometimes life is fun.*

A weekend before Thanksgiving we camped at Cheaha State Park, the highest point in Alabama. We arrived in the evening and set up a tent and laid Chad (6 months old) and Paige (2-1/2 years old) down for the night. Patsy insisted, in the middle of the night, that I warm a bottle for Chad who was sleeping. It was very cold, and we had no camp stove or tent heater. I tried to gather wet wood to start a fire. I gave up to her dismay. To go back to sleep seemed the right thing to do and said, "If he wakes then I will give it another try." For the first time he slept all night. Mother nature is wonderful. In the morning water puddles had turned to ice. We cut our camping trip short.

Chaparral Missile testing was one of my projects that was interesting for an unusual reason. One of the tests consisted of conducting vibration tests on the loaded missile with a warhead in its case while at low and high temperatures. The vibration equipment would not operate at extreme temperatures. I came up with an approach that required the test be completed once started. After starting the test, a weather report stated we were in the path of a tornado on the ground 10 miles from us. I was faced with a live missile being vulnerable to becoming active and the tornado. I also knew the missile would save Army lives in the Vietnam War and MICOM our Army customer needed to field the Chaparral Missile as soon as possible. I asked the technicians to hang in hoping the tornado would lift and go over us. It did. I subsequently drove to Memphis, Tennessee and flew to New Mexico on a jet sleeping all the way, after having little sleep because of around the clock testing.

Patsy with Chad (age 7 months) and Paige (age 2-1/2 years) flew from Memphis to Hobbs, New Mexico two weeks earlier. Because of a bad storm including fog and snow, it took them 24 hours to arrive at her parents. The stewardesses were of little help and would not even warm a bottle for Chad. They had to fly on prop aircraft zig zagging from one out of the way airport to another. She ran out of diapers and bottles of milk. Several airports had closed cafes, etc. She could not resupply. Some kind fellow passengers were going to Hobbs by car from Big Springs, Texas. The next plane to Hobbs was the next morning if the weather cleared as well as no place to stay. They voluntarily asked if she would like to join them for the hundred-mile trip. She arrived exhausted and hoarse.

We had arranged a baptism service at the Episcopal mission, St. Timothy's, in Eunice on Christmas Eve. The church had been the hospital in Eunice when my appendix was removed six years before. Dr. Hanns, my surgeon, owned the hospital and had given it to the four Episcopal families when he retired. The operating room was the largest room in the six-bed hospital. The families converted the operating room into the church sanctuary. They installed beams to give a cathedral ceiling appearance and added paneling. The sanctuary was beautiful. It still amazes me that our children were baptized in the room where my appendix was removed and where I had temporarily died.

We returned via a DC-9 jet. The stewardesses could not have been more helpful to my requests, to Patsy's dismay. We arrived in Memphis to find out my pickup had been totaled. We had parked at a friend's home on the street. A load of teens going around a corner fast collided into the back of the truck shoving the bed into the cab and bending the frame. The good news was it could be driven. The other good news was that a friend in Huntsville purchased the pickup. With the insurance money and selling the beast, I came out ahead.

Brown Engineering Company had nearly 4,000 employees at the time. Most of the employees were engineers and scientists. This would change over the next few years as the NASA "moon race" need for engineers fell off. In 1967 Teledyne, Inc purchased Brown Engineering and the name was changed to Teledyne Brown Engineering (TBE). *So long to 1967, another great year for this family of four.*

Chapter XI - 1968–1971

During the latter part of the 1960s, the Test Lab would enter a new era and be transformed. The Test Lab number of employees would be reduced from 120 to 20. The two cost-plus contracts with NASA that were the mainstay of the Lab were completed. Don Martin, the Test Lab Manager, was transferred in the company and would serve with distinction in line and program management positions. Jim Hammons, one of the Lab Branch Managers, was promoted to Test Lab Manager. Jim had a classic management style. He was a quiet gentleman who made good decisions and was able to lead a group of strong, sometimes stubborn, employees with unique personalities and talents. I learned much from this good man. The engineering staff was reduced to four; Bob Hall, Charlie Gibson, me, and what's his name. "Mac" McCaslin purchased a service station and Buddy Laubenthal took his place as foreman of the technicians. A service station at that time provided full services at the gas pump and had attached garages for changing oil and much more. Much later they were replaced with convenience stores that provided self-service gas pumps.

Each engineer would wear several hats as proposal manager, program manager, project engineer, and marketer. I liked the diversity these various disciplines required. Jim gave us lots of rope and always listened to my crazy ideas. Over time we would go from two cost-plus type contracts to over 50 fixed price contracts at one time. The challenges of competing with other companies and completing contracts within the fixed price were great. One was able to let the creative juices flow. Being a hopeless optimist and lover of finding solutions that others thought were impossible, was fun.

Jim Hammons asked me to prepare the annual budget for the Test Lab, others thought this was a burden. To me it was an opportunity to discover the big picture. The budget included many items including business license fees, administration costs, facility maintenance and calibration costs, equipment, supplies, etc. The budget would define the cost of overhead applied to each hour of labor. I always was concerned with the big picture as well as details of a task. *Knowledge of the budget process would be good to have later.*

I started playing golf. Patsy showed an interest, so I surprised her with clubs, shoes, lessons, etc. for her birthday. She joined a women's league and played a lot of golf. She had also joined a women's bowling league. Patsy was a natural athlete. Nearly beat me on a par three course. *Not good for the male ego.*

The Christmas of 1968, Mom requested that Bonnie, Nancy, me and our families meet in Ramsey, New Jersey at the home of Aunt Marian, Uncle Chet and their daughter Carol. It was a memorable time. We all shared remarkable times together. The first night Patsy and I, my sisters and cousin crossed the main road and strolled down beautiful streets where the Country Club and large picturesque homes were located. Fresh snow, combined with decorated homes, reminded me of winter post cards of Vermont and New Hampshire. The laughter and joy, while catching up on our lives, cannot be expressed with words by this author. *My favorite photo of Patsy.* My aunt and uncle's large home was located on a large pond. They had skates for all adults and older children. On the pond, I believed teaching Patsy to skate would be neat. She had not ice skated before. She skated backwards like an Olympic skater and did circles around me, while my skills were severely lacking. *I must reluctantly admit she was always a better athlete.*

We all visited Grandmud at the Actors Home in Englewood, NJ with our children. Grandmud was bedridden but, true to form, she grabbed center stage as I am sure she often did during her 50 plus years on stage. She could change voices in mid-sentence from a deep Irish brogue to the opposite. Grandmud told us a story from her time of service with the USO during World War I. The actors had to wear soldiers' uniforms and were housed in Army facilities. An Army Major was assigned to escort her to the stage and deliver her back to her quarters. After her performance, he drove the jeep to an isolated area and proceeded to attempt to have his unwanted way with her. She then said, "I should warn you that I have syphilis." The major quickly returned her to her quarters. As she walked to the door, she turned and pointed to the Actors Patch on the upper arm of her uniform. Grandmud was always a treat to experience. She had served for several months and was on the last ship returning soldiers home.

Because of my cryogenic experiences, Jim assigned me a NASA Request for Proposal (RFP) to test a large liquid hydrogen (LH2) flying saucer looking vessel. The "flying saucer" was designed for the purpose of testing large seals for LH2 fuel tanks on Saturn missiles. Hydrogen becomes a liquid when its temperature is reduced to 423 degrees below zero. Hydrogen is colorless, odorless, highly flammable and the flames are not visible to the eye. I proposed installing a 2,000-gallon tank and surrounding it on three sides with an earthen berm 30 yards from the Lab. The open side with no berm would be away from the Lab, so if the tank or test item blew up, the explosion would be directed elsewhere. We were awarded the contract. *Now the fun began.*

The facility would have to be approved by NASA before they delivered LH2. I designed and supervised the installation of a concrete foundation to support the tank, adjoining concrete pad for the test article, necessary piping system, a 30-foot stack to vent hydrogen from the relief valve, and the berm. The vent stack was needed because the tank would be over pressurized due to the surrounding tank's external temperature relative to the tank's internal cold LH2. The relief valve would allow hydrogen gas to bleed off through the stack keeping the tank pressure at an acceptable level. I had a K bottle of helium gas connected to the stack in the event of a stack fire. By letting the inert helium into the stack, the fire could be snuffed out. After the 2,000-gallon tank, plumbing, berm, etc. were installed and ready to receive LH2, I called NASA to inspect the site. The NASA personnel were impressed as they said, "This is the safest and best designed LH2 facility they had seen and that it was better than any system located at MSFC." *My chest stuck out a little.* Within a couple of days, they delivered a load of LH2. One morning a technician came to me a little out of breath to inform me there was a stack fire. Likely, lightning during the night had ignited the escaping gas. I asked if he had opened the helium valve to snuff out the fire. He said, "No way I'm going down behind the berm to the tank and stack." You could not see the flame but could see the heat waves above the stack. I walked down to the tank and opened the helium valve. The fire went out as I had designed it. No big deal. *The good news is that they thought I was brave.* I did not think so because I was confident my design was sound. *Besides, I am immortal.*

Soon after we were ready to receive the test article, NASA decided to test the "flying saucer" at one of their facilities. The good news is they covered all our cost and we had expanded the Test Lab capability. The very bad news was that two technicians were killed at NASA when attempting to test the item and it exploded. Based on the reason determined as the cause for the accident, that would not have happened at our facility. I certainly wished they would have let us do the testing, not for the extra profit, but to prevent the needless loss of life and family suffering.

The USS Pigeon was the lead ship of her class of submarine rescue ships. The Alabama Dry Dock and Shipbuilding Co., Mobile, Alabama launched the ship in 1969. Pigeon was the first seagoing catamaran warship built for the Navy since Robert Fulton's twin-hulled steam warship was built at the close of the War of 1812. The Deep-Sea Submersible Vehicle had to be lowered between the two hulls by a complex crane system. TBE engineering group conducted a feasibility study concerning the crane for the Navy. As a result of TBE's findings, the primary shipyard bidders were encouraged by the Navy to use TBE to design and build the crane system. I was assigned the task of testing the system to ensure that Navy specifications were met. The project included reliability testing, environmental testing and sea trials. The complex task was a challenge for me, and I was especially looking forward to the sea trials. The TBE president, Joe Moquin, requested to review program management, engineering, manufacturing, and testing approaches and estimates. He only approved my approach and estimate for testing. Joe told the others to find a way to reduce the price or we would not be awarded the contract. Fortunately, I had gained experience in fixed price contracts vs. cost-plus sooner than the rest of the company. The Test Lab contracts on NASA work ended first, causing us to be more competitive. The experience of others was primarily on cost-plus contracts, which were inherently inefficient operations and created bureaucracies. They could not adjust, so the ship builders were forced to seek a different contractor. To say I had been excited with the idea of conducting sea trials would be an understatement. I was disappointed possibly because my nickname was Skipper and I had an active fantasy mind. It would also have been an adventure and another learning opportunity.

An aero company, Continental Motors in Birmingham, developed and supplied napalm dispensers for B-26K bombers. A cluster of dispensers were to be mounted to the inside of the bomb door of the aircraft. The long doors could be rotated to open over a target area so the dispenser napalm cartridges could be released one at a time or all together. The door would then be rotated to the closed position while returning to base. The Test Lab was awarded the contract to conduct the qualification tests. Many thought some of the testing could not be conducted. This ENMU engineer believed otherwise. To test the bomb door loaded and unloaded in both the closed position and open position while in flight mode was a challenge. To conduct the vibration test with the loaded dispenser upside down was going to be very expensive, if not impossible. The fixture weight needed to support the test item above the vibration shakers was beyond the shaker's capability. Because of the length of the test item, two large vibration shakers would have to be attached on one side of the long door. Testing the bomb dispenser door in its closed position was relatively easy. We were able to control the shakers by operating them in phase during lateral and vertical tests and out of phase when vibrated at each end. Being out of phase allowed one shaker to pull and the other to push. No one, not even the shaker manufacturer, thought the shakers could function properly upside down. I could not see a technical reason why they would not operate in the upside-down mode. Therefore, I decided to design a four-foot-thick wall that was sunk four feet below floor level, eight feet above floor level and 10 feet long. The wall skin was made from one-inch thick steel and had one-inch steel rod grid spaced one foot apart in all directions. The steel plate on one side contained a grid of several threaded holes to attach items. The container was filled with concrete. The shakers were then mounted to the wall. The low weight fixture used in the bomb open door test was used with the wall mounted shakers. This would allow the bomb door to be suspended from the shakers to simulate the open bomb door dispensing mode. The vibration test setup operated better than in the normal position. One day a customer on a different project walked by the setup and said, "Who was the idiot that came up with that hair-brain idea?" I answered, "That would be me."

Patsy attended the *"Seekers"* class for adults at church to prepare for confirmation. She was confirmed in the parish on April 9, 1969 by Bishop Murray of the Episcopal Diocese of Alabama. Chad was now a toddler.

In 1969 Chrysler, located in Huntsville, won a contract with MICOM to build TOW missiles as the second source. I submitted a bid for the Test Lab to conduct all preproduction qualification testing. As the program manager and project engineer it was a challenge to accomplish the component, subassembly, and system testing on schedule and at a profit. My favorite memory was firing the missile on Redstone Arsenal and successfully hitting the target, a tank. The Chrysler program manager and engineers were a delight to work with and we made a good team.

Once again, we celebrated Christmas in New Mexico with family. I headed to Ruidoso to go skiing following the holiday season. This would be our last time to head west for the Christmas holidays. Skiing the first day was an effort at Ski Apache near the Sierra Blanca Pike (12,000' elevation). I discovered that evening I was sick. The next morning, I decided to return to Monument. The 190-mile road to Monument was covered mostly with one foot of snow. I had a high temperature and could only drive for 15 to 20 minutes before my vision would be too blurry. After resting for a few minutes, my vision became acceptable. Literally no one was on the road because of the deep snow, except in both cities I had to pass through. It took all day which normally would take three hours. My temperature was over 104 degrees when arriving in

Monument.

Each December the company had an awards ceremony. I received a call from work while in Ruidoso at the motel before heading to Monument. I was barely able to speak. They told me that I had been awarded one of the company's top awards. I had received several certificates of achievement previously. The plaque was awarded for the most unique cost reduction idea of the year. The napalm dispensers for B-26K bomber was the basis for the award. Considering that TBE had thousands of employees that were mostly engineers and scientists, I was surprised to receive an award. *A great way to end 1969.*

TBE won a contract from Lockheed to supply the buffet lavatory (BL) for the Air Force's largest plane, the C5. The buffet galley was on one side of the cube and the opposite side housed a lavatory. The structure was to be built on a standard Air Force aluminum seven foot by seven-foot palette for easy loading and unloading on the C5. The electric operated toilet supplier had to be qualified by the Test Lab. Charlie Gibson, our electromagnetic field (EMF) expert in the Lab tested it in the screen room for the supplier. The toilet failed the EMF test and the supplier engineers were not sure how to redesign the toilet so it would qualify. Charlie provided a simple solution. He was good but had to survive a lot of ribbing for his toilet effort. The Test Lab was responsible for the reliability and environmental testing. Being responsible for the testing, I visited Lockheed's facility in Marietta, Georgia to see the manufacturing line of the C5, attended a design review and gathered interface data. Very impressive and a real treat. Our Test Lab capability had to be expanded to accommodate the seven-foot cube. The most challenging tests were developing a centrifuge large enough to apply nine Gs uniformly to the test item and a shock machine that could apply the required sine wave shock. I certainly enjoyed the project, especially designing the shock machine. I designed a steel cart to hold the seven-foot cube test item, with a reinforced three-foot diameter flat bumper and an inclined track. I also designed a large solid reinforced concrete barrier with a discarded large steel vibration shaker casing with a three-foot diameter flat surface imbedded in the concrete and attached to the reinforcing steel. A weight was mounted on the cart to simulate the test article. While experimenting, by letting the cart roll down the incline into a rubber surface attached to the cart bumper of different thicknesses and varying distance for the cart to roll, the desired sine wave shock was achieved.

The project was fun for several technical reasons in addition to working with several engineers and manufacturing personnel in TBE. We usually tended to work too much in our own kingdom.

TBE prepared a proposal and bid for the solar array panels for America's first space station, the Skylab. We were teamed with the prime contractor, McDonnell Douglas (MD) of Huntington Beach, California. TBE's task was to design and build the panel structure and purchase the photovoltaic cells and mount them to the panels. During the preparation the TBE team would travel to Huntington Beach several times to ensure the Solar Panels would integrate and interface with the Skylab correctly and to review our approach. Billy Barnes, a good friend in the design group, was scheduled to present the testing details to MD in Huntington Beach. He had a death in the family, so I was sent in his place. The MD personnel occupied a large presentation room with microphones at each station. This was my first experience in addressing such a crowd. They started firing detailed questions during my presentation. I knew the proper answers but was unsure how Billy would have answered the questions. After a bit, MD suggested we caucus overnight and start fresh the next day. The other TBE members told me to stop worrying about Billy's response and to give the answers that I was comfortable with. The next morning, I provided my answers and surprisingly MD personnel were more than happy with my approach. They volunteered to support me during the test program with equipment and help if it was needed. They had not expressed a willingness to support other phases of the project. One of my TBE comrades said, "You had them eating out of your hand."

Back in Huntsville the TBE president, Joe Moquin, reviewed the estimates provided by program management, engineering, manufacturing, and testing. Each time he reviewed the estimates, Joe would tell everyone that their estimate was too high. He would state my estimate was the only acceptable one, but for me to be available. Each time the others returned for Joe to review the new estimates, they were higher, not lower. I was at TBE around the clock for three days to be available. We visited Huntington Beach to present our price. MD said they would reduce our scope of work so we could submit a lower price. Clyde Ivey, our TBE project leader and a division head visited Teledyne, Inc in Beverly Hills to get approval for us to reduce our price consistent with the reduced statement of work. Because our manufacturing division had lost money on two previous contracts, they refused to let us reduce the price. Clyde Ivey was so upset he invited one of the Teledyne, Inc individuals to the parking lot. MD was appalled with our position and said they would drop us, but not our photovoltaic cell supplier. Clyde Ivey called my room at midnight and asked me to join him downstairs for a drink in the bar at the Marriott Hotel. He said, "Joe Moquin told me to bring the troops home on the first flight in the morning, that we were finished." Clyde asked me not to tell anyone else until morning. *Why he called me to join him in the bar was a mystery.*

TBE funded a ram jet project, based on the opinion of a respected propulsion engineer in the research division. The ram jet, if developed, could exceed Mach IV speeds. If the project was successful, then many lucrative applications should follow. The ram jet had a nozzle inside the front end of a long cylinder. The nozzle would create a thrust to propel the ram jet engine forward. My task was to design and build a chamber that would allow the ram jet to demonstrate this feat. The Test Lab had a 2,000-gallon liquid nitrogen tank and eight large gas storage bottles. The nitrogen liquid to gas converter would allow the bottles to be pressurized to 15,000 psi. The Test Lab existing nitrogen capability was combined with a large Venturi nozzle I designed. The Venturi nozzle was attached to the front end of the cylindrical chamber I designed. This created a wind tunnel to achieve the Mach IV speeds required to test the item. During the test the ram jet would not achieve Mach 2, but a flame was still active. The TBE engineering team returned to the main building to analyze the data. I called them to tell them that I suspected the Venturi nozzle of the chamber had in effect taken over the role of a ram jet. The ram jet had become a nozzle causing the chamber to become a ram jet. After further thought, they agreed. The ram jet project was continued but was never successful. Having no skin in the project, I enjoyed the project and learned a lot.

Gene Engler and Bud Burlinghof had been sent by Teledyne, Inc to serve as Executive Vice President and Manufacturing Vice President of TBE, respectively. Gene basically ran the company with little sense of humor. The first decision he made was to fire 70 individuals in the G&A part of TBE. Gene shaped up the company in short order. It was overdue. He was fair in my opinion. If you performed you were treated well, if not you went down the road talking to yourself. Within two months he called the division leader to his office who had invited someone to the parking lot at Teledyne, Inc. He gave him two hours to turn in his automobile keys and be gone and not to return.

A company specializing in rubber type mounts for equipment requested a proposal and bid to conduct reliability test on a 10-inch-high and six-inch diameter mount. I requested TBE's top and highly respected mechanical engineer to design a fixture to test the mounts in all six axes in each cycle. After trying for a few days, he said, "It cannot be done." This ENMU engineer could not accept that answer. After several hours I found a way. I included the approach with drawings and price in our proposal. Later we were informed we would not be awarded the contract. Months later I was at Wyle Labs and walked by a room and saw through a door where my exact unique design was functioning. A Wyle employee quickly closed the door saying I was not allowed in that area. Wyle would wine, dine, etc. to get a contract. That was not our approach, we competed based on the integrity of our ideas.

I began an MBA program at the beginning of the summer of 1970 at Alabama A&M University located in Normal, Alabama adjacent to Huntsville. The Wharton School of the University of Pennsylvania consistently was rated as having one of the top two MBA programs in the country. The top rating between Harvard and Wharton changed hands often. Wharton gave A&M $50,000 worth of books, hired instructors/professors and set up the same program they had at the Wharton School. The MBA program consisted of night courses. The student would take two semester courses each quarter for eight quarters over a two-year period. No management program was offered in any of the Huntsville universities, so the students consisted primarily of executives from MICOM, NASA and local engineering companies located in Research Park. Straight A students who had just completed college could not compete and typically dropped out. TBE paid for the course. I would not get a promotion after graduation like those who received Masters in engineering. TBE was, after all, an engineering company. However, it provided me with the tools to advance throughout my remaining career to levels I had not envisioned.

Having outgrown our home on Kirkland St. and looking for a better school, we moved to a larger home on Whittier Rd. in August 1970. The home was within three blocks of Chaffee Elementary, one of the top three schools in Huntsville. The home was in the Whitesburg

Middle School and Grissom High School districts. Roger Chaffee and Gus Grissom were two of the three astronauts killed in the Apollo 1 fire on January 27, 1967. Ed White Middle School in NW Huntsville was named after the other astronaut. These schools were built in 1969. I remember that each student in Chad's fourth grade class had at least one parent with a Master's degree. This was typical in the Chaffee classes. Paige was due to start kindergarten. The benefits of the neighborhood included being surrounded by engineers, scientists, and several children the same ages of Paige and Chad. The house was within walking distance of school, a park (including tennis courts, ball fields, etc.), swimming pool, and shopping. The housing area was isolated from through traffic.

One of my fondest memories during the fall was reading from a collection of poems Mom had given me one year for Christmas entitled *The Treasure Chest* compiled by Charles L. Willis. I was reading with tears to Paige, who was sitting on my lap under a tree in the backyard. The poem was "What is a Girl?" by Alan Beck. Later I would read to Chad the poem, "What is a Boy?" by Alan Beck, with emotion. The emotion would be different but equally intense. As you might have observed, there is a difference between boys and girls. *The Treasure Chest* belongs in every home. It is a collection of quotations, poems, sentiments, and prayers from great minds of 2500 years, published in 1965. I still have the signed copy. Mom knew Charles Willis.

In 1970 Patsy and I decided to start our own tradition by celebrating the Christmas season at our new home in Huntsville rather than traveling to New Mexico. Mom would join us for Christmas, a treat. For the first time we were able to attend midnight mass on Christmas Eve at the Episcopal Church of the Nativity. Paige and Chad enjoyed spending time with their new friends during the holidays.

At work our main competitor was Wyle Laboratories located in Huntsville. Each time we had a test project requiring an acoustic chamber, reluctantly we had to subcontract that test to them. They charged much more than the test should have cost. That got under my skin. I decided to design and build a modest size chamber that would cover 95% of our needs. My design required a steel reinforced concrete chamber with a ribbed steel exponential horn to be mounted as a door on one end of the chamber. The acoustic driver mounted on the small end of the horn would be powered by nitrogen supplied from the 15,000 psi storage bottles. Manufacturing fabricated the exponential horn I designed. The chamber was lined with steel on the inside at different angles. The steel was welded to rebar. The outside had a temporary form to hold the concrete. Knowing our Vice President, Dooley Culbertson, would not approve the project, I charged the many loads of concrete to the TBE facilities maintenance account. When we subcontracted to Wyle, they always needed a waiver for particular acoustic frequency bands required to meet the test specification. Our acoustic chamber did not need a wavier as it met the specification requirement at all frequencies. The chamber, with the exception of the concrete, was paid for by the first contract.

Now, the rest of the story. The Executive Vice-president, Gene Engler noticed a spike in the cost of TBE facilities cost one month. He called the manager of TBE facilities to find out why the extra cost. He had not noticed. He discovered what I had done and reported back to Gene. Dooley Culbertson, our VP was now on the carpet for a royal chewing out by Gene. Dooley called the Test Lab manager and me to his office to pass down the heat. Humbly apologizing, I promised not to do that again. I smiled all the way to the bank, so to speak. We made a lot of money with the chamber.

Gene Engler asked all division heads, including me, representing the Test Lab to present their business and marketing plans for the future. I was the last to present our business and marketing plans, which we had implemented with some success. He stated, "No one has a plan for their future except Skipper, so everyone else go back and plan a future or find another job." *Gene never took prisoners.*

The Test Lab won a contract to conduct safety testing on ten automobiles. I served as the program manager and project engineer. Our facilities were capable of conducting most of the tests. I had to redesign some of our equipment capabilities to accommodate the automobiles. One of the automobiles was a Jaguar XK-E V12. While idling during a test, the sparkplugs inside would be covered with carbon within 30 minutes. I would drive on a new four lane limited access road, rarely used, to blow out the carbon. That Jag would go 150 miles per hour. *I would do my duty.*

In the fall of 1971 Bud Burlinghof, our current Vice President, requested Jim Hammons, Bob Hall and I join him in the executive conference room. He informed us that the Test Lab would be closed, and they were going to use the resources to start a new product line,

Environmental Management and Consulting. With all the new environmental regulations he believed that industries would need expert help to achieve their goals. He said while we would bring in $3.5 million per year the new group should bring in $30 million. He offered to sell the Test Lab equipment to us for $100,000 but we had to have a certified check on his desk in six weeks and not a day later. He also wanted us to vacate the building in three months. We were stunned but said we would get back to him.

Five of us in the Test Lab met to come up with a plan to purchase the equipment worth about $2,000,000. The others were trying to figure out how to get Gene to reduce the equipment price. I realized quickly that the priority of the others was misplaced. I also thought that any profit spread over five people was not worth the risk. I believed finding the $100,000 capital and a new facility should be the top priority. I bailed. The others elected to proceed; Gene Engler promoted me to Test Lab Manager. He thought that Jim continuing as the manager was a conflict of interest. Jim was given three months' notice and an office in a different building. I now had the task of completing 50 contracts and telling repeat customers our services would no longer be available. Jim and the others were unable to negotiate a lower price. In the last week they started looking for financing. They discovered a Small Business Loan was the only possibility and that could not be processed in a short period of time. Gene did not give them an extension. Gene was a man of his word.

My new VP boss, Bud Burlinghof, said that no one would be laid off but raises normally given in January would be delayed until they transferred to another part of TBE. This would provide more money for others during the normal review period. Raises given at other times of the year did not affect that period or pool of funds.

We attended the 1972 New Year's party at our next-door neighbors, Rose and Russ Costanza. I met Mark Smith at the party. He was working in his garage on a high-speed modem design. He was planning on starting up a business to sell his modems. He needed state-of-the-art oscilloscopes for the planned business. Because the Test Lab was closing, we had 15 that met his requirements. We negotiated a fair price and I gave him the name at TBE to contact to finalize the acquisition. Mark seemed like an introvert, but we enjoyed the evening talking shop, while everyone else partied. Mark would sell his new company to Motorola a few years later for many millions of dollars. In

1986, he started a second company, Adtran, Inc., a major supplier of communication products he invented. An international company, Adtran now trades on NASDAQ and in 2016 had $636.8 million in revenue with headquarters in Huntsville. The talent in Huntsville is incredible. Many engineers started companies that became very successful. Some became Fortune 500 companies. Years later Forbes magazine had an article naming Huntsville the Entrepreneur Capital of America. *Time to leave 1971.*

Chapter XII - 1972–1974

As the Test Lab needs were reduced, while completing the 50 contracts, I scoured the company to find jobs for the Test Lab employees and was successful for all but four. The personnel department member assigned the task to find all Test Lab employees a position was useless as always. He would be blasted by Gene Engler, but that did not get them a job. The hardest task was having to lay them off after being unsuccessful finding them a job. Each was the best in their field in all of Huntsville. The problem was their skills were not needed elsewhere in TBE.

In early March, Bud Burlinghof was suddenly transferred to Teledyne Continental in Mobile as a vice president to solve some serious problems. Now I reported to Gene Engler, the Executive Vice President. He was demanding and tough, but fair.

On a Friday in late March, I told Gene there was only one contract left to be completed and the two employees working on the project were scheduled to transfer to the electronics group when they were finished. They could transfer early and take the project with them or I could remain in the Test Lab and see it through. He said, "Transfer them and the project." I then expected to be laid off. I had looked high and low in TBE for a new home. The company was laying people off and Lady Luck was not to be found.

He asked if I had found a job in TBE. My answer was no that I had only one encouraging possibility with Dr. Harry Watson, the Optics Department Manager in the SETAC Division. Harry had told me that the only way to get their customer to agree to a new slot was to give the prospect an occasional task to be conducted for the customer. The customer would then send steady funding, if impressed. Harry further added he had no way to pay the employee during that phase. While I sat there, Gene called Dooley Culbertson, a vice president, and asked him if he had found me a job. Obviously, Dooley had not. He then gave him a tongue lashing as only Gene could do with great force. Gene told him I would be in Dooley's office Monday morning and he better have me a job. Monday morning, I reported to Dooley's office and he told me to report to Don Martin, manager of the BATS program, for a three-month task. I reported to Don, who seemed to be unaware of my reporting to him. He suggested I join John Wencil, his project engineer. John gave me a run down on the program and the possible task. About an hour later Don told me to report to Dooley's office. I asked if I should take my personal items. He said yes. Dooley told me that Gene said to stop jerking me around and for me to report to Harry in the Optics Department and that Harry should not worry about funding me. Harry assigned me a desk and gave me an advance infrared optics textbook to study until something came up. He said if I had any questions, ask anyone for answers. I was now in a group of mostly PhDs and I thought optics was something you put on your nose. It turns out that the significant optics field that these fellows were practicing in was the most complex field in engineering or physics. In short order it occurred to me I was in over my head.

When Bell Telephone Laboratories (BTL) in New Jersey withdrew from the defense business, TBE recruited Steve McCarter, previously the head of their missile-defense radar unit, and several other senior engineers and scientists from the BTL unit. They had the top people in the country concerning missile defense technology. In 1971, Steve McCarter led TBE in winning the highly sought-after System Engineering and Technical Assistance Contractor (SETAC) with the Army Ballistic Missile Defense Agency (ABMDA). TBE formed the SETAC division, which was headed by Steve McCarter, the Senior Vice President. Reporting to him was Herb Barnard, a vice president who was Harry's boss. The SETAC division would grow to about 1,000 outstanding employees.

I had not received a raise when I transferred. When Bud Burlinghof temporarily returned from Mobile to his office to collect some personal items, I walked into his office to congratulate him on his new assignment. I also reminded him that when Test Lab personnel were transferred, they would be considered for a raise. I told him that this *turkey* did not get one. I added that I may not have earned one. If not, that was fine, I just wanted to be sure that consideration had not simply fallen through a crack. He said, "I will speak with Gene Engler." A week later I was given a pink slip showing a raise. Harry was concerned that they might not have funds to cover me and talked to his boss, Herb Barnard. Herb said not to worry. One day I saw the Director of Personnel in a hallway. He said, "Skipper, you received the largest raise that I have ever seen at TBE." *Thank you, Gene Engler.*

My first opportunity with the Optics Department's main customer, the Army's Advanced Ballistic Missile Defense Agency

(ABMDA), was to travel to Pittsburgh, Pennsylvania. The GE facility there was developing a ground based infrared telescope. I was to report on their technical progress. While at GE they were having a cryogenics problem that had them stumped. I asked a dumb question about the setup which led to the solution. The customer, Larry Hayes, seemed pleased with my contribution and report, even though I knew little about the technology except for the cryogenics involved. Larry then arranged for me to visit the Ground Based Telescope (GBT) at White Sands, New Mexico to assess the status of the system. The technician assigned full time to operate the infrared telescope was a true New Mexico desert rat. I say that with reverence. *Damn it was good to be in the Land of Enchantment.* In addition to my traveling and new role at work, I was completing my final two months of MBA classes. I would miss more than one week of class time due to business traveling. I had to study for a written test covering the whole MBA program. Patsy did the right thing taking Paige and Chad to New Mexico until my studying and testing was complete. I would have not been fun to be around with my middle name being "Pressure." I survived and they returned to see me walk across the stage to receive my diploma.

Gene Engler offered me the position of Sub-Contracts Manager with the intention of me replacing the Director of Purchasing in a few months. This appealed to me because it gave me the chance to use the skills learned in the MBA program. I wanted business experience to compliment my technical experience. I agreed to accept the position. Gene had an office prepared for me on executive row. Company policy stated your current management had to approve a transfer. The Sr. Vice President, Steve McCarter asked me to his office to tell me that he was refusing to release me. He said he was indirectly funding most of the money for that position and he wanted an attorney to fill the position. Steve further stated that he sincerely believed I would be better off in the long run to stay in my current job. *Later, he proved to be correct.*

Later Gene Engler offered me a job to start up a new facility in College Station, Texas to produce precision steel structures for the nuclear power industry. He said I would be responsible for every aspect of the operation. That would include working with banks, hiring 100 employees, laying out the factory, marketing, etc. He was *generously* going to loan me the top manufacturing engineer in the company for two months. That was it. Gene also would want me to familiarize myself with all aspects of the operation in the TBE nuclear stainless-steel operation in Decatur, Alabama headed by Don Martin for two months before moving to College Station. I asked for two weeks to consider the opportunity. I believed Steve McCarter would not likely stand in my way as he had no skin in the game with this offer. I also suspected my heart would not last six months working directly for the very demanding Gene Engler. I reported to him within the two weeks that I believed my contribution to TBE would be greater in the long run by staying put. He politely disagreed and said he would not hold my refusal against me. *He did not.*

A different customer in ABMDA, Gene Sanmann, asked me to visit Philco-Ford Corporation in Newport Beach, California to audit the Fly Along Infrared (FAIR) II quality program prior to a project review. I was able to report to Gene and Philco-Ford that I had never seen a better system. One of the benefits of the audit and review was getting to know an exceptional group of engineers, scientists, and managers. Rockwell International Corporation, located in Anaheim, California, was the supplier of the optical sensor for the FAIR II program. Due to my extensive vibration experience, Gene asked me to visit Rockwell because the sensor assembly was failing the vibration test. After reviewing their setup, I was at a loss to identify a problem. I asked, "Who supplied the vibration test specification?" They said, "The Air Force supplied the specification that came from the Atlas missile requirements." I asked where on the missile was the vibration data gathered? It turned out it was from the engine end of the missile, not the payload area where the sensor assembly would be mounted. Applying the reduced vibration test specification solved several problems, except for the detector. A smaller capillary tube that supplied cryogenics gas to the small detector would vibrate significantly at a particular frequency thereby interrupting the cryogenic gas flow. They were at a loss as how to fix the problem. Previously, in the Test Lab days, I remembered reading an article in a paper produced by the US Bureau of Standards located in Boulder, Colorado. The article had mentioned that, at certain vibration modes, an acoustic oscillation in a small capillary tube could occur at its particular frequency mode that would interrupt the flow of gas. The fix was shorting or lengthening the tube. I suggested they shorten the tube 1/4 of an inch. Problem solved. Temporarily, I was a *SAVIOR* to all on the program. Not only was the technical solution important but also the significant costs and program schedule that were affected. Gene was pleased with my contribution and invited me to join the FAIR II program full time. *Thank you, Harry Watson, for giving me the opportunity and believing in me.*

TBE engineers and scientists provided support to the ABMDA customer. The Optics Department and the ABMDA customer were made up of brilliant individuals. There was much to learn from these remarkable people. They became an important part of our social circle. Life was good. Gene Sanmann, the government's FAIR program manager was the most intelligent person that I had worked with. He was bathed in common sense and management ability that could inspire all on the program to work as a team and give their best. At the time the FAIR acronym was classified secret. Many program details were classified Top Secret, therefore, my secret security clearance had to be upgraded. The FAIR program was funded at forty-million dollars (a quarter of a billion in 2019 dollars) and would be ABMDA's most successful program. The TBE engineer who served as Gene's project engineer, Norm Cowden, left TBE. Having been on the program for a while and learning a lot, Gene asked me to take Norm's place. Now I was really in over my head. Fortunately, Rex Louis, a TBE engineer was the expert on the FAIR II sensor.

Clyde Ivy, the division head that had departed abruptly, after Gene Engler had arrived at TBE, had gone to work for NCR Corporation in the Chicago area. He called to offer me a job as head of their development group with a huge raise and more perks. He said the unit currently had 70 engineers and needed to expand to 250 engineers within a year. Clyde gave me two weeks to report back with an answer. Patsy, as always, deferred to me on whether to accept the offer. She said she would be okay with the move if I was. I rationalized to myself that I did not want to raise Paige and Chad in Chicago, that it was much colder, did not want to leave friends, church and that we would be even further from family. So, I turned Clyde down. *In two years, I would discover this was a good decision for an unfathomed reason that would surface.*

I would take 26 business trips one year, mostly to Newport Beach, California. I would go to Anaheim, Vandenberg, California, New Jersey, Monterrey, California, Air Force Academy, and Washington, DC. Many of the trips would be with Gene Sanmann. On one trip to a conference at the Naval College in Monterrey, Gene introduced me to Roy Nichols. Roy presented a paper at the conference, which was the most articulate, informative, and dynamic speech I had ever heard. He worked for McDonnell Douglas in Huntington Beach, California. Later Roy transferred to Huntsville.

Each time, after returning from trips, I told Patsy about the great restaurants I was experiencing. *Dumb, I know.* Patsy let me know that she was taking care of the children and did not want to hear about these wonderful experiences again.

Gene directed me and Rex to take our wives to California for a series of launch readiness reviews starting in Newport Beach, on to Anaheim, then Vandenberg. The Philco-Ford program manager hosted a dinner party at his house to give Patsy and Pat, Rex's wife, an opportunity to meet the people we had been working with. The trip lasted three weeks with lots of free time. We had dropped Paige and Chad off in New Mexico with Patsy's parents. We visited Disney Land, Knott's Berry Farm, San Luis Obispo, Santa Barbara, Solvang, Lompoc, Monterey, Carmel, missions, museums, and ate in great restaurants. The three weeks with Patsy and no cares in the world was fantastic. *As I would discover later this was very important to us.*

One spring ABMDA was faced with a funding crisis. They asked TBE to find other work for those working on the ABMDA support contract until funding was restored. About that time Bill Giardini, the Vice President of a different division in TBE, asked me to take the lead on a three-month study they were awarded from Eglin Air Force Base in Florida. Eglin wanted to know if a facility could be built to test "stores" mounted below aircraft with several environmental conditions occurring at the same time. Stores could be bombs, missiles, disposable fuel tanks, instrument pods, etc. It seemed to me that my whole career, up to this time, had provided me with the tools to make this a reality. This was going to be fun, but a challenge considering the schedule and technical issues to be solved. I was able to gather an exceptional staff that gave this a chance of being successful. Eglin wanted a facility that would apply the following conditions simultaneously to stores; shock, vibration, acoustics, temperature extremes, being hit by lightning, high altitudes, and at flight velocity. The idea seemed impossible to most. Ever the optimist, possessing a can-do attitude and a great staff, we charged ahead.

A month into the study, I was required to brief the customer and his boss at Eglin AFB. I tagged along on a four-seater charter flight going to Eglin. Unknown to me, Joe Moquin, the TBE President, would be sitting beside me in the back seat of the loud aircraft. I had many one-on-one meetings with Joe over the years and he was always a gentleman and helpful. I still was intimidated making small talk with him for two hours. He asked who I was visiting. He was going to meet with someone else. *Thank goodness*. However, he later decided to show up at my meeting. The customer and his boss, a division head, had not understood how much work needed to be accomplished to complete the study. Joe, near the end of the briefing, directed me to take no vacation or be sick until the study was finished. That meant I would lose vacation time, as I was at the limit on how much could be accumulated. Teledyne, Inc policy dictated that with no wiggle room. I told Bill what Joe had said. I wanted to be paid for the vacation time I could lose. Bill arranged for me to get an extra week of pay. That violated policy. He was always a great man.

One adventure during the study was a trip to a facility in the Midwest that tested all USA aircraft with lightning strikes. Dr. Al Froelich joined the study team as the lightening expert. Al had visited the facility while attending Notre Dame working on his Ph.D. in Nuclear Physics. Walking into the large lightning facility reminded me of an early Frankenstein movie. Large old electric equipment and spiderwebs gave the facility an eerie look. The lightening guru there did help that image.

At the end of the study, I returned to Eglin to give an oral report to the customer in addition to the written report. The team had identified the massive amount of equipment and building design required including office space that could successfully conduct the required testing of stores. I expected to just flip through a hard copy of viewgraphs across the desk of the customer. He said, "I have reserved the Eglin Auditorium for the day and invited everyone at Eglin to your presentation." He then informed me the purpose of the study was to settle a huge debate at Eglin and that half of them strongly believed it was impossible. *I wanted to run home.* On the stage, he introduced me as being an expert in five different engineering fields. *Could have fooled me.* I briefed the 300 attendees for five hours. There was one obnoxious civil servant that kept rudely interrupting making statements implying I was wrong. I calmly answered his concerns and that defeated his points. Afterwards, several civil servants apologized for his behavior. I think his behavior helped me convince the rest that the chamber was feasible. Not everyone has a unique opportunity to perform with their accumulation of experiences to accomplish a task others thought impossible. I cannot help remembering with fondness and joy that rare experience.

Paige, Chad, Patsy and I continued with many normal activities such as church, camping, fishing, T-ball, gymnastics, swimming, school events, etc. Paige was fearless, especially on the balance beam, and would compete as far away as Chattanooga, Tennessee. Patsy and I happily concentrated on activities with our children and never considered spending time away from them overnight. We did attend the theater, movies, concerts, bridge events, live night club entertainment, etc.

With our high energy children now in school, Patsy decided she wanted to become a nurse. The University of Alabama Huntsville offered a four-year BS program. Calhoun College offered a two full year program whose graduates actually had a better chance of passing the state boards. Patsy was amazing to watch while earning A's. She believed her best would be C's. I always knew she was smart even if she did not. *Watching Patsy's confidence and joy grow was a beautiful thing to behold.*

Gene attended Oklahoma University to finish his Ph.D. starting in August 1973. Chris Horgen, with ABMDA, took over the FAIR II program. Visits to California were important at this time because launch of the Atlas missile with the FAIR II payload was nearing. In late 1973, Chris, Rex, myself, Philco-Ford Corporation key people, as well as Rockwell key people, traveled to Vandenberg for the launch. Gene, having a lot to offer, also joined us from Oklahoma for the launch.

The evening before the launch, we ate at the Far Western Restaurant in Guadalupe, California. It had one of the best steaks in the country, if not the best. One of their policies was a free 22 oz steak if you finished the meal. Gene was the only one to accept the challenge and he received the free meal.

The following night I was located in the bunker close to the launch site. Most of the others were located miles away to observe the data as it came in during the flight. TV monitors showing the engine areas and launch pad showed the fuel as it flowed through the engines just before firing. The abrupt load roar of the engines and the TV monitors suddenly going blank made me think the Atlas had blown up. Inexperience on my part showed through, all the others in the bunker were cheering. The other good news was that no one noticed my reaction. The flight was a huge success. We had to wait for a limited analysis of the flight data before heading home.

Not knowing when the launch would occur, Chris, Rex and I had no reservations therefore flew standby to Huntsville. When we reached Memphis, Tennessee that night there were only two seats available to Huntsville. Rex and I were going to flip a coin to see who spent the night in Memphis. Chris, our customer, insisted we odd-man-out. We said no because he was the customer. He insisted we were a team, thus odd-man-out left Chris in Memphis. Harry, our boss, was not amused that we left the customer in Memphis. It did not help that we knew Chris was okay with the outcome.

Along with Patsy and me, Roy and Sue Nichols, Gene and Bobbie Sanmann, Chris and Nancy Horgen started a bridge club. We rotated homes each month for bridge. It was always a pleasure to be with these very exceptional individuals. It was fun to play with really good bridge players.

Several families in our neighborhood were Episcopalians attending the nearby St. Stephens Episcopal Church. Because several of our children's friends went there, Patsy suggested we go there instead of the Church the of Nativity. I reluctantly agreed. As an adult, for the first time, I did more than attend church on Sundays. I became an usher. *Not much, but a beginning.*

The TBE Optics Department had expanded significantly since joining it in April of 1972. There were currently three branches. Harry, Rex Lewis, and Hugh Morgan fielded TBE's first response to Harold Bates from the Army McMorrow Research Laboratory of the Missile Command (MICOM) on Redstone Arsenal proposed for a Manufacturing, Methods and Technology (MM&T). The Optics Department subsequently received a contract with MICOM to conduct the MM&T study on the Hellfire missile semi-active laser seeker. Harry created the fourth branch, Optics

Application Branch, with the MM&T contract as its first task. He promoted me to be manager of the newly created branch. I was amazed. To have landed in this department with some of the best minds in the country as a branch manager was a huge WOW! Branch managers received several perks such as a parking place, an annual executive physical, etc. I asked my good friend, Dr. Nick Passino, a branch manager and the Optics Department Deputy, why he thought Harry selected me to head the new branch. He said Harry's main reason was because I had a knack for spotting opportunities for the department that he had rarely seen. I did not know that about myself. *That unconscious mind again raising its head.* The Optics Application Branch successfully completed several projects; only the most memorable will be mentioned during my tenure.

Incredible core of individuals such as Dr. Al Froelich, Hugh Morgan, Chuck Whaley, Manfred Segewitz, and Jim English joined the branch. Al received his Ph.D. in Nuclear Physics from Notre Dame, and was exceptionally productive and could come up with ten ideas to everyone else's one idea when brainstorming, but someone else should pick the idea to pursue. Hugh Morgan, a past race car driver, had a BS in Physics from Georgia Tech and nearly finished his Ph.D. at Johns Hopkins University, was methodical and one could be sure he would produce a reliable result. Chuck Whaley graduated from the University of Tennessee, was an excellent electronics engineer and an accomplished artist who could always be counted on. Jim English was a solid electrical engineer who joined us for a short time from McMorrow Research Laboratory. Later he decided working in the government was best for him, so he returned to McMorrow Labs. Manfred Segewitz had worked with NASA in their wind tunnel, and later for years supervising a large group of skilled technicians, and in the TBE optics laboratories for years bringing a lot of practical experience to the table. He had an electrical engineering degree in Germany, was employed by Siemens before coming to the US and had an electrical engineering degree from UAH. All were characters in an entertaining way, worked well as a team and advanced the state of art in several areas. They would make me look good. They all were more intelligent than me and knew it.

A semi-active laser seeker would guide a missile to a target that had a laser beam focused on the target from a tripod or helicopter. This meant someone had to hold the laser source on the target until the missile arrived. The customer was with the US Army McMorrow Research Labs located on Redstone Arsenal.

The customer of the MM&T program thought we would be successful if we could save 20% on manufacturing cost of the Hellfire missile seeker. We would have to actually build seekers to demonstrate the technologies. After listening to the team ideas, I asked the customer to give us the leeway to make significant changes in the design. He gave us the go ahead. We would concentrate for the next two years on meeting our ambitious goal. As a team, we were able to reduce the seeker head cost by 85% and improve its performance. More later on results.

I was in a Monday meeting on October 28, 1974 in California and was summoned to take a call from Patsy, my wife. She informed me that she had discovered a lump in her breast the previous night after my departure for California. She had seen her gynecologist the next morning, Monday, who immediately referred her to Dr. Joe Akin, a surgeon. He had her check into the hospital that day to conduct a biopsy the next morning, Tuesday. She said there was no need for me to be there. I caught the redeye that night and arrived just before she went into surgery. Being hopelessly optimistic, I was expecting a benign tumor. I had never known anyone to have cancer at that time in my life. Joe came out during the middle of the surgery to inform me that it was malignant, and he was going to do a modified, radical mastectomy. Patsy had told him to go ahead if the tumor was malignant. I was in shock, being hit with that sledgehammer. After surgery, Joe believed he had gotten all the cancer cells. The pathology test would reveal that 15 of the 17 lymph nodes removed under the arm were malignant.

At the time, the medical field suspected some estrogen produced by the ovaries could cause further problems. Joe suggested conducting an oophorectomy to remove the ovary. He said that would also allow him to explore for other possible cancer cells. This was scheduled two weeks later while Patsy was still in the hospital. Her parents, brother Joe and his wife, Charlotte, had arrived from New Mexico. Mom had arrived from Texas. Following the surgery, Joe said no cancer cells were found. I went back to the waiting room, gave an okay gesture and quickly escaped. I walked outside the hospital for several blocks before I returned. My violent bawling, caused by the good news, had run its course. It was hard to comprehend that Patsy at 33, Paige at nine, Chad at seven, and me at 36 could have our lives turned upside down. Our lives would never be the same. Patsy would start stretching exercises in the hospital to gain strength and flexibility in her arm. She would also start chemo treatments with Dr. Parker Griffith, the only oncologist in Huntsville. 1974 began with so much promise but ended in anxiety.

Chapter XIII - 1975–1977

1975 started with addressing the needs of the family. Patsy would have to get a wig and a prosthesis. She never complained. We were going to fight this demon and win. Patsy and I believed the best way to protect the family was to continue normally and not deviate from basic activities or functions. Patsy would continue interacting with Paige and Chad in a normal way, such as hiding cookies from the sugar demon. Of course, I knew where, because Patsy and I shared the secret. My instincts were to treat Patsy as if nothing serious was at hand. She was grateful for this effort and it was an effort. Her main concern expressed to me was that I might not be happy with her not having a breast. I sincerely expressed to her that I had not considered that. My only concerns were her health and healing. A truer statement could not have been stated. The priest of St. Stephens Episcopal Church had moved leaving a vacancy. Patsy suggested, under the circumstances, we should move back to the Episcopal Church of Nativity where there was a priest. *My heart had never left.* We all had many supportive friends that made life much easier.

Patsy would suffer through chemotherapy and its several side effects with a smile, humor and hope. While still receiving chemotherapy, in less than a year, lymph nodes on the left side of her neck were growing. Dr. Joe Akin removed them and sent them to a pathologist in Birmingham. About four days later while we were sitting at the table for dinner, the den phone rang. Joe was calling to say the pathology report was not as we had hoped. I asked, "What did that mean?" He said, "Patsy never had more than a five percent chance of living three years." No one had been that blunt before. I knew it was important to hold it together for the others and retreated to my study to get my act together. I returned to the dinner table and said it was a friend that called. After the children were in bed, I told Patsy that the path report indicated they were all malignant and would never mention Joe's other remark.

Dr. Parker Griffith's specialties included oncology and radiation. He suggested Patsy receive radiation treatments and to try a different chemotherapy. The previous chemotherapy had run its course and had shown it was not effective anymore. She had the same side effects (mostly hair loss and nausea) from the radiation treatments.

Again, she persevered with a smile, humor and hope.

Chad would start playing football in the YMCA 65-pound league. Chad was the smallest player at 46 pounds. He had outstanding coaches who were fathers from the neighborhood. It was a joy to attend practices and games. In addition to watching Chad or Paige play sports, I got to know other dads from the neighborhood. At some time during the season, a colleague from work was telling me that a friend of his from NASA, who was coaching a team, had described with enthusiasm a small kid on his team as being the hardest hitter. I realized he was talking about Chad even though no names were mentioned. Chad would not tackle a player by hitting him at the knees if he knew the kid had a knee problem. This made me feel as proud as being the hardest hitting player. Chad did not have a mean bone in his body. I remember one game that it was raining buckets and coming down at about a 45-degree angle. Chad was playing middle linebacker and halfback. He kept tackling them for a five-yard loss. When our quarterback was hurt, the coach asked who wanted to take his place. Little Chad was the only one who volunteered. The coach did not want him to hand the ball off. On the first down he gained 15 yards up the middle. The next down he gained 10 yards up the middle and so on until the other team limited him to a yard or two. After the game the opposing coach came over lifted Chad over his head and said, "You're one fine football player." Never saw an opposing coach praise a player before or since. Paige was a team cheerleader. Subsequent years she would be a mentor to cheerleaders. Paige was always good with children and a good athlete.

We continued with camping trips to Fall Creek Falls, Smoky Mt. National Park, Guntersville State Park and more. One spring, Mom joined us, and we tent camped at Disney World Campgrounds with several boat trips to the Animal Kingdom. Mom would go on the Space Mountain with Paige and Chad while Patsy and I waited. Mom had a passion for rollercoasters. We all had a great time.

Rosalind and Col. Duncan (Retired) who had earlier helped trick me, back in 1964, into loving the game of bridge, now lived within a mile of us. Paige and Chad would start taking piano lessons from Rosalind. They became the surrogate grandparents of Paige and Chad as their grandparents lived far away. Chad loved being with Col. Duncan in his woodworking shop, while Paige was receiving her lesson. A kinder couple did not exist. When Rosalind became terminally ill, Paige and Chad started taking piano lessons from Judy

Bell on our street.

One day when we were meeting with Dr. Parker Griffith, Patsy asked if she should get a second opinion. Parker said, "You will not receive a different medical opinion. Because you ask you must. I will set up an appointment with MD Anderson in Houston, Texas." We traveled to Houston with a stop in New Orleans to enjoy a good seafood dinner. The testing at MD Anderson was in 1976 on May 27 and 28. They discovered nothing new. They did have an experimental chemotherapy program available. We elected to proceed with the program. (Later the program would be discontinued because it did not prove effective.) They said they would send the medicine to Parker to implement. We proceeded to Bonnie's for a visit. On the way we stopped to visit with old friends, Travis Durr and Mack McCaslin and their wives near Huntsville, Texas. They had purchased an oil field that was near its end. It was fun to get a tour of their poor boy wells. We traveled to MD Anderson again in early September 1976. The third time her mother, Lucille, wanted to join Patsy in Houston in late November 1976. I thought it would be a nice opportunity for a mother-daughter adventure and I would be a third wheel. Lucille kept making comments to Patsy about how thoughtless I was to let her fly to Houston by herself. Patsy finally said, "Skipper gives me hope by letting me do things on my own, so please stop the comments." When Patsy arrived home, she told me the group of doctors bluntly told her there was no cure for her cancer and there was no reason to return. It was the first time she was very upset and was giving up. I responded with all the technical reasons why we were going to prove them wrong. The next day we visited Parker Griffith to pass on MD Anderson conclusions. Patsy was still very upset. He gave us the same technical reasoning that I had stated the night before. Parker then said, "You may be ready to give up, but I am not." She perked up and never looked back. He gave her the hope she needed to hear. During the 1974 thorough 1977 period Patsy would undergo removal of lymph nodes in the neck, a lumpectomy, more chemotherapy, another mastectomy, and more chemotherapy. The time of effectiveness of each treatment was shorter between each event.

Patsy, Paige and Chad would make the annual trip to New Mexico to visit family and friends without me for the first time. Activities at work were a problem and Patsy needed to know she was up to standing on her own. I reluctantly stayed home.

Roy Nichols and Chris Horgen would start a new business, Nichols Research Corporation (NRC). The business was founded mostly on Roy being one of the top minds in the country in his field, if not the top. Chris, along with his technical expertise, had a firm grasp of business details. He had a two Masters in Engineering and an MBA. There were only three employees including Roy and Chris. I helped them move office equipment into a small office one night. In 1996 they would have more than a billion-dollar business backlog along with five hundred million dollars of options.

Following are a few of several goals to reduce cost and improvements concerning the MM&T semi-active laser seeker task. The coils driving the spinning mass motor activation sequence were changed reducing the seeker coil cost and weight by 30% and eliminated nutation present in previous seekers. The diamond turned precision machined stainless steel beryllium aspheric mirror cost was $200 when made in large quantities. The aspheric mirror was replaced with an injection molded polycarbonate mirror coated with gold that cost three dollars. The bulkhead and casing holding the drive coil had previously been constructed of several precision stainless steel parts. These parts are replaced with one injection molded engineering plastic part. I would travel to Keene, New Hampshire many times to visit Sid Davis of Miniature Precision Bearing (MPB) the company helping with the design and manufacture of the exceptionally precise gyro parts. The electronic section housing and mounting portions were replaced with a single piece made from injection molded engineering plastic. Other precision stainless parts were also replaced with injection molded engineering plastic technology. All these changes made the seeker head lighter and more stable and performance more consistent. Every part of the seeker was improved concerning cost and performance. We validated our design by building a few to demonstrate the significant performance improvements and cost reductions. The project was completed in May of 1976 meeting contract cost and schedule requirements.

In 1976, the president of Teledyne, Inc, Dr. George Roberts made his first visit to TBE since purchasing Brown Engineering in 1967. He was scheduled to be at TBE for only two hours. Several displays were set up in different buildings. I was asked to display the MM&T seeker and be available to answer questions. Dr. Roberts had his PhD in metallurgy. He was interested in our project because we had successfully made so many material changes. We visited for a pleasant 45 minutes. This prevented him from completing his tour. *Oh well,* I was honored to have the attention of the president of a two billion dollar a year company.

At the conclusion of the MM&T program I was asked to brief the Hellfire Office, Navy personnel from China Lake, California, personnel from Eglin AFB, and the prime contractor for the Hellfire seeker, Rockwell International located in Anaheim, California. The Air Force and Navy were attending because they were interested in using the seeker on one of their missiles. In fact, the AF requirements were driving the design specification and costs. The Pentagon had decreed that a Tri-Service seeker was to be used on the Army Hellfire, the AF Maverick missile and possibly on the Navy Bulldog missile. The Army was planning to purchase a minimum of 25,000 and the AF only 2,000. The Navy was not sure their Bulldog missile would proceed or use the Tri-Service seeker. My customer had discreetly kept me informed of the technical, cost and schedule problems that Rockwell was having. I subtly presented the approaches we had taken in our design to avoid problems that Rockwell's design had. No one knew I had knowledge concerning the Rockwell problems. After the presentation, my customer gave me the impression of those attending the briefing. Rockwell, he concluded, was completely embarrassed. He said the Hellfire office was impressed and wanted a copy of my view graphs so they could give a presentation to a four-star general visiting from the Pentagon next week. The AF staff were more impressed with the performance of our design and not particularly interested in the cost saving. The basic Hellfire seeker had been a modification of the Sidewinder missile seeker developed by the Navy at China Lake. Their lab manager was still significantly involved with the Sidewinder development. The Navy was the most impressed. He said every time they tried to change the design it had made the performance worse, even by just changing the paint on some minor part. According to the Navy man, this small team had accomplished more in a short period of time than hundreds of engineers had in over a decade. *I was indeed proud of the team of rascals.*

The Hellfire office did brief the general as scheduled. He was thrilled and was looking for an opportunity to drop the Tri-Service seeker approach because the AF specifications were driving the Army costs to levels they could not live with. The general said this would give them the ammunitions to kill the Tri-Service approach, which he passionately never liked. He did go on to accomplish his goal. My customer set up a meeting for me with the Hellfire Program office. Herb Barnard, our VP at the time wanted me to brief him first. He gave me some great pointers. I wanted to present an insurance program idea in the event Rockwell could not produce. I laid out a program using our design. I suggested a two-million-dollar sole source contract. They agreed this would be money well spent.

Herb was promoted to be President of Teledyne Hasting Instruments in Hampton, Virginia. Later he was promoted to a group president over five or more Teledyne companies. I was encouraged to throw my hat in the ring more than 15 years later when Teledyne, Inc. was looking for a new Teledyne Hasting President in 1993.

I met with Harry Watson and our new vice president, Bob Rieth, to discuss approaches on how to proceed. I said, "I can successfully convince the Hellfire office, but did not have a clue on approaches to use in the Pentagon or others in Washington. This could lead to hundreds of millions of dollars but that the Washington crowd could kill our program. We need to pull out all the stops." They picked, against my objections, a fellow in our marketing department to handle Washington. I simply did not believe he had the experience to be successful and I considered him a bullshit artist. *Sorry about my French.* I suggested Joe Moquin, TBE President, who was highly respected at Redstone Arsenal, meet with his contacts to show our support and commitment. He did. He reported that we had solid local Army support.

The Army held a Christmas celebration for 300 each year in the Officers' Club on Redstone Arsenal. The event was attended by the top brass, local company presidents and other executives. One was expected to bring an escort, *preferably their wife.* Joe Moquin, our President could not attend due to a conflict. Because I had the largest contract with the Army at Redstone Arsenal, I was asked to attend in his place to represent TBE. My fondest memory of the occasion occurred after dinner where the tables had been removed and all were invited to dance. Normally the dance floor was full, but during one dance I realized everyone else had migrated to the edge of the dance floor and were watching us dance. *Patsy could dance.* We were doing the North Texas Push, a form of jitterbug, that was from the 1950s and the main dance at ENMU as well as many other parts of New Mexico.

That is one memory that will never die. A good note to end 1976.

Six months later, I received a call from Martin Marietta in Orlando, Florida. They invited me down to talk about helping them on a new contract based on a recommendation from the Hellfire office. I was to learn they had been awarded a 10.2-million-dollar sole source contract to perform the effort I had initially proposed. Reporting the phone call to Harry, I was bumped-up-the-ladder to meet with our Sr. VP, Steve McCarter. I suggest he go with me to Orlando to explore the possibilities. I told him that I wanted a piece of the action and was not interested in giving away our ideas through a small contract. He agreed. Driving around the Martin Marietta parking lot looking for a parking space, I spotted a reserve parking spot with the four-star general's name that the Hellfire office had briefed in Huntsville. I asked Steve if he knew why the general had a parking spot. He said the general went to work for Martin Marietta a month ago. *Now the bright light came on.*

Steve met privately with one of their VPs, while I was introduced to the program manager for the new contract. He invited several key engineers to our meeting. The project engineer presented their design for the seeker. When he was finished, I turned to the program manager and said, "That design has no chance in Hell of working." He and the engineers agreed and wanted to give us a $100,000 contract to provide them with our design. I said, "We are only interested if we received a contract to produce part of the seeker." I pressed for information concerning the Hellfire office role. He stated they had no interest in pleasing the Hellfire office that they were interested in keeping people in Washington happy. They got the required check mark from the Hellfire office by agreeing to meet with us. After finding Steve, we headed for home. Neither of us was surprised with the outcome. Martin Marietta would eventually receive over a billion dollars to deliver Hellfire missiles.

I received a call from Norm Andrade of McDonnell Douglas (MDAC) located in Huntington Beach, California in the summer of 1976. He said the Navy lab leader in China Lake had suggested that he team with my group in TBE to pursue an active laser seeker program to be awarded by Eglin AFB. I expressed an interest, so he flew to Huntsville to discuss the program. An active laser seeker (ALS) would provide an ability to fire and forget, unlike a semi-active seeker, and to hit a target even if the target aircraft released flares. The Sidewinder heat seeking missile would be fooled when hot flares were released by the target aircraft. The laser would be located in the active laser seeker.

We reached an understanding with MDAC on which parts of the seeker would be ours and theirs. My next step was to seek funding during the proposal phase of the procurement. Steve McCarter approved funding and authorization to proceed. The proposal phase required us to design and build an active laser seeker referred to as Pave Prism to be tested at China Lake. Norm and I would visit several places during the proposal phase. I would learn a lot from Norm on how to compete for a program.

Norm and I traveled to Eglin AFB, Davis AFB, Texas, Washington, DC, Naval Station, Pentagon, and Nellis AFB to promote the program and learn more about performance requirements. Norm met me in Las Vegas with a McDonnell Douglas VP to join us for the 7:00 am meeting at Nellis AFB. We spent the night casino hopping rather than sleeping. Just before going to the meeting the VP became ill. He went to bed, Norm and I carried on without him. Our meeting was with the pilots of the "Red Eagles" who operated Mig-17s, Mig-21s and Mig-23s and the pilots of US combat aircraft. The two groups were adversaries in the air. On the ground they were a team. We told them our goal was to learn firsthand from their knowledge and get their suggestions to improve missile capabilities. They were helpful and appreciated someone asking for their input for the first time. We returned to the hotel to find the VP had eaten a full breakfast and won $750 dollars at a one-arm-bandit in the cafe. *I want to be a VP.*

We visited the Pentagon to ensure funding would be available and to promote the benefits of an ALS missile. The other visits were mostly to determine user needs. They apparently had not been asked. We reported these findings during several visits to Eglin AFB, who appreciated the input. They apparently favored our winning the competition. Following the Pave Prism phase, we won the Active Laser Seeker (ALS) contract.

Paige would be confirmed at the Church of the Nativity in March 1977 by Bishop Stough. That summer we made our annual visit to New Mexico to visit family and friends.

In July 1977, Patsy had exhausted all the chemotherapy treatments available and had been declared free of cancer. Patsy, Paige, Chad and I would meet with Joann and Bill Archer from Knoxville at Opryland over Labor Day weekend. We journeyed to their home. The following day we all would go to the Ocoee River to ride the rapids.

Patsy had intended to go down the rapids with us, but said she was tired and would greet us at the bottom. This was unusual, but we had filled the previous days with many activities. We arrived home on Thursday. Saturday morning Patsy was not feeling well. From the study, I called Dr. Parker Griffith at his home and relayed her symptoms. He said, "I will meet you and Patsy at the hospital in 30 minutes. Skipper, she may not come out this time." Having been told six weeks earlier that she was free of cancer, his statement was shocking. I had to go outside behind bushes to get my act together. I returned to the breakfast table and calmly told them Parker wanted Patsy to meet him at the hospital. Chad had a football game that morning, so I called a neighbor Jesse Stutts, whose son, Jay, was on the team. I asked him to take Chad and Paige to the game. Paige was the cheerleader mentor.

At the hospital, Parker checked her in. I wanted to stay, but Patsy insisted I must attend the game, or the kids would be worried. Reluctantly, I agreed. At the game, I stood at the fence at the end of the field rather than on the sideline with everyone else. I knew it was not possible to keep it together and knew by now everyone knew of Patsy's trip to the hospital. Jesse joined me and I did not keep it together. Jesse, a true gentleman and friend, helped me survive the game. On a Thursday morning nearly two weeks later, Parker made his hospital rounds before 7:30 am as usual. When he was through his examination, Patsy asked, "How much time do I have?" Parker asked, "Why do you want to know?" She said, "Because I need to talk with Skipper." He responded, "It does not matter if you have four hours or forty years, you need to talk to Skipper." After he left the room Patsy said, "I do not ever want this topic brought up again." She proceeded to tell me briefly the flowers she wanted, dress to wear, and which earrings she wanted her mother to have and the ring she wanted to give Paige on her 16th birthday. She said everything else is up to me. End of discussion. The next day, Friday, it did not look like she would make it through the weekend. I walked across the street to our bank and asked them if our joint account would be frozen if she died. They said yes. They said I could create a single account in my name, transfer the balance in the joint account to my new account, and all checks written on the joint account would be routed to the new account. I wrote a check for the balance in the joint account and deposited it in the new account. I did not want Patsy to think I had given up, so I elected not to tell her. If she was to write a check, it would simply be covered by the new account.

To everyone's surprise, on Monday she had gained enough strength to return home. Parker had given her a shot that long ago had been used to treat breast cancer. Patsy would be in and out of the hospital five times. She would accumulate fluid in her lungs and the cancer was throughout her abdomen. At home she could not lie in bed because of the fluid in her lungs. I purchased a recliner for the den that seemed to allow her to rest. I also purchased a new television. The old one we had purchased when first moving to Huntsville in 1964 did not have a great picture. Patsy had wanted a fireplace, so I had a zero-clearance fireplace installed in the recreation room. I bricked the fireplace myself. I wanted it done right.

Bonnie visited one week to be with Patsy. Patsy was unable to do much and needed help that I could not provide from work. Forty years later, Bonnie emotionally told me she had been very close to many good people and that no one came close to being as good as Patsy.

One evening in October, I came home from work to find Patsy very upset with me. Someone had given her the mail including our joint bank account statement. She had seen the check I had written. Patsy thought I had paid for a cemetery plot, casket or whatever. She stated that she thought I had given up hope. Patsy further stated she relied on my hope for her hope and promise. Kneeling by her chair, I assured her that was far from true. I asked her to recall the day in September when we were all concerned about the chances of her surviving the weekend. I said it was necessary to create an account to ensure that funds were available to feed our out of town guests. She was relieved.

On another occasion while kneeling by her chair, I started reminiscing about times past. She said, "Stop, don't do that again, it sounds like you have given up." I would not make this mistake again. *My main selfish regret later was ignoring her for my sake, not hers. I would like to have had the memory of sharing with her my love by sharing times past. I did not tell her how much I loved her afterwards because she might take it wrong.*

On the third anniversary of her diagnosis at the end of October, Patsy and I went out to dinner. She barely had the energy for me to carry her to the car. At the restaurant I drove very close to the door and helped her inside. We enjoyed the dinner and the first opportunity to be alone for a change.

On November 16, 1977 my grandmother, the drama queen died. Three days later Patsy went in the hospital for the last time. It was 2-1/2 weeks before she died. Paige and Chad would spend the next to last weekend with Lee Tidwell and Erin, her daughter. Patsy had met Lee during the nursing program. Lee was Dr. Joe Akin's nurse. On the last Sunday, on the way home from church, the children and I stopped by the hospital to see Patsy. At the end of the visit, Paige and Chad stopped in the short hallway at the door and motioned that they wanted a moment before going out to see their grandparents and other relatives. After they departed, I closed the door again and returned to Patsy. She said, "Please do not bring them back. I do not want them to remember me like this." Later in private, Paige asked me to promise her that I would tell her if I learned that her mom was going to die. Reluctantly, I agreed. *I did not keep my promise.*

Early on Wednesday morning, *Pearl Harbor Day in 1977*, Patsy would go to sleep after rounds. During the morning several nurses independently and quietly stood at the end of Patsy's bed with tears. Her breathing became slower all morning and at noon she took her last breath. After kissing Patsy, I was asked to wait in the hall while Dr. Joe Akin, who happened to be on the floor, and his nurse, Lee Tidwell, went in the room to pronounce her dead. Lee would tell me that Joe, after leaving the room, told her to call his office and cancel his afternoon appointments. Joe went home. Father Emile Joffrion would perform the sacrament of extreme unction.

Emile wanted to be with me when I told the children of their mother's death. I told him I wanted to tell them privately, but he could stop by 30 minutes later. Chad would walk home from school first. He sat on my lap and I told him the sad news. He screamed and shouted a short phrase. I did my best to comfort him. Before Paige was due home, I asked Chad to go visit with Mike his friend next door and not tell Paige. It was okay to tell his friend. Paige sat on my lap screamed and shouted the same exact phrase as Chad. I also tried to comfort Paige. Emile stopped by and talked with each of them. He was and still is the best priest I have known. After a decent amount of time, family returned to our home. Family members were staying with us. Each night, for months, I would tuck the children in and give them an opportunity to let loose and try to answer their questions. There was not always an answer. The first night Paige thanked me for not keeping my promise to let her know that her mother was close to death. She said, "I do not think I could have handled that." I had been wrestling with not telling her because I had not lied to her and Chad before. I did not want to destroy my integrity. They needed to trust me more than ever. Paige's comment took a huge weight off my shoulders. I will always be grateful to her for this gift.

On Thursday, Lucille, Patsy's mother, saw the dress that Patsy wanted to wear for her funeral. Lucille was very upset and said no way was her daughter going to be buried in that. She wanted to buy a dress. Knowing Patsy would want to comfort her, I agreed. Sue Nichols approached me in the living room to tell me that Lucille was bad mouthing me to everyone. I thanked her and said I would take care of it. In the den, I knelt next to Lucille's chair and asked her to help me decide which casket to use and showed her two photos. She said for me to decide. There were no more complaints. I knew everyone grieves differently. Lucille was falling apart, and I was not. That upset her, she thought I must not care.

Thursday evening a visitation was held at Laughlin funeral home. Many came by the visitation that night including Dr. Parker Griffith who was visibly upset and barely able to utter, "We should have been able to do more." Lee Tidwell graciously sat with me for a while after everyone else had departed.

The funeral was on Friday at the Episcopal Church of the Nativity. I will always be grateful for all the friends from church, work, nurses, doctors, social friends, as well as friends of Chad and Paige who attended. The church was packed, and the service was special. I was surprised to see the TBE president and vice presidents at the funeral. I knew their schedules were packed. The journey out of the church was very difficult because of the love that radiated from those in the pews. I mostly held it together, but not internally.

Attending a very small Baptist church in New Mexico, Lucille was unfamiliar with an Episcopal church service was nervous about the funeral. After the funeral, she thanked me for a lovely service. It was as if a huge weight had been lifted from her shoulders. During the burial service at Maple Hill Cemetery, it was very cold and windy. Paige had an appropriate coat on, but Chad was not dressed for the occasion and shivering. I cuddled him inside my overcoat which gave me a different kind of warmth. *The things one remembers.* Several friends joined our family at our home which was comforting.

The next morning Patsy's parents, brother and wife headed back to New Mexico. Mom asked me if I would like for her to move in and help take care of Paige and Chad. I said, "I would like to try on my own." She suggested staying through the holidays and then discuss the possibility again.

On Sunday, Paige, Chad, Mom, Aunt Marian (Mom's sister) and I attended Lessons and Carols service at the large beautiful stone Chapel at the University of the South in Swanee, Tennessee. The University of the South is an Episcopal seminary. It was a beautiful and moving service conducted at the beginning of Advent. For years after I would attend the service as my way of getting spiritually into the Christmas season. I would ask various friends each year to join me. Not all were Episcopalians, but all seemed to love the service. Sometimes there was a good covering of snow that made the campus all the more beautiful.

On Christmas Day Sue and Roy Nicolas invited Mom, Paige, Chad and me over for Christmas dinner with their family. They also had longtime friends, Pat and Jim Kyser. After dinner in the middle of the afternoon, we were all sitting around, when the loss hit me full force like a freight train. It finally hit me that my best friend, lover, biggest fan, confidante, best critic, and source of joy was gone. *I had just entered Hell.*

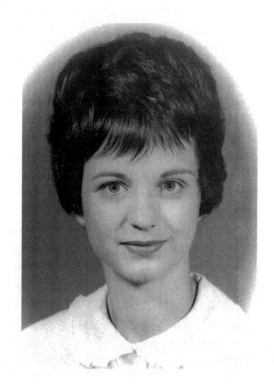

Chapter XIV - 1978–1981

Hell would continue through February when light would start to shine again. Friends, family and church got me through this period. The subject of me taking care of the children by myself, after the holidays, was not discussed with Mom or anyone again. Emotionally, I was not capable of taking care of myself, much less Paige and Chad. Mom was an anchor for us all. She was unique in her spirituality, optimism, energy, example and never gave advice unless specifically asked. *I should have asked for more advice.*

On my first business trip (there were direct flights from Huntsville to Los Angeles) I could not stop crying on the flight. The loss of Patsy was front and center. This was the first time I was not surrounded by family and friends. A very nice stewardess knelt by my seat during much of the flight trying to console me. I will never forget her kindness. The tears did not stop until we landed at LAX.

Sue Nichols would become close to Mom and was always available to listen. One day Sue said none of her much younger friends could keep up with Mom. Mom would retire by 7:00 pm to allow us to have our time together. She started reading by 3:00 am until 6:00, go for a two mile walk and return to fix us breakfast. After we went on to work and school, she did the house chores and proceeded to volunteer for a variety of organizations and do research at the library. She would return before the children arrived from school. One day when Sue was visiting, the subject of my Dad came up. Mom, skipping into the kitchen said, "He had a twinkle in his eyes." Sue and I displayed huge grins at Mom's expression of joy.

There would be many days that it seemed impossible to go on. I knew the impact on our children if I did not go on, so I persevered. At church each Sunday, there was so much love I wanted to attend all three services. I knew this would not be a wise move for our children. Paige and Chad were very involved at church. In fact, they would each earn a scholarship to Camp McDowell in the Episcopal Diocese, the following summer. A scholarship was awarded to the most active youth in each age group. In addition, the Acolyte Masters, John Cotten and Wally Reynolds were especially helpful with Paige and Chad. Helpful for me was attending a church history class each Sunday night taught by John Hendrix. Another thing that was therapeutic for me was going to the church each Saturday morning. Tut Clements, Phillip Arnold and I would perform handyman tasks at church for a few years, including stripping many layers of paint and refinishing the very old kitchen cabinets.

The Nichols, Horgens and Sanmanns asked if I would like to continue with the bridge group and that we could play any game if I desired to keep going. I was delighted and full of gratitude for their support and friendship. In January, my good friends Bobbie and Gene Sanmann invited me to attend an opera in Chattanooga, my first. It was a break I needed. I must thank them for exposing me to a new love. The bridge group was a big part of the reason I survived.

For much of the first year and more, I believed that life was not bearable without a loving wife. We had a great marriage which allowed me to believe I was capable of loving again. *This would prove to be correct.*

A new will needed to be prepared to ensure Paige and Chad would be cared for in the future. I wanted a couple who would raise them in a Christian family environment, with love and with education at the forefront. Sue and Roy Nichols were the ideal choice. Although they had three daughters, they agreed to accept them into their family. *A huge blessing and relief.* I knew Paige and Chad would be loved by exceptional people.

At work I was able to be functional in meetings, but reading documents, not so much. I would read a paragraph and could not tell you one word read. Harry and the branch team carried me through and back from Hell. Another branch manager, Dr. Nick Passino was always available to listen. He would become my best friend for 35 years until his untimely death.

Norm Andrade, my McDonnell Douglas counterpart, was leading our team effort for the Active Laser Seeker (ALS) program to be awarded by Eglin AFB. He was especially helpful. Norm had also lost his first wife while in his thirties. She had a heart condition. He gave me some good advice. He said, "Do not get married again until you are comfortable being single. You will then get married for the right reasons." It would take me three years to be comfortable being single. He also advised never, never date anyone from work. Norm had a bad experience before learning the importance of that wisdom. Later when I considered dating, the idea of introducing them to Paige and Chad seemed like a bad idea. I did not want them to get attached and then have to deal with more grief.

Mom, Paige, and Chad gave me a fortieth birthday party. The second one in my life. It was very special. They invited the bridge group (Bobbie and Gene Sanmann, Sue and Roy Nichols, Nancy and Chris Horgen) and Lee Tidwell. They had decorated the recreation room and tables set up with checkered tablecloths and candles. When I arrived home from work, they were all hiding in the living room.

Lee and Erin joined Paige, Chad and me during spring break to tent camp at Fall Creek Falls State Park, Tennessee. There were various activities to occupy our time which gave us many opportunities to laugh and have fun. The break provided us with a family life we had experienced numerous times in the past. After returning home, I tucked Paige in bed. She said, "Dad you should marry Lee." I knew they both loved Lee and Erin. Lee and I were just good friends and romance was not going to happen. She was beautiful, intelligent, full of life and a dozen years younger. I assured Paige this was not possible even though we all enjoyed being together like a family.

Each year the four branch managers would meet and decide how to divide up the raise pool of money pool. Every year I was able to persuade the others that all my staff should receive above average raises. That meant the other branch managers had to dip into their allotted money. One year, Jerry Edwards, a branch manager asked, "How do you manage that crazy bunch?" I shrugged my shoulders. *It's still a mystery.*

TBE decided to identify nine product lines. One of those product lines was optical seekers and I was designated the Product Line Manager and would report to Steve McCarter, the Sr. VP. I had the sense that my regular boss, Harry, did not appreciate me reporting two levels above him. I would not have liked that in his shoes. Harry never mentioned that anomaly as a problem. It was never a conflict. Steve occasionally asked me to report the Seeker Product Line status. One time he asked if I was worried about anything. I responded yes, without stating why. Steve asked if I could do anything about the concern. My answer was no. Steve said, "Before my recent heart attack, I worried about too many things and then realized that accomplished nothing. If you can do something, do it, if not, move on. Do not worry and you will live longer."

MDAC was the ALS prime contractor and our customer, but it felt more like a team with Eglin AFB, the customer. TBE was responsible for the ALS gyro optics head assembly including the detector and part of the appropriate electronics mostly located behind the head. TBE did not make the 8-element Silicon detector. MDAC was responsible for the overall system, laser and signal processing requirements. Our joint team was not responsible for the missile, propellent, etc. We were to assume the ALS would be mounted on a Sidewinder missile.

Each member of our Optics Application Branch participated in the design and construction of the ALS with overlapping responsibilities. This was easy because the team worked well together. The laser beam had to be routed through the gimbals and pointed at the target. The returning signal that bounced off the target had to be captured by a mirror that focused the beam through a Fresnel lens and second mirror to a quadrant sensor. The sensor electrical signal was sent to the signal processing electronics. The electronics section would point the gimbals and provide guidance signals to the missile.

The dividing line of responsibilities between the seeker design was somewhat blurred but generally as follows; Chuck Whaley had the electronics; Hugh Morgan had the optics and part of the mechanical structure; Al Froelich had the spinning mechanism and the bulkhead; Manfred Segewitz had the quadrant sensor and pre-amp; and I took on the gimbal structures. Each area included support equipment that had to be designed and built such as jigs for gimbal assembly and alignment jigs for other parts of the head. Precision optical alignment equipment had to be designed as well as methods to test and calibrate the electronics. In a few cases this was as complex as the seeker parts. None of the areas were simple. An example was the pre-amp which was to be designed by the electronics division. They assigned the task to their best engineer, Ed LaBudd. After some effort, he said it could not be done, that it was impossible. Manfred disagreed and said he would like to take on the task. I said, "Go for it." Manfred succeeded in advancing the state of art. Our team would travel to MDAC several times to ensure the TBE gyro optics head assembly design would interface mechanical and electronically with MDAC portions of the ALS seeker. We produced two units. I negotiated with MDAC for TBE to keep the second Unit. I wanted to have the unit for marketing, demonstrations and sentimental reasons. I could not have been prouder of our group for advancing the seeker technology. We had a lot of fun. Team members would work many hours on their own to meet schedules and solve many technical challenges. The project spanned about three years including the Pave Prism and ALS phases.

In the spring of 1978, the Active Laser Seeker program gave the bidders the opportunity to test their concept at the Navy facilities at China Lake, California. We fabricated the Pave Prism seeker head, a crude configuration that could be mounted on a motorized tracking platform. McDonnell Douglas (MDAC) provided most of the support equipment along with the electronics needed that would implement the algorithms needed to lock the laser on the target and guide a missile. The Navy provided the target fighter aircraft. At least one other competitor, Xerox was set up at the site. Their system produced no results, while our Pave Prism had limited success, but success nevertheless compared to Xerox. We were told the jet would approach from the distant mountains. Standing beside our tripod, my eyes started watering as I concentrated on the spot in the mountains. All of a sudden, I thought a spot was closing on us. It seemed like the fighter jet passed over us at a few hundred feet or less in a couple of seconds after visually being spotted. The plane was flying in the full military power mode. It was scary how fast the target had approached. Made me glad for the decision when graduating from ENMU not to join the Navy as a fighter pilot. If you cannot spot the enemy, not knowing where he was coming from in the vast sky, you would be nuts to be a fighter pilot. Of course, the plane had radar and more to help, but still. *Thank you someone up there for my decision.*

During one of the China Lake visits the Optics Department Manager, Dr. Harry Watson joined us. He needed to be back in Huntsville so I drove him to Los Angeles International (LAX) so he could catch the redeye flight home. The following morning, I met with Steve McCarter for breakfast at 7:00 am. Steve was visiting Teledyne, Inc headquarters in Beverly Hills. He wanted to review a few points concerning TBE negotiations with MDAC and the division of work for the ALS. During the negotiations everything was going smoothly until MDAC wanted to conduct some of the analysis needed to design the seeker head. I became stubborn. This discussion went on for a while. One of my team members suggested we caucus. He suggested we accept the MDAC position so we could move on. We returned to the negotiations and standing my ground explained we needed total control of the head design. They backed off. The meeting ended with everyone happy and expecting to win the ALS contract. We were awarded the contract.

The children and I would go skiing during spring break of 1979 to Vail, Colorado. The following spring break we went to Aspen. At Vail, Paige and Chad would attend ski classes. Each day they would beg to drop the classes and go with me on the mountain to show me their stuff. After the third day, I gave in. We skied the intermediate runs and they kept begging to go on the black diamond expert runs. On the last day, we stopped at a black diamond run with their begging at its peak. Relenting I said, "You'll go first, and I will follow and pick up the pieces." At the bottom of the run, they turned around and waved for me to join them. The first mogul got me, and I slid down to them on my back. *I am a role model.* The next year at Aspen, on the last day, we skied mostly the black diamonds. Paige did not fall, but the two male hot dogs fell a lot.

In the summer of 1978 Paige, Chad and I visited New Mexico seven months after Patsy's death. Lucille said to me, "Now I understand." She was referring the doubts she had about me caring for her daughter. Ebb had recently had colon cancer surgery. It never occurred again. He would live to be 101 years old. We had a good time as always visiting family and friends.

Paige and Chad continued with sports. On one occasion Paige, about 14 years old, was playing her last game of softball for the season. She would be moving up to a new age group the next year. Coaches for the following year were at the game scouting. In the top of the final inning the game was tied, and the bases were loaded. Paige was playing third base. She caught a fly ball, tagged third base (the runner had started for home) and tagged the runner coming from second. She got all three outs by herself. In the bottom of the last inning, she knocked in the winning run. The scouting coaches gathered around me wanting Paige to play on their team the next year.

One afternoon during Chad's confirmation classes, Nancy Lacy was walking around outside of the church. I happen to arrive, and she said your son is driving the instructors up the wall including her. Chad did not understand how he could have been Baptized as an infant without his permission. I would find out later that Mom had explained to his satisfaction the reason. *It was more of a commitment by parents and Godparents to raise him in a Christian environment.* So, in April 1979 Chad was confirmed at the Church of the Nativity by Bishop Stough. During the same service Dr. Parker Griffith was confirmed. In late fall of 1979, the three survivors would find their photo in the church directory.

I had been elected to the Vestry at church and Father Joffrion had firmly suggested that I attend a Cursillo weekend at Camp McDowell. I could not think of a reason to refuse. I attended in May 1980. Paige and Chad stayed with friends because Mom had gone to Kansas to visit my sister, Nancy, and her family. Following the weekend, Nancy called with the news that Mom had a stroke. She said the doctors indicated stress might have been a contributing factor to the stroke. Paige asked me not to let Mom return to living with us. Paige said she did not think she could control her ability to maintain a stress-free environment. She seemed to think she caused Mom's stroke. The Kansas doctor's diagnosis of a stroke proved to be incorrect. Stress had nothing to do with her condition. Likely Paige's self-esteem suffered until the correct diagnosis was discovered. In my opinion, Paige's self-esteem continued to suffer causing her to act out.

A couple of weeks later the doctors cleared Mom to drive her beloved VW Beetle back to Huntsville. She unintentionally wandered all over the map on the way home. Within one week, she was deteriorating. In Huntsville Hospital, after preforming a scan, they discovered a brain tumor the size of an orange that caused her to become totally paralyzed. She could not even blink her eyes or squeeze your hand. She had a five percent chance of improving if the neurosurgeon operated. In her condition there was little to lose by trying so I authorized the operation. The operation occurred on July 2nd. Nothing changed, the tumor was malignant. Mom would reside in a nursing home her last months. I tried to stop by on my way to work each day and on the way home. *In addition to my deep concern for her, I now had no help being a single father.*

On a Saturday evening, October 27, 1980, I was rear-ended by a car going 40 mph. I was going less than 10 mph with no headrest. This would cause long standing issues. That night at 2:30 am I received a call from the nursing home that Mom was near the end. I called Father Emile Joffrion. He met me there. She died less than 30 minutes later. Emile, who had become very close to Mom, planned and conducted the funeral service. Again, the church was packed. As a long-ago Episcopal Nun, who was filled with spirit, she would have been delighted with the service. Mom's best friend, Sparky from West Palm Beach and Aunt Betty from Coral Gables respectively attended the funeral and invited us to visit during spring break. Her body was flown to Carlsbad, New Mexico to be buried next to Dad. My sisters, Bonnie and Nancy with their families attended a memorial service conducted by the priest from Grace Episcopal Church. Mom had made many friends in the short time she lived in Huntsville. Nearly 40 years later people still volunteer that Mom was special and made a difference in their lives. She had made her mark on many during her life. Mom lived life to the fullest. *There could not be a better Mom.*

After attending to Mom's affairs, I was not sure that real laughter or joy was possible. I was emotionally burned out. In December a ski brochure arrived in the mail offering a trip to Innsbrook, Austria. I persuaded a good friend, Charlie Gibson, to join me. He had never skied and was also single. Paige and Chad stayed with neighborhood friends. Our 10-day adventure started January 17, 1981. We stayed at the Grauer Bär (Grey Bear) Hotel in the heart of the historic section. The nearest skiing was a 10-minute city bus ride to Igls, a small ski village. The first day we ventured to Igls to rent ski equipment and enroll Charlie in a ski class. We met a beautiful Swiss woman, Bridgette, and her mother. Mother did not ski. *Oh well.* I came to the rescue suggesting we meet the next morning at the ski rental shop. The beautiful natural blond (an apparent identical twin of Cybill Shepard), with hair to her waist, did not disappoint. We would ski every day under a blue sky. Austria reportedly had the best snow in 25 years. It snowed every night leaving the trees heavy laden with fresh snow and sparkling everywhere. Bridgette had a lovely voice and often skied singing to me. She also taught me some German. At the day's end, we could ski down to the rental shop, leave our equipment and go next door to a pub. Charlie met an attractive lady from London in ski school. They were invited to the Annual Ski Instructors' Gala that evening, after the first day of skiing, and could bring a guest. Bridgette and I joined them for a memorable night of entertainment. The ladies' hotel was in Igls and the door was locked at 10:00 pm. Only guests could enter after ringing the doorbell. After midnight and escorting the dates each night to their hotel, we took a cab and sang all the way to our quarters in Innsbrook. *Glühwein and spending time with lovely ladies does encourage singing.* Each night there was a unique entertaining event. At all times, laughter fed on itself.

One night the group including Bridgette's mother rode on a chairlift to a beautiful building high on the mountain. The large hall ceiling was more than two stories high, had a narrow balcony on one side, a small semi-round balcony at one end over a dance floor and a wall of glass facing Innsbruck at the other end. I learned to polka. An oom-pa-pa band was on the small balcony. We formed a snake dance, went up the stairs at one end of the narrow balcony, down the other stairs, and over the long-occupied tables. After midnight I rode down the long toboggan run on a small sled with Bridgette's mother. *Great fun.* The last day we (not mother) rode down the Olympic bobsled run with a professional driver and attended an international ski jumping competition at the Olympic facility. Cybill *(oops, Bridgette)* and I were never alone except when skiing. Even so it was a romantic adventure never to be forgotten.

The ski trip story was important to mention because all who come after me should know that joy can be right around the corner and a surprise. I learned that life and joy were possible again and that it was important for me and the children to have a break from each other. This unconscious dude had not considered the importance of a break. Paige and Chad wondered why I was so tired after a vacation. I did not volunteer that I rarely received four hours of sleep. I started the tradition of bringing the children a present when visiting a new country. Paige would receive a classic doll attired in that country's costume. Chad would receive either a goofy or collectible present.

Back to work. One day, John White, who served on Harry's staff, entered my office and asked me to be one of four project managers on a new contract about to be awarded to TBE. He was to be the program director of the System Technology and Material Program

(STAMP) and would report directly to a VP, rather than Harry. The four projects included different Soviet missiles and equipment. I would be responsible for repairing eight hundred SA-7 Soviet Union missiles for Egypt. (The heat seeking infrared shoulder fired missiles were first used by Egypt in the war with Israel. They were similar to our Redeye missiles.) I would be able to accept this challenge and uphold my branch manager responsibilities because much of the branch staff would join me. The task was to staff the project, design the repair line, design each test station, prepare procedures, determine test requirements, order parts and equipment and repair the missiles on an impossible schedule. The SA-7 missiles had to be completely reverse engineered due to the lack of documentation and several repair stations designed and built before the repair line could fully commence. Both the customer and TBE knew the schedule requirements were impossible. The Foreign Military Sales (FMS) required 300 missiles be delivered to Egypt each quarter. MICOM would be issuing the contract. Knowing the schedule was critical, I laid out an overall design for the repair stations and prepared a list of staff needed before the contract was signed. Each subassembly and sometimes components needed at least one repair station. The propellants and warhead sections would be inspected and repaired at a different facility. The reverse engineering was the highest priority. I researched and studied the Soviet approach to manufacturing missiles. Their approach was quite different then the USA approach and would significantly impact the repair approach.

Paige, Chad and I found ourselves knocking on the door of Sparky in West Palm Beach. Her daughter, Janie, answered the door. She no longer was the skinny 10-year-old, when I had last seen her. The home was actually hers. Her mother Sparky and daughter, Jackie also lived there. Jackie was five years old and had been one month old when her father, a Philadelphia banker, was killed in Nicaragua in a small plane accident. The home was being refurbished by Janie and it had a large pool. The home was about two blocks from the Coastal Waterway. Everyone had a great time. We headed to Betty's in Coral Gable to visit. A very different kind of visit but still fun. We stopped by Janie's again for two days. Within two blocks, when heading home, Paige and Chad both said, "Dad, you need to marry Janie." I had not exposed them to anyone else before. It turns out Janie and I would date, on and off, for 18 years.

The STAMP contract was signed. I first invited Manfred Segewitz to start the reverse engineering of the A-7 missile. Staffing ramped up quickly. Eventually 200-300, including support staff in other divisions, would work on the project. I organized two twelve-hour shifts to work around the clock seven days a week. The project would be housed in four buildings, two would be in facilities on Redstone Arsenal. The main activities were in one of those buildings and the propellant in a different building. None of the missiles would leave the Arsenal for security (the program was classified Secret) and safety reasons. I would have five offices including my regular branch office. During this period, I have not included projects ongoing in the branch.

Retired NASA German legend, Dr. Walter Häussermann, was hired as a consultant for the STAMP for a different missile project than the SA-7 missile. The morning he reported to work, no one seemed to know why he was there. I happened by and asked him if he would provide a suggestion on a reverse engineering problem that was giving us headaches. He said he was willing to do his best. I found an empty office in an out of the way location. He would solve the problem within three days. His reputation was that he had no technical limitations. I moved him to one of the buildings on Redstone Arsenal before he might be discovered. A couple of months later, Joe Moquin visited the main repair line and spotting Walter sped across the room and all but genuflected before Dr. Häussermann. He was a key person in Wernher von Braun's inner circle that took us to the moon. He was head of the Astrionics Division of what is now Marshall Space Flight Center. The Astrionics Division had 3,000 employees and reportedly had two billion dollars of subcontract work. He had also been the Director of the Guidance and Control Laboratory. He led electrical, computer systems, guidance, and navigation systems for the Saturn V. He received the *Decoration for Exceptional Civilian Service* in 1959. He was truly a quiet, humble genius.

The first status review was conducted in Cairo, Egypt and hosted by an Egyptian four star general, the head of Air Defense. Nine of the TBE/MICOM team were in attendance. The night we arrived I became very sick, not being immune to Egyptian bacteria. They had the same problem when they visited Huntsville. The next morning, I was on the agenda first, after John White provided an overview. After we sat down around the conference table, I asked our secretary, seated on my right, to please scoot up that I may have to leave suddenly. She looked at me and said, "You should leave now." They later said I staggered from the room. Splashing water on my face and arms seemed to help. I returned to my seat just as John mouthed, "Are you ready?" I nodded. He then turned the floor over to me. Somehow it went well. The General offered us box lunches of KFC chicken and Sport Cola. The chicken had been fried in camel fat or worse. The Sport Cola was an attempt to copy Coca Cola with no quality control. Ramadan was in full swing. *I joined their fasting.*

The group of nine Americans attended a Belly Dance performance where she was reportedly the top dancer in Egypt. *No argument from me.* Four days later, after fasting and feeling slightly better, we headed home. Ray Watson (a past TBE VP), Jack Blessing and I detoured through Copenhagen for two nights at Hotel d'Angletterre. Ray then headed home. Jack and I headed for London for a couple of days. We watched the rehearsal of Diana and Charles's wedding procession from St. Paul's to Buckingham Palace. We watched from our rooms in the Strand Palace Hotel on the Strand. Millions invaded London for the occasion. The next day, July 29, 1981, while the real wedding took place, we flew home from a nearly empty airport. *Life can be enjoyed.*

The missiles were in pitiful condition. A bullet was even imbedded in a warhead. With much effort, about 78 missiles were repaired for the first delivery, far below the requirements, but more than expected. We had picked the easiest missiles to repair. I was congratulated by the customer for a significant achievement.

Knowing the team had spent several months working 12-hour days seven days a week, I invited all of them and their spouses for steak and beer in the TBE Park. I asked Ed Seigler to purchase the best steaks as well as plenty of beer and soft drinks. He took care of all the details and as always, put on a great celebration. The cooks prepared the steaks over coals to your specifications. They also prepared baked potatoes and provided chips. The spouses had earned all we could offer and more for putting up with tired missing partners. The German legend Dr. Walter Häussermann, the quiet humble genius, introduced me to his wife, Ruth, as his "boss." *I was overwhelmed and surprised.* The event was unusual at TBE and was a big success. The bonus was the new friendships developed as a result of the relaxed atmosphere.

A military cargo plane carried the refurbished A-7 missiles and Manfred to Cairo. To our surprise, an Egyptian general wanted to randomly pick and live fire three missiles at targets. Manfred sat next to him and, as a devout Catholic, quietly prayed. The general told him, success or not, that it was in Allah's hands so do not worry. Fortunately, all missiles hit the target. *Thank you, Pope.*

Paige, Chad and I made our annual trip to New Mexico to visit family and friends during the summer of 1981. The Eunice High School reunion was special as always on July 4th. We had a great time as always.

Janie and Jackie joined us for Thanksgiving. Nice to have a better cook than me prepare the dinner. Paige, Chad and me, of course, did not like to see them head back to Florida. *In hindsight we all were falling in love.*

Our customer had been promising Washington more than was possible. He had received a lot of heat for not delivering the promised number of missiles. We received a letter from MICOM, through contracts requesting how many missiles we would deliver on the next plane three months down the road. I suggested that we give an optimistic number, but much lower than required. My rationale was that we would be protecting the customer from himself. Unknown to us he had already stuck his neck out in Washington. He now took the position that TBE had a management problem, me. He had words of praise for me the day before to TBE executives.

The customer staff tried to push me to do things that would cause significant delays. I went to the mat to make sure the greatest number of missiles could be delivered. They simply did not know the difference between the Soviet design philosophy and US design approach. The customer said they would not sign additional funds ($40,000,000) next week if I was not replaced. Bob Rieth, our VP, invited me to join him in his office to tell me to return to my branch duties immediately. He said, "We know the customer is the problem and you were doing the right things, but the big dollars are critical. Joe Moquin (TBE President) made the decision to secure the funding. This will not be held against you by anyone including Joe." I asked if I could address my staff to thank them for their contribution to the project. Bob said that was not possible. John White gathered them and said, Skipper's talents are needed elsewhere." Manfred was very upset and walked out of the meeting. *His action was appreciated by me at a time when I was down and still is remembered with gratitude.* John replaced me with three individuals. One of them immediately implemented the customers recommendations. Six weeks later, John White's deputy, Rodger Watson told Bob Rieth that I had been right on every point. Bob told Rodger that he knew I was right. They did not deliver one missile that quarter.

At the time, the pressure from Washington, the Pentagon and Embassies did not make sense. Egypt was not being threatened or attacked. No one ever hinted why there was an impossible schedule. I assumed the missiles might be going to Iraq during their eight-year war with Iran. Years later, when I saw the movie "Charlie Wilson's War," the light came on. A scene showed Charlie negotiating with the Egyptian President, Muhammad Mubarak, concerning the 800 SA-7 missiles. They were going into Afghanistan to knock down Soviet aircraft. We did not want US hardware to show up on the battlefield, only Soviet hardware. According to a report by the Federation of American Scientists, during the 1980s, in an effort to topple the Soviet-backed government of Afghanistan, the U.S. government provided mujahideen with Soviet-made SA-7s.

In December, when relieved from the project, I arrived home early and said, "The 12 hour and longer days and nights are over." They both leaped with joy. It was a blessing to be totally free to participate in the children's activities. We attended the 1981 Christmas Eve service and celebrated Christmas without Mom, who died a year ago. That meant I was picking presents without help. *Not sure if they faked enjoying Santa's presents.*

Chapter XV - 1982–1986

Life raising two teenagers was always interesting. It is amazing how dumb parents become and how teens know everything. Paige was suffering in high school years. She was acting out. Knowing she needed help dealing with losing her mother and grandmother, I obtained counseling for her. The first was a poor choice. The second, David Barnhart, EdD was much better. In my presence, he told Paige I was a loving father doing the right things. In hindsight, neither counselor addressed the cause, they only tried to change behavior. I regret not recognizing the difference. Father Joffrion, who had three daughters, said to me, "It is too bad we cannot put our daughters in a deep freeze at fourteen and take them out when they are 20." *I might broaden that age range.* Chad was continuing piano lessons and wrestling. Paige was expanding her artistic talent. *Quite the artist.*

Because of being rear-ended on the eve of Mom's death, my neck continued to be a problem, even with physical therapy. It reached the point of needing an operation because of the pain down both arms. Dr. Don Maccubbin, a neurosurgeon, performed two operations to remove disks about the time school was out for the 1982 summer. Janie and Jackie came up from Florida for the summer to take care of the three Colins. I had to lay on my back for more than two months. I could not hold a book or watch TV. Janie, an avid reader and teacher, would read books to me, which prevented me from going crazy. *Some might think she failed.*

The Optics Application Branch concentrated on contracts with Eglin AFB and MICOM, while some members were still working on STAMP. My duties as branch manager were not as demanding as in the past, but still challenging.

Charlie Gibson was asked by someone who was going to be interviewed by me, what could he tell him about me. His reply was, "He works hard and plays hard." Finally, remembering Charlie's comment solved my problem of a book title. *So, Charlie you can take credit or blame for the book title.*

Bob Schwanhausser transferred from Teledyne Ryan Aircraft to TBE to be Vice President of Advanced Programs in 1981. Swany was credited with bringing in two billion dollars of drone business to Ryan. Swany proved to be a hard charger. Soon after he arrived, he asked three of us from different departments to meet with him concerning his desire to expand our business in Egypt. He asked if the existing Soviet A-22 "Atoll" missile could be modified to improve performance. The Atoll missile was similar to an earlier version of our heat-seeking air-to-air Aim-9 Sidewinder Missile. The Sidewinder Missile was used on fighter aircraft in the Air Force, Navy and exported to several allies. Two of us reported back with some ideas. He asked me to develop a program plan and to document the performance improvement ideas and compare them to the current version in the Egyptian inventory.

Swany and I visited Davis Air Force Base, near San Antonio, the Pentagon, the State Department and other locations to ensure Foreign Military Sales (FMS) funds were available and that the performance enhancements were not a security issue. He then headed to Egypt to meet with the head of their Air Force. His plan was to repair their inventory and enhance the performance. Following the meeting, he called me and said, "Skipper, I need your help, get your rear-end over here. Prepare viewgraphs, then fly to Europe and spend a couple of days to shake off jet lag. I will meet you in Cairo and you will brief the head of the Egyptian Air Force." I asked, "Where are you?" He said, "I am in Verbier, Switzerland (a "Jetsetter" destination ski village) 100 miles from Geneva." I responded, "Geneva sounds like a good spot to linger. We could fly down to Cairo together. If that works for you, what hotel do you recommend in Geneva?" His answer was the Ritz-Carlton de la Paix (a five-star hotel). I thanked him and we hung up. Ten minutes later he called me and said, "Beverly just kicked my rear-end for not inviting you to stay with us at our chalet in Verbier. If you would like that, I will pick you up at the Geneva airport." *Who am I to argue with a VP?*

I spent three days, nearly around the clock, refining technical details and preparing viewgraphs. TBE President, Joe Moquin, asked me to give him a dry run. I was exhausted. It would be the worst briefing I, and perhaps anyone, had given to Joe. It certainly was the worst I had presented to anyone. He wished me well and I headed for the airport. I fell asleep on the taxiway.

In late November 1982, Swany was waiting at 6:30 am at the Geneva airport. Several friends attended a birthday party for Beverly at the Ritz-Carlton the night before. We picked Beverly up at the Ritz-Carlton and proceeded on a beautiful drive around Lake Geneva to their chalet. After eating lunch at a lovely French Restaurant in Verbier, we ascended on a lift to the top of the mountain to check out the snow and observe the skiers. There was no snow in the village. Their chalet had 13 beds. Their deck overlooked a beautiful valley with snowcapped peaks all around. They planned to take me on a brief tour to Italy, France and Switzerland the following day. Alas, just before he was going to grill some thick filets, I became miserably sick. Beverly graciously nursed me for the next two days. Feeling slightly better she drove Swany and me down the mountain to the railroad station which took us to the Geneva airport.

The meeting with the head of the Egyptian Air Force included several generals. At the end of my briefing after answering their questions, I asked if they had helmet sights. If not, how did the pilot aim and fire the Soviet Atoll missile? They did not seem to understand. "Top Dog" suggested we meet the following morning at their military AFB. They invited me to sit in a Soviet MIG hoping that might answer the question. I said, "Sure, that would be useful," internalizing my excitement with a straight face.

Our Egyptian agents were two retired four-star generals. One was a national hero for winning the Yom Kippur War in October 1973. The rest of the world thinks Israel won, but not the Egyptians. In 1972, Sadat had expelled 20,000 Soviet advisers from Egypt and opened new diplomatic channels with Washington, DC. Our agent had been responsible for acquiring a much-needed arsenal of weapons after Egypt lost the 1967 War. He acquired them from the Soviets, hence he was a hero during the Yom Kippur War in October 1973. I asked our agent if he could arrange for me to take pictures of the cockpit the next day for engineers back home. He made some calls and received permission. I would have to give the film to the Air Force, and they would release the film to me in two months. I told our agent that would not work because we needed to perform some engineering tasks immediately. He said, "Take two rolls and quietly keep one."

Swany suggested I stop in Greece for a couple of days, then go to London for a few days after I finished in Cairo. *Who was I to argue with a VP who was going to sign my expense report?* He gave me the telephone of Stavros, a taxi driver, who would pick me up at the Athens airport, get me a hotel, show me the sights and return me to the airport. He recommended a hotel in London that Henry Singleton, the Teledyne, Inc Board Chairman, and Dr. George Roberts, the President and the vice chairman of the board, and of course Swany always stayed in when in London. Swany said he would call the hotel and vouch for me because it was an exclusive hotel and only accepted former guests. Swany headed back home.

The next day a brigadier general had the task of carrying my camera in a small plastic shopping bag. He was at my shoulder regularly asking, "Now?" My answer was always, "Not yet." I sat in the Soviet MIG-23 cockpit with the Atoll missiles spun up. The pilot had to have the target inside a small simple gun sight before releasing the missiles mounted under the wing. It seemed to me like sitting in a Model A Ford era airplane. The pilot was not going to win any dog fight. I told them we could significantly expand the launch window. They were very pleased. I wondered how many Americans had sat in a Soviet MIG. This was long before the Soviet collapse. *I had to pinch myself to see if I was dreaming.*

The taxi driver, Stavros, met me at the Athens airport in a large new Mercedes on Thursday. He said, "All taxi drivers are on strike, but not to worry, I owe Swany a huge favor." The first stop was at a very nice 15 story hotel. It had a large pool on the roof. The desk said they were full. Stavros asked me to give him some of the monopoly money I had gotten at the airport. He knew someone. He did and I was assigned a very nice room. He would take me to many sights in Athens and to a shopping area that was void of tourists. The quality of items was better and less expensive. Friday night he took me to a Taverna. We were escorted to the best table. It was in the center next to the stage. He ordered our meal (his recommendation) and a bottle of Ouzo. When we finished the meal and too much Ouzo the entertainment started on the stage. After midnight and having finished more Ouzo he dropped me at the hotel. The next morning, I wished I had never heard of Ouzo. Saturday morning Stavros drove us southeast along the coast about 70 miles. This was a very beautiful and different Greece. He dropped me at the hotel about noon. I joined many people at the pool. There was only one vacant lounge chair that faced a thoroughbred racetrack. Every 30 minutes there was a new race. I noticed a sign when getting off the elevator that said no nude bathing allowed. Not all women read the sign. Sunday morning Stavros dropped me at the airport.

The hotel in London consisted of 13 suites and no other rooms. The suite was furnished with remarkable antiques and consisted of a parlor, dining room, bedroom and of course a bathroom. They served in your suite the traditional "Tea" including lovely pastries in the afternoon. They had no breakfast menu. They brought a breakfast fit for the Queen to your suite. The breakfast was served on a silver tray with a silver cover. I used this hotel on many future visits. *Sometimes I know I am the luckiest person ever.*

Back home, Swany asked me to return to Egypt and meet with the head of the Egyptian Air Defense and other four-star generals to present our suggestions and get their comments. During a layover at Kennedy International in NYC an attendant upgraded me to First Class on the flight to Cairo on a Pan Am 747. They did know how to pamper. I was served one of the top five meals I was ever to eat. For the first time, I did not travel in a suit. Because of the length of the trip, for the first time I wore Levi's, a knit shirt and tennis shoes on an airplane. Of course, they lost my luggage. I could not even get a toothbrush, much less underclothes or clothes washed overnight. I was unable to shop as my meetings were scheduled while stores were open. I had to meet the gracious generals in my bohemian attire. They said not to be concerned, they also had experienced luggage problems while traveling. After four days my clothes smelled like the natives. My luggage arrived on the fourth day. On the Pan AM return flight home, I sat in business class when leaving Rome next to an Irish Catholic priest who had spent the previous six months in the Vatican and would spend the next six months in Mexico City. *Never try and match drink for drink with and Irish priest.* The good news, he introduced me to Priest Bailey's Cream after dinner.

The program forming in my mind consisted of two phases after a TBE study. The study would require many technical inputs from Egypt. The first phase would mean a $40,000,000 contract to TBE and be funded with FMS funds. The second phase would expand the contract to $200,000,000. I recommended a Memorandum of Understanding (MOU) be prepared to protect both our interests. They suggested I prepare a MOU and return to Cairo. They volunteered that Egyptian Industrial Relations group would have to bless the programs.

I returned to Huntsville. Swany suggested I prepare a briefing and return to Cairo to meet with the head of Industrial Relations. Our agents set up the meeting for May 1983. When I arrived, the head man was out of the country. It would be two weeks before he returned. The agents always furnished me with a driver and car around the clock, so I made the best of the situation. I toured the pyramids and rode a camel.

One night I attended an impressive light show at the pyramids. I visited the Egyptian Museum, a mosque, the Citadel, the Coptic Christian area and the Khan El Khalili Market in the Hussein District in Cairo. One day the driver headed south along the Nile river to show me the Step Pyramids. It was an interesting drive and experience seeing rural and agricultural parts of Egypt. Cairo had a population of 18 million without an adequate infrastructure. It took five hours to cross the city. My driver was resourceful. He would drive on sidewalks scattering pedestrians to cut time. *Sometimes business travel is fun.* The meeting with the head of Industrial Relations was brief and positive.

Back at TBE, I presented my program plan to Swany and the need of $300,000 funds for the study. Due largely to Swany's solid reputation with Teledyne, Inc, funds were approved.

I prepared a draft MOU for Swany expecting him to return to Egypt to negotiate a final version. No, he delegated that task. Off to Egypt again. John White, the STAMP program manager had convinced Joe Moquin, the TBE President, that he should accompany me during the negotiation. He convinced Joe his experience with STAMP would be helpful. I could not think of a believable or tactful reason to counter the suggestion. We headed for Egypt in December 1983.

John headed for the only chair close to the general and gave him a present. This was my event and John was getting in the way. The general suggested we start negotiations with his staff the next day. The negotiations were going well until we came to the exclusive clause. They did not want the clause in the MOU. We debated for hours discussing the clause. John never spoke during the negotiations and suggested we caucus. Outside, John suggested I drop the clause and move on. I said, "There is no way I will return to TBE without protection for our investment. My conscience will not allow that." We returned to the room and I told the Egyptians, "No one in this room will remove the clause. Those we report to will have to agree to removing the clause. After the study is completed, TBE could go to Iraq with a program using the data collected from Egypt. The clause protects Egypt as well as TBE."

The next day, meeting with the general who had reviewed the modified MOU, he made a point of being pleased with the exclusion clause and that it must be included. The general approved the MOU without changes. John returned to Huntsville. *Oh well! My ego was intact.* I stayed in Cairo until all pertinent parties had reviewed and approved the MOU. On Thursday, I was told that President Hosni Mubarak would have to sign the document. He was out of country and would not be home until Saturday. Friday was their weekend. Someone would go to his home on Saturday and get his signature, just a formality. I would not be allowed to go to his home, but not to worry. The Egyptians said I should go home, and they would overnight, via DHL, the approved document to Huntsville and it would be there by Monday. I had been in Cairo eating bad food, missing Paige, Chad, and friends. I hopped a flight home.

Monday morning a message was waiting for me that Hosni Mubarak had not signed the MOU. One person on his staff opposed the idea, which could have caused a potential political issue for President Mubarak. I crawled, my head down, into Swany's office to give him the news. He asked, "What did you learn?" I responded, "Never leave without a signature?" Swany with a smile said, "Good, let's move on." Learned a lot from Swany by his example. A good friend and mentor.

In April 1983, on a Thursday, I was asked if I would go to New Delhi, India with 48 hours' notice. They wanted me to play tourist and quietly meet with an operative that had missile parts needed for STAMP. The parts would have been obtained from under a lamppost in Moscow. My task was to determine if they were the needed parts. Money would exchange hands somewhere, then parts would make it to Huntsville. Of course, the adventure was accepted. I planned to take Paige with me. Friday morning Paige and Chad visited the Madison County Courthouse with birth certificates, class pictures, etc. The clerk prepared and signed the passport applications and sealed envelope for each. I gave the envelopes to a friend going to Washington, DC on Sunday evening. Monday morning, he gave them to another friend, who walked them through the State Department. He gave the passports to the friend returning to Huntsville Monday evening. I never got the word to head east. *Great disappointment for several reasons.*

Janie and Jackie came to Huntsville to see Paige graduate from Grissom High School on June 24, 1983. Paige informed me she would not go to college, because I wanted her to attend. She traveled to Hobbs, New Mexico to start a new chapter with her grandparents, Ebb and Lucille. Janie suggested that she and Jackie move to Huntsville. My brain told me if I encouraged her to make the move, it would be a serious commitment on my part. I did not encourage the move. Janie and Jackie returned to West Palm Beach. Soon after, Janie gave up on me. I then realized too late that my heart wanted them to move to Huntsville. Paige called her from New Mexico very angry with Janie for leaving me. We did keep in touch occasionally by phone. Paige still stays close to Janie and her family. Chad and I visited New Mexico in August and met Mike Sampson from New Hampshire at a fish fry at the home of Ebb and Lucille. He was working at the Hobbs Hospital expansion. He and Paige were dating. Later he moved back to New Hampshire.

On a Monday in 1983 I met with Swany at noon. He told me only his secretary knew what he was going to tell me, and I must not tell anyone. He said, "I returned home Friday night after winning a large contract whose details I have shared with you. It turned Black when the contract was signed. We cannot discuss the subject again. I had a message to call Joe Moquin as soon as I arrived home. I assumed Joe wanted to congratulate me on getting the contract. He briefly offered congrats. Then said for me to call Rutherford at Teledyne then call back. Rutherford then told me I would be President of Teledyne CAE in Dayton, Ohio. I called Joe back who asked what my answer was. I responded, I did not hear a question from Teledyne. Swany then told me, "A Teledyne jet will pick me up tomorrow morning to take me to my new job." He did not tell his staff until late in the day. I never thought he had much respect for some of his staff he had inherited. *Neither did this dude.*

On a Sunday evening in October 1983 I drove Chad to EYC, a youth group at church. An attractive blond lady, Diane Dutton was waiting for EYC to start. She was one of the EYC sponsors. We chatted while waiting for EYC to start. I decided to wait at the church to drive Chad home. After the EYC adjourned, Chad asked if he could borrow the car for a little while and return for us to go home. Diane volunteered that she could drive me home and Chad would not have to return to the church. She was driving a Nissan 240Z sports car. *Great ride home.* I decided getting to know her was a good idea. She had a nursing degree from UAH and worked for TVA in a management position. A couple of months later we visited Grand Cayman Islands to go scuba diving. While she was an avid scuba diver, I had never been before. Diane had two sets of scuba gear. With her certificate we rented two bottles of air. Loving the water and swimming, it was great seeing the coral and many varieties of fish. We saw a large barracuda each day. Stuart the dive shop operator said that barracuda was the granddaddy of them all. On the last day of diving, I rented an underwater camera. With the last frame of the roll Diane was excited because she had captured a closeup of the barracuda on film. She was an award-winning photographer. We began swimming to shore a few feet from the bottom. I looked up to see the barracuda coming straight at us like a bullet. Diane had not seen him. I peeled off hoping to distract him. He was after her but veered off at the last moment. I was out of air so headed to the surface. Diane followed. I informed her of the barracuda's behavior. She still had air, so she swam under the surface while I swam on the surface. The granddaddy circled us all the way to shore. We asked Stuart why he had not bothered us all week but now was aggressive. He informed us that they did not like bright light. The camera strobe likely upset him. *Thanks for giving us a heads up.*

1984 started with Diane and me spending two weeks in Innsbruck, Austria. After arriving home, Chad and I enrolled in a scuba diving class at the University of Alabama Huntsville (UAH). It was a great opportunity to share with Chad a time of learning. I quickly learned how stupid and dangerous it was to dive without being certified.

In April of 1984, Vice President Bob Rieth asked me to be the proposal manager on a large program. The Tank Weapon Gun Simulator System (TWGSS) program Request for Proposal (RFP) was scheduled to be released in two months by Program Manager of Training Devices (PM Trade) in Orlando, Florida. It was closer to four years before the RFP was released. Bob said he had signed a teaming agreement with a German company, Eichweber GmbH. (KEHA). They had a similar system called "talissi" which had been mounted on tanks in Germany, Switzerland, Netherlands and on American tanks at Ft. Carson, Colorado. Bob said he would assign a marketing man, Chump (not real name), who had an engineering and law degree. I pleaded with Bob to let me handle the task without Chump. He said I had no choice in the matter. Chump had been barred from Eglin AFB and other customer organizations. I did not need to have that kind of help. Mr.

Chump had no common sense or people skills. I did enjoy visiting with Chump when business was not on the table.

Rudy Walther, the American representative of Eichweber based in Huntsville arranged for me to visit Ft. Carson to observe the "talissi" system in use and to learn about the system. Chump insisted on going with me. The base commander assigned his sergeant major to help us and demonstrate "talissi" mounted and operated on tanks. I had never met a more capable, professional and cooperative soldier. He was articulate and well informed. He promised to send us documents I requested. Two weeks later, unknown to me, Chump called him and badgered the sergeant major because we had not received the documents. The sergeant rightly told Chump not to contact him again along with anyone else from TBE. So much for a valuable source and promising friendship. Bob Rieth would not reassign him, he basically said, "Live with it."

The TWGSS had several subassemblies mounted on a tank. A laser was attached to the gun and retroreflectors mounted on the tank at strategic positions. The laser would send and receive a signal to a target tank with a TWGSS also mounted. A computer in the TWGSS system attached inside the tank would consider the type round selected by the gunner, calculate the trajectory of such a round and target distance based on the TWGSS retroreflectors mounted on the target. The computer would instruct the laser to send data as to where the target was hit. If the target tank was hit in a vulnerable spot, its TWGSS unit would then be made unable to fight. A red light mounted on top of the target tank would be turned on and the smoke cartridge ignited.

My first visit to Hamburg, Germany was in April 1984. This would be the first of perhaps 40 visits. Hans Peterson was my KEHA counterpart. The hospitality could not have been better by Kurt Eichweber and his staff. The only downside was they did not want to share design details TBE needed to prepare a credible proposal. They did provide a lot of information.

The president and owner of the company, Kurt Eichweber, had an interesting background. After World War II, nearly starving, he noted that spare parts were not available for many items. Being an entrepreneur and possessing an inventor's mind, he started making replacement parts for equipment. He would create many groundbreaking inventions, resulting in many patents. Reportedly, by 1960 Kurt had $60,000,000 in the bank and a thriving business. KEHA concentrated on military customers in several countries.

Hans Peterson drove me to Haderslov, Denmark to see where Granddad was born. The city had recently purchased the house with intention of it becoming a museum. A lone worker was there who let us tour the four-story mansion on our own. Grandad was born and lived there until going to America. The large foyer had two symmetrical staircases on each side of the foyer rising to the next level. I was able to purchase an architectural book that included the family home.

After we returned from San Francisco in May 1884, Diane moved to Chattanooga. My car decided it did not have enough mileage, therefore added many miles on weekends. She rented a home on a bluff with over two acres giving me opportunities to spend time outdoors doing yard work. *Did I mention that is not quality time?* In July we returned to the Cayman Islands to dive.

Bob Rieth, the VP I reported to, and his wife were invited to the annual KEHA Christmas party always on the first Friday in December. Bob asked me to take a date and attend in his place. Diane joined me on my fourth visit to Hamburg. I presented Kurt Eichweber with a custom made set of six pewter mugs that I had an American company create with his company crest engraved on one side and his initials formally engraved on the other side for his 61th birthday. He did not open the gift. Kurt rented an excellent restaurant for the night that also had a bowling alley in the basement. Only employees and no spouses attended. The head table was elevated and occupied by the officers of the company. Diane and I, as guests, sat at the head table. The party started at 3:30 pm with coffee and cake followed by beer, then wine and a several course dinner. Then drawings for door prizes, everyone would receive a prize including us. Diane won a very large hanging sausage that she gave to Hans Peterson. Then company annual awards. Then entertainment. Then dancing. The party ended Saturday at 5:00 am. Diane gathered a crowd all evening and charmed everyone. The result was that no more design details were held up or held close to the vest. They now trusted me. *Go figure.* Spouses and dates are important contributors to success.

We were invited to the home of Kurt Eichweber Saturday night at 6:00 pm. Rudy and his wife were also invited. Rudy gave me a heads up on the agenda. Kurt opened the gift I had given him early in the week and seemed very pleased. He gave us a tour of displays made by employees in the machine shop and served cocktails. The items on display were elaborate, complex and functional. One I remember was a complex steam locomotive with no detail missing. The engine was fully functional as a steam engine. He had other displays driven by operating steam engines that he demonstrated. Every part was designed and machined in the KEHA shop. Kurt was proud of each item added every year as a surprise by his machine shop.

Kurt had two large Mercedes hired to take the six of us, including his wife Herta, to a private club for dinner. In a private room, each place setting contained an unbelievable number of silverware pieces and crystal. Kurt selected six different types of drinks to be consumed before, during, and after dinner. He also selected our meal which included several courses. If you took a drink of wine or water, a white gloved waiter stationed behind each couple would fill the glass almost before being set back on the table. This was the best meal I have had in my entire life. Kurt was an engineer's engineer, held many patents and was a tough businessman who took no prisoners. That night no business was discussed. Surprising to me, Kurt was exceptionally charming and entertained us with many stories until after midnight. Many of his stories were centered around his extreme dislike of "Stasi" (the East German intelligence spy group). Diane and I had to drag ourselves up at 4:00 am to catch our flight home.

In June 1985 Chad graduated from Grissom High School. Chad wanted to attend the University of Montevallo just south of Birmingham. We walked the beautiful campus, which was very emotional for me because his mother was not along for the visit. With a few hidden tears, I believed she was with us. Chad and I visited with the Registrar who recommend that Chad not attend until he spent a year in between high school and college working. That motivated his son who was then ready to study and did well. Chad would work for the first year after graduating.

Paige and Mike Sampson had become engaged and were to be married in New Hampshire. In July, Chad accompanied me to Hamburg. During my meetings at KEHA, Chad explored Hamburg. We had a great time in the evenings. The sunlight did not go away until midnight and dawn would start about 2:30 am. We returned via Manchester, New Hampshire so we could attend Paige's wedding. Walking our beautiful daughter down the aisle was very special and will never be forgotten. *Why do I shed tears?*

Gene Timmons was hired to be a Division Vice President of

hardware programs in mid-1985. His division included Engineering, Manufacturing, Logistics, Marketing, and Program Management departments. Because of the potential of TWGSS/PGS, I reported directly to Gene on the program.

In September of 1985, Manfred Segewitz was needed full time in Hamburg. He knew the language, was a very good engineer and always became indispensable in a "heartbeat." Before Manfred arrived, I had been learning to read German bit by bit. As a result of him being there, my learning German came to a screeching halt and I lost ground. He contributed significantly being at KEHA full time rather than relying on my visits. I had my hands full making appropriate contacts in other parts of Europe and on the home front, as well as managing efforts at TBE.

In 1986, after several more TWGSS related trips, Dr. Harry Watson, the Optics Department Manager, said it was time for me to choose between the Optical Application Branch Manager and the TWGSS Proposal Manager position. For me it was an easy decision due in part to my adventurous spirit. The TWGSS program was challenging and had the most potential. I had become addicted to the international travel and meeting interesting people in several countries including America. The technology pushing the state of art was another attractive factor. I also liked wearing three hats: proposal manager, systems/project engineer and marketing. Chump continued to be dangerous and had other activities, so I made most outside contacts. Hugh Morgan became the branch manager. Six months later Hugh said, "I had no idea what you did for us." *It was an affirmation I greatly appreciated.*

Gene Timmons was hired to be a Division Vice President of hardware programs in mid-1995. His division included Engineering, Manufacturing, Logistics, Marketing, and Program Management departments. Because of the potential of TWGSS/PGS, I reported directly to Gene on the program.

Paige presented us with my first grandchild, Jason Michael Sampson, on September 4, 1986 in Nashua. Janie and Jackie traveled to New Hampshire for the occasion. We were all there for the new arrival. Janie and I were not dating at the time, however, later that changed. Paige decided to return to Huntsville with Jason after about six weeks. They deserved much better than Michael Sampson, who had serious problems. After returning to Huntsville, out of the blue, Paige said, "Dad over the years you were not at fault, I was out of control." My heart nearly burst with hope for her well-being having turned an important corner.

My previous boss, Dr. Harry Watson, died of stomach cancer in October 1986. He was a pure gentleman who was loyal to a fault. *He is still missed.*

Chad joined the Navy in October 1986 and I attended his graduation from the Great Lakes Naval Training Center. He received awards; I could not have been prouder of him. He has always had a great work ethic and wanted to do the right thing no matter the difficulty or pain. We mucked around Chicago for a couple of days doing nothing in particular, just enjoying each other. Paige, grandson Jason and I would spend Christmas on Signal Mountain with Diane.

Diane and I traveled to Jamaica in late November 1986 for a grand week. The scuba diving was not as good as at Grand Cayman. We did enjoy many other activities including pina coladas and dirty banana drinks.

At the beginning of 1986 I did not have a clue of the major events that would occur during the year; giving up the Optics Applications Branch, reporting directly to a Vice President in a different division, having a grandson, Chad joining the Navy, Harry's death, and Paige and Jason under my roof.

Chapter XVI - 1987–1992

I would continue traveling often to Hamburg, Germany; Orlando, Florida; Fort Knox, Kentucky; Fort Benning, Georgia; and England. Also traveled to Grafenwöhr Training Center in Germany, Greece, Netherlands, San Angelo, Texas; Washington, DC; Ft Worth, Texas; Ft. Eustis, Virginia; Ft. Hood, Texas and the Pentagon. Fort Knox was considered as the heavy armor (tanks) user; it therefore had significant input to PM Trade's specification. Fort Benning was the Bradley Fighting Vehicle user command and supplied PM Trade (the potential customer) with specifications needed for the PGS (The PGS was the same type system as the TWGSS). The basic system could be mounted on either vehicle with different brackets and software.

On one trip to Fort Knox, I briefed a major general on the benefits of the TWGSS system. He was skeptical, tough as nails and in a bad mood. He wanted to know who set up the meeting. He did. He argued with nearly every feature and benefit presented. After he cut the meeting short, I was told the major general did not want the system and no one could change his mind. The good news was that he personally was not a player in the decision. Nevertheless, it was not a fun day.

On another occasion, I was asked to brief a major general at US Army Garrison Grafenwöhr, Germany near Nuremberg. The general was cordial, appreciated my traveling to Germany, and liked the TWGSS system early. I had set up a meeting in Hamburg the following Monday morning. Before the meeting, Diane and I checked out Nuremberg. After the meeting we headed for Innsbruck, Austria, Italy, Lichtenstein, Switzerland, the Black Forest, followed the Rhine River and on to Hamburg. *Good business scheduling of meetings*. We traveled about 3,000 miles in the complimentary large Mercedes. Nice upgrade from the VW reserved. On the autobahn, while Diane was dozing, I enjoyed pushing the Mercedes to 225 km/h (140 mph). *Always liked driving fast cars and racing motorcycles.*

On one trip to Ft. Benning I was given a top speed, white knuckling, rough ride in a Bradley Fighting Vehicle through forest, crossing streams and leaping ditches. Soldiers more than earn their pay. Another benefit of the trip was attending an Auburn basketball game starring Charles Barkley. As I remember Barkley destroyed the backboard during the game. He would go on to be in the NBA Hall of

Fame.

The British Army was interested in our system along with the other US companies pursuing the TWGSS program. Near 10 Downing Street in London, I gave a briefing to British generals and staff. They could only purchase from a UK company. We were to team with Royal Ordinance and KEHA. British Prime Minister Margaret Thatcher had sold all Royal Ordinance divisions except the military portion. Later we would be asked to adapt our system to a British tank for a demonstration. I was impressed with Royal Ordinance Professionalism and hospitality. I subsequently visited their facilities in Manchester, England. They took me to a private club outside the city for a great meal, my first edible food in England. Years later restaurant food improved considerably.

PM Trade gave each of the four bidders an opportunity to host them at each European team member facility for one day. Each US company had to team with a European company as no American company had developed the technology. The customer had a team of nine representing the government's ultimate user, development organization and NATO. We upstaged our competition by convincing PM Trade that four days with us would be well spent. I promised them private meeting time with the Netherland army including a demonstration of the KEHA system purchased by them, and private time with German and Switzerland army personnel. All had experience with the KEHA system. Gene Timmons (my VP) and I met them in Amsterdam on Friday and proceeded to visit the sights of Amsterdam and socialize on Saturday and Sunday. On Sunday evening KEHA arrived with a plush bus to take us to a hotel near a Netherland Army base. KEHA arranged a feast in the dining room to be remembered. Key Netherland Army personnel joined us. By now it became public knowledge that my passport had grown legs and escaped. Our new Netherland Army friends arranged for me to enter the base the next morning in spite of my passport being AWOL. After much hospitality and discussions, Gene, KEHA and I excused ourselves to allow the potential customer team to have a private exchange with the Netherland Army Officers. This was greatly appreciated by all, as was the subsequent demonstration on the heavy armor firing range.

We boarded the nice bus and headed to Germany. When we arrived at the German border, the customs gentleman boarded the bus to check passports. The KEHA Germans had a plan to smuggle me into

Germany. I was to sit near the back of the bus. One of our German friends joked and bantered with the customs gentleman until he finally said you are good guys, got off the bus and waved us on. *Humor makes the world run smoothly.* A few days later I entered the US Consulate in Hamburg at 8:00 am and walked out 50 minutes later with a new 10-year passport. *We have been blessed with a great country.*

Arrangements were made for the German and Swiss army to have private discussions with our potential customers. We then conducted the one-day briefings and tour of the KEHA facility. The customer team went on to visit their fourth bidder (Saab) for a one-day meeting. Great four-day adventure all around with the customer and individuals from other countries.

Gene and I returned to Huntsville feeling we had made a solid impression with the potential customer. Short lived. I received a call from my counterpart in the government with his voice breaking with anger believing we had stabbed them in the back. They had received a call from the Pentagon in the middle of the meeting with Saab causing their one-day meeting to be shortened to put out the fire at the Pentagon. I told him that neither Gene nor I had talked with the Pentagon since we had seen them in Germany, but I would try to find out what happened. I discovered through a friend in Washington, DC that Chump, the marketing guy (who I had not wanted near the program but was forced to accept), had gone to the Pentagon and gotten into an argument with an Army officer, leaving the impression the program was not necessary. I told Gene what happened. He said, "Chump was now removed from the program." I suggested calling the customer to explain what happened and that Chump would not be seen again. Gene said, "No, get on a plane and go to their office in Orlando to tell them." I did and apologized. When I told them Mr. Chump was removed, they were greatly relieved. *So was I.*

In December 1987, I requested Gene Timmons approve the purchase of an Apple Macintosh computer. He could approve the accessories and software, but not the computer. Bob Rieth had become TBE President on September 1, 1987. He had to approve a computer purchase. The only personal computers the company had purchased were for secretaries to use as word processors. Many engineers at the time had purchased Mac computers with their own money and brought them to work. I found out from the accounting department that there was enough year end funds to cover the cost of one computer. So, I gave Vivian, Bob's secretary, a purchase request and asked her to get his approval. About that time, Bob stepped out of his office and said, "Skipper what the hell do you want?" I explained in detail that I needed a computer to prepare the TWGSS proposal. He said, "If I approve this will anyone else find out? I do not want to set a precedent." I said, "What computer?" He signed the purchase request. On a separate purchase request Gene approved all other items. *Life is good.*

The TWGSS Request For Proposal (RFP) was released in January 1988. We had about six weeks to respond. Thanks to a dedicated group of individuals the proposal was delivered on the due date. Members (Hugh Morgan, Chuck Whaley and Manfred Segewitz) of the Optical Applications Branch had transferred from the SETAC Division to the Engineering Directorate in the Business Development Division. Without them we would not have achieved the quality proposal submitted. *Did I mention that loyalty is a strong trait of mine?* Of course, many others contributed significantly to the effort in several areas of TBE.

During the preparation of the cost section of the proposal, the KEHA team from Hamburg arrived in Huntsville to negotiate their portion of the effort. It consisted of Kurt Eichweber, owner and president, and several of his vice presidents and other support personnel including Claus Loges, their program manager. Off to the side before the meeting, Kurt's staff said he was firm on KEHA fabricating the laser-transceiver subassembly and could not be moved. This violated our teaming agreement. Knowing this point would not persuade Kurt, I took a different approach. I had developed a spreadsheet that contained each subassembly detail cost based on where it was fabricated. While chairing the meeting I presented a total contract cost with a viewgraph of the spreadsheet developed on my new Macintosh computer showing the cost if KEHA fabricated that subassembly. I then suggested we take a brief break while I changed the fabrication location of the laser-transceiver to TBE in the spreadsheet. The cost was reduced by $27,000,000 (66 million in 2019 dollars). Obviously, the team would not have a winning bid if KEHA fabricated any portion of the system. Kurt gave up his dream. The Apple Macintosh computer paid for itself many times over in this meeting.

One of the four bidders, Loral Corporation, was late delivering their proposal, therefore was disqualified. They protested; therefore, a Government hearing was scheduled in Washington, DC. Also attending were the company presidents of the other bidders (Raytheon and Xerox) accompanied by their attorneys. I attended with two attorneys, who were considered the second-best law firm in Washington, DC. Loral said they could not deliver the proposal because they underestimated the time to transport the proposal. At no time in the government history had they accepted a late proposal according to attorneys accompanying me. The attorneys spoke for me when I was given the opportunity. They spoke elegantly concerning applicable laws and the dangerous precedent the government would set if the Loral proposal was accepted. The Government ruled that they would accept the Loral Proposal. My attorneys said Loral had the number one law firm and that they were owed a favor by this arm of the government. *Now the waiting period to find out who was the winner.*

After completing a project for Diane, she stated that I was very creative. That had never occurred to this unconscious person. Upon thinking back on engineering tasks and management decisions completed, it occurred to me she might be right.

Diane and I attended a spiritual seminar for a week at Kanuga (an Episcopal retreat and camp) near Hendersonville, North Carolina. The "Dream Seminar" was based on Carl Jung's teachings and the application to personal spiritual growth. We arrived a day early to take the Myers-Briggs test. The results were interesting in that Diane and I were total opposites. The knowledge I gained provided a greater understanding of how individuals at work, friends and family reacted and made decisions. Each individual is locked into his or her categories and should be considered when interfacing with them. While I had relied on common sense and respect in the past, this new knowledge proved important. The week was very informative about dreams which could reveal much about one's own self-discovery. Only the dreamer can interpret their dreams. Others do not have the knowledge of all current issues needed to analyze a person's dreams.

My 50th birthday was celebrated with Diane, who pointed out that Superman had almost been born on the same date. Both Supermen are doing well, thank you. Early in 1988 Diane and I parted on the best of terms. We had a great run together, but it was time to move on for both of us.

In July Chad's ship, the AS-18 Orion, arrived at the Naval Base in Charleston, South Carolina from the Mediterranean Sea. The ship was a Fulton-class diesel electric nuclear submarine tender, based in

Sardinia, Italy. I had not seen Chad in nearly two years. I met him in Charleston when he was available to disembark. I was proud of Chad; he had received numerous awards while serving in the Navy. He was able to wrangle me a tour of his ship even though it was in dry dock for repairs. His discharge would not occur until October 18. We had a great time checking out the sights of Charleston and decommissioned Navy ships including the USS Kitty Hawk Aircraft Carrier. Being with Chad, always a gentleman and fun to be with, was a special treat.

In July, PM Trade invited each of the four companies submitting proposals to a mandatory oral examination. Each company would be questioned for one day concerning the proposal technical volume and a half day on the management volume. We were first up on a July Monday morning for the technical exam to be followed by Tuesday morning for the management volume. I selected nine key individuals to accompany me to the exams. Some were selected for their TBE position, such as Bill Myers (TBE Manager of Quality Assurance), Lum Brantley (Director of Logistics), Gene Andrzejewski (TBE Contracts Officer), etc. Others were selected for their program specific position such as Chuck Whaley (Project Engineer) and Colin Gordon (TWGSS Logistics Manager). A director in the division joined us against my objections. The vice president, Gene Timmons, could not attend and wanted him to attend on his behalf to represent TBE. The good news was the director only stated the TBE eagerness to provide a good product to PM Trade and never spoke again at the exams. The Director had a Jekyll and Hyde personality and had an 80 percent turnover rate in engineering. He was unpredictable and had ruined several excellent engineers' careers.

I arranged a suite at a Marriott Hotel which had a large dining table that allowed us to meet on Sunday to prepare for the exams. The two-hour review went very well. The team appeared confident and ready. One thing stressed was that I would field all questions because of my years of interfacing with the customer and their team. That experience provided me the knowledge of the customers desires and concerns. I said that I would hand off questions to individuals for their input for two reasons: one, I did know the answer and two, to give the customer confidence in the whole TBE team. At the end of the Monday exam with the significant customer team, I was sure we had answered all concerns and that they were impressed with our team. On Tuesday I fielded all questions, although I asked Gene Andrzejewski to confirm some of my answers to the customer. We returned to Huntsville to wait for an award decision. *Sometimes life requires extraordinary patience.* The DE reported back to VP Gene Timmons that my performance was extraordinary. He never blew up on me again. *I have to admit it was good the DE accompanied us to the orals.*

On August 23rd Gene Andrzejewski, TBE contracting officer, received a call that we had won the award, but were not to reveal that knowledge. Gene and I were to arrive in Orlando on August 24th, then review and sign the contract on the 25th. We were advised to stay on the other side of Orlando at a hotel until called to visit them for the signing. We spent too much time at the hotel swimming pool waiting on the call that finally came at 5:00 pm. *Sunburns can hurt.* The reason for the long delay was because tradition dictated that our US Representative had to announce the award first. After reviewing and signing the contract, we called Huntsville to announce the contract award was completed. The contract value was approaching $110,000,000 ($273,240,000 in 2019 dollars). They could now let the cat out of the bag. Their response was that the US Representative had made the announcement at 2:00 pm, and they had been celebrating since. *Gene and I had to celebrate alone with a bottle of champagne.*

Gene Timmons arranged a reception at the downtown Hilton Hotel for all who participated in the proposal preparation. After we were relaxed sufficiently, Gene gave a speech thanking everyone for their contribution to the proposal followed by asking me to step forward. He then cut the new tie in half that I had purchased that day. He said I was now the first member of the "100 Million Dollar Club" and my tie would be mounted on a plaque and hung in the main lobby of the company. *I was later shown the plaque, but of course, it never was hung.* While the celebration was continuing, Gene asked me to accompany him to the Heritage Club for dinner. *Once again not going to refuse a VP.* Over dinner Gene asked me to be the TWGSS Program Manager and said that I would be a director. Being a director was a significant position in Teledyne, Inc's eyes. He then asked me what the biggest challenge would be concerning my position. I silently thought about program issues. Gene said, "Train someone to take your position so that you can be promoted and not be indispensable to the program." I picked Ed Seigler as my deputy. Gene did not like Ed and said he was a poor choice. Gene was fired years later, and Ed was promoted to Vice President of Administration. Gene was wrong; Ed would prove invaluable to me and the program in many ways. I am still amused with that outcome. Ed demonstrated he was very effective in his role as a VP. Ed always had been an outstanding contributor to TBE.

Ed informed me I was expected to select Executive level furniture from any source in Huntsville. These were the kind of things that did not occur to me. *Have to confess it was good for the ego.* I was able to assemble a great program management staff that served me and the program well.

One of the items I assigned to Ed was creating a detailed Work Breakdown Structure (WBS) tied to individual charge numbers for the program after providing him with the overall concept. Ed created a WBS that would be a great tool to track every subassembly cost and progress. Ed and I presented the WBS to Gene expecting him to be impressed and provide his blessing. Gene blew up and attacked Ed, his favorite target. He dictated we supply each director with four charge numbers and let them manage their work. He said my task was to get a million dollars added to the contract (Soon after, I actually had $1,500,000 approved by the customer). Gene had stripped the tools necessary to successfully manage the contract by the program office and each functional manager. I seriously considered stepping down as the TWGSS Program Manager but decided being a quitter was not a good idea. *Right or wrong, I felt like I had given birth to the program and that would be like a father giving up on his son.*

Gene, two months after contract award, surprised Ed and me by telling us to add department bureaucracy management cost to the program. In the past, those costs were always included in the department overhead budgets. That motivated functional managers to control their management cost so as to be more competitive on all contracts. Overhead rates were added to basic labor rates, hence higher overhead rate increases labor estimates. Changing this culture would leave the department bureaucracies no incentive to hold down management cost. Coupled with an ineffective work breakdown structure, the program office and functional managers did not have the tools to monitor cost and progress. *A disaster in the works, I once again considered stepping down as the Program Manager and should have followed my instincts.*

In October 1988 Chad was discharged from the Navy and Paige married John Moore. I would have the occasion to babysit with two-year-old grandson, Jason. We would have a grand time dancing to Elvis

Presley. I was amazed at his balance and athletic ability. Later I remember walking with him, holding hands, when we met a policeman on a sidewalk and Jason in a very joyful way said, "Hello Mr. Policemen." *Memories are great.*

The TWGSS program was occupying too much of my time. I would attend the I/ITSC (The world's largest modeling, simulation and training event) conference each year. This year it was held in Orlando and the first after winning PM Trade's largest contract, I needed the break and opportunity to receive congratulations *(good for the ego)* from competitors and others for being awarded the contract. While the contract went through many changes before its end in 1994, my story will mostly concentrate on personal adventures along the way.

In early December 1988, Janie joined me in Hamburg for the 1988 Awards/Christmas party. We arrived on Saturday morning and explored Hamburg during the weekend. Each workday I visited KEHA at 8:00 am for the day while Janie explored the city sites. Each evening we attended a different KEHA department Christmas celebration at wonderful restaurants. The celebrations always ended well after midnight. Janie firmly suggested we spend Thursday evening at a nice restaurant alone. On Thursday in addition to reviews at KEHA, I was to meet with two Greek Army officers who had traveled to Hamburg to meet with me to discuss providing the systems to the Greek Army. At noon Kurt Eichweber, KEHA President, invited key personnel on the program, including the Greeks, to lunch at a private club on the Elbe River. In the middle of the afternoon six of us slipped out because we had a lot of tasks to complete that day. All six of us piled into a taxi. It was crowded so Kurt Eichweber's attractive secretary had to sit on my lap. *Life has its hardships.* The meeting with the Greeks did not conclude until 8:00 pm. When I arrived back at the Hotel Europäischer Hof, Janie had been sitting in a chair dressed for the evening for two hours. *Groveling is necessary at times.*

The KEHA party, without spouses, always started at 3:30 pm on Friday with cake and coffee and ended about 5:00 am Saturday. Kurt always reserved a complete restaurant for the event. During the party much wine, beer and more were served along with a several course dinner, door prizes for all, KEHA awards to particular employees, entertainment, and dancing until the end. As always, we were required to sit at the head table with all KEHA officers. Prior to dinner the president, Kurt, gave his annual speech and proclaimed that I was the reason that we had won the TWGSS program. Janie was liked by all.

Kurt invited Janie and me to his home for dinner the following night. Kurt again showed us his latest fully operational model steam engine powered device given to him as a surprise from his machine shop. After cocktails he treated us to a several course dinner at one of his private clubs. As usual on these occasions he was charming and filled with many stories until after midnight. We had to head for the airport at 4:00 am. Later Janie said," Now I understand why you are exhausted when you return from Hamburg."

In March 1989 my second grandchild was born in Huntsville. They wheeled Paige and her baby out of the delivery room. Paige announced a baby girl had arrived and would be named Patsy Gail after her grandmothers and would be called Patsy. This new Patsy looked just like my late wife Patsy. My first thoughts were that it was going to be painful looking at my granddaughter and calling her Patsy. That pain lasted a few days. Then I was thrilled. Paige could not have blessed her mother more and given me a new Patsy to adore and love.

I celebrated my 51st birthday on March 22, 1989 with Lavon, Marie Kieffer (Miss Guatemala), and Bob Heath (a very successful commercial developer and entrepreneur) at the private Heritage Club, arguably the best meal available and atmosphere in Huntsville. *Where did the time go?*

I would travel often on business to Europe for a variety of reasons. One trip was to England in May 1989. When first arriving in London, I was instructed to immediately catch a train to Warwick, England. I was greeted by representatives of Royal Ordnance and immediately taken to a VIP site on an army base. A semi-annual VIP live firing demonstration for dignitaries of the British government was about to begin. We were all ushered to a small grandstand built into the side of a slopping hill that might hold about 25 individuals. Every British Army weapon was subsequently demonstrated firing at targets in the valley starting with the smallest weapon and concluding with large weapons such as fighting vehicles and tanks. Some of the targets were pop-up silhouettes of soldiers and actual retired tanks. One demonstration consisted of snipers firing at pop-up silhouettes several hundred yards away in the valley. To our surprise the snipers stood up in their camouflage including twig, bushes, etc. They had been in the grass about 10 yards from us from the start. Two British Harrier Aircraft flew over demonstrating their unique ability to take off and land vertically. To put the icing on the cake two awesome American A-10 Thunderbolt fighter-boomers snuck up behind us then fired at the retired tanks. The American pilots circled and repeated firing. *Fantastic demonstration. Once again had to pinch myself to see if I was dreaming.*

Following the demonstration, the British Army formally met with our Royal Ordnance personnel to learn more about the TWGSS system to help them decide on going ahead with a program. Being a foreigner, I was not allowed to attend the meeting, however Royal Ordnance personnel kept coming out to my sitting area for answers to questions that were asked. After several trips, the British Army requested that I join the meeting. Reportedly this was a first for a foreigner. The meeting was a success. The Army suggested we mount/integrate our systems on British tanks in the Southwest part of England on the coast.

Chad and Angel were to be married on June 10, 1989. I had received an invitation to attend a large AUSA formal banquet in Orlando on that day. I told the VP, Gene Timmons, my boss, that I could not attend because of the wedding. Gene said, "It is mandatory you attend the banquet. You lease a jet, rent a tux, get a date and go after the wedding." I billed TBE for a new tux and all accessories including shoes. I rationalized keeping the tux was an earned benefit. Of course, the wedding started late, and I discovered Chad had invited Diane, my old flame. *An awkward moment introducing her to my date, Lavon.* The photographer had not shown.

Diane, an award-winning photographer, volunteered to step-in. She would give Chad and Angel a beautiful album as her wedding gift. Lavon and I departed the reception early and headed for the airport. This was before cell/mobile phones and we were running an hour late, so I called the pilots from the church to have the jet warmed up. We arrived at a small airport in Orlando and climbed into an auto at the bottom of the jet's steps and sped off to the hotel where the AUSA banquet was being held. The reception had already started. In our room we quickly changed into our formal attire and walked into the reception just as they were opening the doors to the banquet hall. On subsequent visits to Orlando the customer asked about the mermaid lady. Her evening gown had nicely fit her beautiful frame resembling a mermaid. I insisted the next morning we leave on the jet by 9:00 am. Lavon and the pilots wanted to leave much later, but my sister, Bonnie, had traveled from Texas for the wedding and I wanted to spend as much time with her as possible.

While traveling through the Atlanta airport I was paged and requested to answer a public telephone. An officer I had visited in the Pentagon some time ago asked if I could help get funding restored in the PM Trade budget. Our program was not affected but nearly all other programs were not funded. I said, "I will try." After calling my VP, who was not available, I called VP Charlie Granger, TBE's main liaison with Washington. He contacted the Teledyne, Inc staff member Jim McGovern. Jim was a graduate of the Navy Academy, Top Gun school, law degree from George Washington University, served as a staff member for Senator Powers, had served as an Under-Secretary of the Air force and had been Acting Secretary of the Air Force. Jim was able to get the funds restored as a result of his powerful contacts.

In November 1989 I attended the large annual I/ITSC conference in Ft. Worth, Texas. One day the officer who had contacted me in the Atlanta airport, thanked me profusely for getting the funding restored. Of course, all I had done was make a phone call. *I saw no point in passing on that point.* Bob Rieth had become the TBE president on September 1, 1989 and had been invited along with several generals, admirals and presidents of large military companies to a reception at the private Cattleman's Club on the top floor of a high-rise building in downtown Ft. Worth. There was no program, just an opportunity for social interaction and to exchange ideas. Bob could not attend and asked me to attend in his place. After standing around visiting with people I knew only from TV, print or word of mouth, we were seated. At dinner, I was next to Tommy Franks, an Army officer. He had attended high school in Midland, Texas, not far from my high school in Eunice, New Mexico. We had a lot in common and enjoyed the evening. He was a quiet, smart, humble man. *I often wonder why I met so many interesting people in my life.* Years later, General Franks would lead the 2001 invasion of Afghanistan and led the invasion of Iraq in 2003.

In the Ft. Worth-Dallas airport following the conference, it was announced at the gate that a tornado had landed in Huntsville near Airport Road in south Huntsville. The current airport was about 20 miles west of the old airport. I called Paige to see if they were okay. John answered the phone and was not aware of the tornado, therefore I knew they were safe because the tornado had missed their home. The tornado claimed 22 lives and stayed on the ground for miles. Many homes, business, churches and an elementary school were damaged or leveled. Years later, in 2003 the home we purchased had had its roof torn off and the large houses on each side of ours were leveled.

On November 28, 1989, Chad became a father when my grandson, Spencer, was born in Huntsville. *At age 51, I am not mature enough to have grandchildren much less three.* Over the years, Janie still was only a phone call away. It was always good to know that she and Jackie were okay and there for me and my children.

In February 1990 Bonnie and Alan moved to Grapevine, Texas. She had designed and created a beautiful home on the large lake. In March, Chad and family moved to Ft. Lauderdale, Florida.

In May-June 1990 I spent five weeks in England while we set up and conducted a demonstration on British tanks. The team stayed in an old Victorian Inn on a picturesque hill overlooking a small bay. Sheep roamed the hills. The small village, bay, and hills could not have been more peaceful. It was a great five weeks and mostly successful system demonstration. No other potential bidders gave a demonstration.

On one long weekend, I rode the train to London to meet Janie and Jackie (13-year-old). They were exploring London and more. I joined them visiting London icons and we attended an Andrew Lloyd Webber theatrical performance of *Aspect of Love* at the Prince of Wales Theater. I had over time seen most of his shows in London theaters. *I am a fan.* We also took a boat ride in a narrow canal from London to the countryside.

Teledyne, Inc. announced that on July 1, 1990 Jim McGovern would be president of TBE. I would have many memorable experiences with him concerning the TWGSS program but will not elaborate to protect the innocent. Bob Rieth had been promoted to Group Executive for Aerospace Group in Teledyne, Inc.

I met with Greek Army officers in Athens, Greece as agreed in our December meeting in Hamburg. They were interested in having the TWGSS system. They were extremely helpful in divulging what should be in our proposal to insure an award. They stipulated they would not work with a specific TBE individual (to be subsequently referred to as Ego) concerning any adventure and explained why. I reported their remarks to Gene Timmons, then said I could easily oversee the proposal and would win the contract based on what I had learned. Gene asked me to invite the Greeks to Huntsville for a meeting. I contacted them at the Greek Embassy in Washington and invited them to meet with Gene and me. Gene invited Ego to the meeting. Gene told them Ego would be the proposal manager. Body language gave away their disapproval. Afterwards I gave Ego my many detail notes on what the Greeks had provided me to win the contract. Ego did not use the information and lost the bid.

During many trips to New Mexico for the Eunice High School reunions held on the July 4th, I fortunately was able to visit Mardy and Jim Manes and their family. They had moved to Hobbs. Jim was a school principal and Mardy was a teacher. Their profession was blessed to have them.

On August 2, 1990 Iraq invaded Kuwait. President H. W. Bush marshaled an international coalition to kick the Iraqis out of Kuwait. Complete sanctions were applied by the world community to Iraq. The first phase of the Gulf War was called Desert Shield. *Little did I know the effect the Gulf War would have on my life.*

On November 5-8, 1990, I attended the I/ITSC conference which was held in Orlando. This was memorable because I called and asked Jim McGovern to fly down and join me for an informal meeting with the customer. He asked me to arrange a date for him. I told him that he was on his own. On the ride to the customer meeting after picking him up at the airport, he made a call in the car to US Vice President Dan Quayle. He had a mobile phone that was the size of a briefcase. I had not seen a mobile phone before. The vice president was not in town, so Jim talked to his chief of staff, Bill Kristol. They bantered awhile and then a meeting was set up for Jim to meet with the vice president. That night Jim attended the large I/ITSC conference banquet with a date, whom he introduced to the keynote speaker at the head-table following the speech. The keynote speaker was an old buddy from the days when they were both staffers on the "Hill" in Washington, DC. The Teledyne, Inc. Chairman of the Board and the President of Teledyne, Inc. would not have approved of his young date. *Maybe I should have found him a date.*

Bonnie and Alan invited me to join them for a tour of the Texas Hill country during the 1990 Thanksgiving weekend. We stayed in unique B&B's and generally had a great time. I will not forget Alan pulling off to the side of the road in the middle of nowhere to chase an armadillo. The good news is that he was not successful. *Not good for his ego having assured us he could catch an armadillo.* Bonnie and I shared a good healthy laugh at his expense.

The next phase of the Gulf War was called Desert Storm and began on January 17, 1991 with the aerial-navy bombardment of Iraq and their forces in Kuwait. On February 24th the ground invasion by the coalition started. On February 28th the Iraqis agreed to a ceasefire. Iraq and the United Nations would subsequently sign a Weapon of Mass Destruction (WMD) agreement.

On March 6, 1991 Chad and Angel were blessed with their second son, Denver, my third grandson. Not to be outdone, Paige gave birth to Joseph on April 10th who would be my fifth and last grandchild. Janie had been back in my life for a while. On one trip to visit her and Jackie in West Palm Beach we attended the SunFest, a large art festival. I purchased a Batik art by G. Nggong. Unknown, to me this would be the second of many pieces of an art collection. However, it was the last purchased before retiring. The first art purchased was in 1962. The still-life painting "*Kettle*" created by DeNice in the mid-1800s was in a frame carved by a slave before the Civil War. Several paintings that Paige had created also are part of my collection. I am biased of course, but many others have been amazed at her talent.

A limited edition of a Honda Gold Wing GL1200 motorcycle found a spot in my garage in 1991. The limited edition had fuel injection, computer, etc. and was created to celebrate the 10th anniversary of the Gold Wing. Fuel injection and computers were not available before or after. My Gold Wing was in showroom condition. *Only downside was that it was hard to find the fairer sex to ride with me.*

The customer asked to meet TBE unofficially with our Vice President, Director of Engineering, Director of Manufacturing, Director of Logistics and me, the TWGSS Program Manager in attendance. The customer brought the same equivalent individuals. Their TWGSS Program Manager opened the meeting with a viewgraph presentation. He concluded with the comment, "You have a management problem and it is not Skipper." *Phew!* Our Director of Logistics was the only other person to escape their wrath. While the others were not pleased, I was grateful for the meeting. I was hopeful some of our problems would go away.

In May 1991, I attended the International Training Technology Exhibition & Conference (ITEC) in Maastricht, Netherlands. KEHA had set up a booth which I helped man. I enjoyed the week, especially a reception in a local cave. Later I visited Ft. Eustis, Virginia to answer questions concerning their interest in our developing the TWGSS concept for other applications. I would return home with a fever of 104 degrees and no potential business. *I should have stayed home.* Because of technical issues and schedule impacts that affected program cost, I was losing sleep.

Chad and family would be transferred by American Airlines to Los Angeles Airport in January of 1992 and to Huntsville in May.

During the mid-1992 summer, Janie drove Jackie to Brown University in Providence, Rhode Island from West Palm Beach, Florida, then picked me up at Logan Field in Boston. We drove along the coast via Salem, Massachusetts and Camden, Maine to Bar Harbor, Maine with several stops along the way. After about two weeks we returned to Brown University by way of Franconia, New Hampshire and childhood New Hampshire farm to tour Newport, Rhode Island with Jackie.

In 1992 a TBE team visited the Army TWGSS customer, PM Trade, to negotiate the final stage of the contract. They returned to Huntsville to acquire final acceptance by TBE officials. The TBE president and Teledyne, Inc had accepted the results. I believed TBE could do better. I reviewed my concerns and an approach to improve our position with Jim McGovern, TBE president. Jim said, "Skipper this is what I have been looking for; you and I are going to visit PM

Trade and you will conduct the negotiation." The TBE Director of Contracts, Gene Andrzejewski, of course accompanied us. My approach considered what the customer could sell to their hierarchy. I believed you had to provide the tools to the customer for this to happen. As a result, we came home with an additional $3,000,000 ($5,641,800 in 2019 dollars). The net profit on a $100,000,000 engineering support contract would be $3,000,000. To say Teledyne, Inc. was thrilled would be an understatement. Jim McGovern attended a conference in a Colorado lodge the next week by all presidents of Teledyne companies. *He was the hero.*

I accommodated the team when the first 16 TWGGS units were delivered and integrated onto M1 tanks at Ft. Hood, Texas and working with the exceptionally alert soldiers as well as seeing our systems at work. *However, I would not add visiting Ft. Hood to my bucket list.*

Chapter XVII - 1993

The first week of January 1993 would find me at the United Nations Headquarters in New York City. In December the United Nation Security Commission (UNSCOM) had asked Russia and the USA to each provide two missile experts to become team members of the UN Weapons of Mass Destruction (WMD) long-term in-country team in Iraq. In December, I had been instructed that only four individuals at TBE (President, two VPs and my boss) and my children could know of my reason for being out of pocket. I did reveal to my priest, Father Rod Murray, what was going on in case things went badly in Iraq and asked him to find out if there was an Anglican Church in Iraq. The Episcopal Church is part of the worldwide Anglican Church. The Episcopal Church Center in New York City reported back that no Anglicans were known to be in Iraq, however St. Christopher's Cathedral and Awali Anglican Church were located in Bahrain.

The USA was to provide one expert from the government and one from industry. I was the industry pick. My experience included launcher systems, solid and liquid propulsion, guidance systems and total missile systems in all phases of design, manufacturing and testing. My experience ranged from man portable to ICBMs and several missiles in between. Fortunately, I had engineering and/or management experience on the Redeye, Stinger, Chaparral, Tow, Hellfire, Sidewinder, Atlas, Titan I, Titan II, Saturn I and Saturn V missiles. The missile experience was years earlier and was consistent with the Iraq missile technology supplied by the Soviets. To top it off, I had been the Project Manager of reverse engineering and repair of 800 SA-7 Soviet Union missiles for Egypt. I had also worked with the Egyptian Air Force to repair and improve the performance of their Soviet Union supplied K-13 "Atoll" missiles.

Specific names of several individuals mentioned herein are not always accurate for privacy or security reasons. Generally full names are accurate and identified in other public publications. There is a limit to the content that I am allowed to publicly disclose. Also, the book size should be limited, therefore many interesting stories are not included.

Ambassador Carl Rolf Ekéus was Director of UNSCOM. Per UN Regulation 687 UNSCOM inspectors had the authority in Iraq to:

"unrestricted freedom of movement without advance notice in Iraq"; the "right to unimpeded access to any site or facility for the purpose of the on-site inspection, whether such site or facility be above or below ground"; "the right to request, receive, examine, and copy any record data, or information relevant to" UNSCOM's activities; and the "right to take and analyze samples of any kind as well as to remove and export samples for off-site analysis."

Iraq was allowed to have missiles for defensive purposes that would not exceed 150 kilometers (90 miles). The presence of and the capability to design and manufacture WMDs such as chemical, biological and nuclear weapons was not allowed. Because missiles were allowed the inspections were more complex. Our team MT-1 (UNCOM-49) would be the first Long Term Monitoring Team to arrive in Iraq and would remain there 2-3 months. Most previous WMD missile teams would only be in Iraq for a few days and rarely two weeks.

The first week in January included members of the mission, Curtis, Azad, Boris and myself. The orientation was primarily given by Scott Ritter and Major John Larrabee; however, several other unnamed individuals or organizations contributed. Nikita Smidovich, an ultimate diplomat from Russia, was the Operations Deputy to Ambassador Ekéus. He was blessed with an incredible intelligence and ability to motivate individuals. Nikita had helped represent his country at the Geneva talks on the Chemical Weapons Convention. He had been head of the USSR Division of Chemical and Biological Weapons Issues from 1989 to 1991. We were briefed on backgrounds of several key Iraqi individuals and their pictures, status of their missile programs, and our need to secure our data and personal security. We were instructed to check our UN vehicles for bombs prior to each use and not to have discussions anywhere that we did not want the Iraqis to hear. We were told that outsmarting Iraqi intelligence was nearly impossible, therefore do not try. If a sensitive discussion was required, the UN airplane in Bahrain would arrive to take us to Bahrain for a dialogue. The last day of the orientation we were instructed to return home and wait for a call to go to our airport and fly to Bahrain. An airline ticket would be at the counter and all we needed were clothes as everything else would be provided. They further said it would be 2-3 weeks before President H. W. Bush stopped bombing Iraq. The UN would send in an airplane to make sure it would make it safely, then we would be on the next UN plane. The night before flying home they gave us a "sendoff" at a very nice local bar. The ambassador and Col. Dave Underwood (chief of the Bahrain UN office) quietly gave me their personal phone numbers to call if I needed anything. We would have no contact with the outside world, just technical and logistics discussions with the UN. Scott promised he would personally provide the Super Bowl results immediately after the game. *However, it would be March when I returned home before discovering the Cowboys won. We were truly isolated from the world.*

Late in January the bombing stopped, and the UN airplane made a safe flight to an airfield outside of Baghdad. I received the call to head for the Huntsville airport. Paige drove me to the airport. To say I was excited would be a huge understatement. However, much later Janie said that Paige cried all the way home from the airport concerned that I might not return. Iraq stories including the bombing were dominating the news.

Arriving late at night in Bahrain on January 23, 1993, we were told a meeting was scheduled the next morning at the UN hangar facility at the Bahrain airport and that our team would fly to Iraq the following morning. A few UN headquarters personnel would accompany us to introduce us to the unsuspecting Iraqis. The meeting was to inform our WMD team of the current status in Iraq, more orientation, issue a temporary UN passport, assign us a lock box (for all our valuables, passport and personal information), and inform us that a second airplane had made it into Iraq carrying the UN support staff (medics, motor pool and communication equipment individuals). After a brief lunch, they left the four of us alone to decide how we were going to conduct our mission. *We had just been thrown in the deep water.* The previous teams had gone in with boots kicking in doors (not always literally), conducting interviews, taking documents and more during short missions. We decided to go in wearing coat and tie, require the Iraqis to give us briefings on subjects identified by us the previous day, then conduct surprise inspections each day. We were required to submit daily situation (SITCOM) reports to UN headquarters and a final report. The other team members believed we could create the final report in 2-3 days at the end in Bahrain. I disagreed so I prepared an outline for the final report. They saw the need to prepare and contribute to the report daily. Later Nikita said it was the best report they had ever received, and it should be required for future UN reports to use the same approach.

The next day, January 25th, we flew to Iraq in a UN cargo plane (C-160) with only two engines, flown by German pilots, on loan to the UN by Germany. The canvas bench seats on each side of the aircraft were less comfortable than any airlines worst seats. The pilot-issued ear plugs were slightly effective. The 2.5-hour flight arrived at the Iraq Ain Assad Air Base about 145 miles from Baghdad. Iraq's largest air force base had been destroyed by US bombs during the Gulf War with the result that many buildings, bunkers and airplanes remained in unreal condition. Iraq fighter/bombing aircraft buzzed us to harass us. We knew they had little ability to train for lack of spare parts and more. The only flight time the Iraq pilots had was for our harassment/benefit. We arrived in time to check-in and dine at the Baghdad Sheraton Hotel. The UN offices were on the top floor of the 16-floor hotel. Every room was bugged as well as all other parts of the hotel including bushes around the hotel exterior. Our UN vehicles were also bugged. Nikita Smidovich informed the Iraq head of WMD that we would have a meeting at 8:00 pm that evening at one of the Iraqi facilities to introduce us and define our mission. The Iraqis were surprised and reluctantly agreed to meet that evening which ended after midnight. They were informed the team would arrive at Ibn Haytham Missile Research and Development Center at 8:00 am in the morning. The facility had the capability to develop, design, produce, and test prototype missile systems. When development was demonstrated and completed, the Center would provide the design to a factory selected by the Military Industrial Commission (MIC). Iraq was not given an option concerning the next morning meeting. Azad was designated the WMD Chief Inspector. He spoke Russian, Arabic, and English. Boris only spoke Russian. Curtis and I only spoke American English. The Iraqis were insulted because Azad was not an engineer. Engineers were the top of the Iraqi culture. Doctors and attorneys were not considered on the same level in the Iraqi society. *Love their culture.*

The team arrived for our first morning at the R&D facility and outlined our approach to achieve our mission. Dr. Ra'ad was the Director General head of Nine Directorates and attended all our meetings. Iraqi engineers all spoke good English. They had received engineering degrees mostly in the West. Some pretended not to understand English to avoid answering questions. Each morning we would expect them to conduct a briefing in the conference room using a computer projection on an overhead screen, covering a subject of our choosing to be followed by a surprise inspection at their facility in Baghdad, or anywhere in Iraq. The missile related facilities were located all over Iraq including missiles that had been allegedly destroyed such as Scud missiles. They had not witnessed a UNSCOM team wearing a coat and tie before. They considered this professional respect for them. At the end of the day we informed them that the briefing subject the next day would be to show their design software and demonstrate with actual data from a missile they were developing. The next day we discovered the software was flawed causing them many headaches. We always had to be careful of the questions we asked to ensure we did not inadvertently point to a solution to the Iraqi problem. *Talking about walking on eggshells at times. This required discipline. Engineers tend to want to solve problems no matter who is at the table.* The surprise inspection of the laboratory revealed a lot of German manufacturing and testing equipment including a German gyro balancing machine with the same model number that I had approved for our Optics Lab at TBE.

Back at the UNSCOM office in Baghdad I started the Final report and Curtis prepared the SITCOM under Azad's supervision. Days later Curtis asked me to swap writing assignments. I had the patience to work with Azad hovering. Curtis and I roomed together. After a week rooming at the Baghdad Sheraton Hotel, we moved to a different hotel (Iraq considered it a five star, we might have given it one). Nearly three weeks after our arrival in Iraq, Curtis received a family emergency call and returned to America. Then it fell on me to write both reports after our day in the field.

Azad would do the niceties each morning in Arabic, then turn the floor over to me to for the topic discussions of the day. My early experience with missile technologies matched the Iraqi's Soviet systems. Having significant experience with two Soviet missiles helped also. When selected as a WMD inspector I had been concerned that my abilities would embarrass me and let down the UN and USA. Soon after starting our meetings with Iraq, I realized my experience was a natural fit for the mission. I was enjoying the task and felt confident my contributions mattered. I was surprised the Iraqi's respected me and were concentrating their technical attention in my direction. Azad with no technical background and Boris only understanding Russian were likely the biggest contributors to this attention. *In any case, it was good for the ego.*

About one week after arriving in Baghdad, the four of us visited a restaurant with large carp swimming in a tank at the entrance. We were expected to pick out the one we wanted to eat. It was a delicacy for the Russians. Curtis also liked carp. *Me not so much.* They served the fish, head included, on a large silver platter. We each carved pieces. The first hot pieces were tolerable. When starting to cool even the Russian supplied vodka did not help. The others continued to enjoy the carp. Because the only embassy in Baghdad was Russian, our new friends were able to get vodka. With a nice tip the waiter poured us our drink from a bottle housed in a paper bag. Alcohol was not allowed in Iraq.

We would discover many lies and misleading information over time. We would visit many installations throughout Iraq. It still amazes me that a handful of UN personnel was a big part in maintaining a stabilized Middle East during this time.

It was interesting to witness the differences between American and Russian engineering approaches. The Iraqi's provided us with all the parameter data necessary to calculate the missile range. Curtis, more analysis experienced than myself, fed the data into our computer software program. The computer ran and ran and finally spit-out the answer to about 10 decimal places. Including the time to enter the data and the computer run time, about one hour was required. Boris pulled from his pocket a folded well used logarithmic graphic with a nomogram to determine the range. The nomogram had lines drawn by hand for each parameter and had obviously been used over time on Soviet missiles. It took him about one minute to determine the range. His answer was within 3% of the computer-generated value. *As they say, close enough for government work.*

After Curtis returned home, I roomed with a member of the chemical team. Daan was from the Netherlands and was a character. The chemical team was made up of members from many countries that supervised the destruction of 30,000 chemical weapons. The chemical team rented one of the hotel rooms near mine. After removing the bed and more, they moved in a refrigerator, sofa and chairs. The refrigerator housed soft drinks, Foster beer (the Australia's had it flown in via UN plane) and vodka supplied by the Russians. They made me an honorary member at no cost and would not allow me to pay for my drinks. *Great bunch!*

After about three weeks I could not put another forkful of Iraqi restaurant food in my mouth. I was losing weight fast. I was not overweight when arriving. I would lose 20 pounds during my stay. I had to add many holes to my belt. I contacted Dave in Bahrain, who graciously sent a case of cornflakes and a case of milk cartons on the next UN plane to Iraq. The milk did not have to be refrigerated until opened. I would put one in the fridge before use. I started stopping beside the road outside Baghdad to buy a sack of navel oranges. *Sweetest and juiciest oranges ever.* I bought dried figs from street vendors. They were mounted on strips of cloth made from dirty yellowish well used looking tee shirts with knots between each fig. They were delicious. I also purchased a small chicken each evening from street carts being cooked on rotating spits. They would split them down the middle and supply a clear plastic bag of over-steamed veggies and a piece of Iraqi bread. The tough bread was about a foot in diameter and 1/4 inches thick. My teeth could not bite a piece off, and I had to tear with my hands. I would eat half a chicken for dinner and the other half for lunch the next noon. *Not good but bearable.* We ate US Army MREs on inspections far from Baghdad when using a helicopter.

The young Aussies of the chemical team flew in lamb from Australia via the UN plane. The only lamb available in Iraq was mutton and barely edible. The Aussies arranged the private use of the hotel kitchen. They served the lamb and properly prepared veggies and more (Foster beer) for the UN team. I will never have lamb this good again. *This was one of the most memorable meals in my life.* The Aussies and Kiwis were the friendliest and most generous individuals I would meet in the UN or anywhere. While the Aussies and Kiwis were super great to outsiders, they were not fond of each other. They also knew how to enjoy life to the maximum. Some of their fun was outside the box.

During our stay two Catholic Churches were bombed not far from our hotel. Reportedly there was little damage, and no one was hurt. We were harassed on occasion. During the night, our phone with a loud ringer would provide us with entertainment about each time we tried returning to sleep. The beeping was very loud when leaving the phone off the hook. There was no way to disable the phone. One time when we were stopped in traffic, an Iraqi smashed our windshield with a bat and ran off. One of our passengers recognized him as a government employee he had met. Never saw him again. A group of the chemical team were walking along a sidewalk and were peppered with ripe tomatoes from a drive by car. A nearby shop owner helped them clean up.

The UN Nissan Pathfinder vehicles were beefed-up for safety and were serious gas-guzzlers. Driving in Iraq was always interesting, "Imshalla," no lights at night, changing tires in the middle of highways with vehicles whizzing by at 60 mph by the locals was amazing. "Big" rules at traffic lights (big trucks did not stop for red) however the helpful beeps gave one a chance to survive. The chariot wheels on trucks are memorial, you stayed away from them. Taxis conditions varied. One might have no floor allowing you to see the ground and no good place to place your feet. Most taxis were a little bit better. Taxi drivers drove small orange autos. Beyond that they were nearly all different. Sometimes they would not let me get in their taxi and others would not let me pay and thanked me for being in Iraq. The latter often had a cross hanging from their key chain. On occasion riding in an elevator I was also thanked, typically by Kurds.

Weddings on Thursday nights, Iraqi Saturday nights, generally had us staying inside because of the lead rain. AK-47s going off throughout the night. Noise in the hotel from wedding parties consisted of terrible loud music that lasted most of the night. We saw the ugliest dogs in the world, perhaps that is why the Iraqis did not like dogs. Very large pictures of Saddam Hussein were everywhere. One picture we saw each day when visiting the Ibn al Haytham Missile Development Center was smiling Saddam with 64 teeth that we could count.

One of the sites inspected was the University in Baghdad. I discovered a large computer with the same model number we had at Teledyne Brown Engineering in Huntsville. We used it for many complex design and analysis tasks requiring a powerful computer. They claimed they purchased it to analyze boilers that had failed. *Not in my world would you purchase such a computer for this purpose. You would to develop missiles.*

One day at the request of the chemical team, the Iraqis bussed us south to Babylon on the Euphrates River. It had not been open for some time. The gate was locked with a chain and large padlock. The museum section had a lot of dust, etc. The museum contained many artifacts and a good model of Babylon. We explored the ruins. The ruins were reportedly the fifth city of Babylon. The first was created in the 19th century BC. It had been destroyed and rebuilt five times at the same location. Babylon was the first city in the world to have a population of 200,000. *Quite a day. A rare day of not working.* Another day, we visited the Great Mosque of Samarra from the 9th century. The mosque was a ruin except for 180-foot cone-shaped minaret tower. We climbed the external spiraling stairs with no railings to the top. Impossible for anyone with fear of heights.

Fridays were Iraqis only day off and viewed like our Sundays. In Baghdad on a Friday, I attended a flea market. It was on a parking lot larger than a football field. Individuals were walking around elbow to elbow trying to sell everything from used bent nails to an arm full of watches. I had previously purchased two Soviet made 1084 mm cassegrain telescopic lens for a camera including several filters and leather cases from a photo shop. After negotiating, I purchased two 35 mm Soviet cameras for $10 each. After returning to my room, I discovered the cameras did not have through-the-lens light sensors. The telescopic lens blocked the external sensor. The next Friday at the flea market I had fun selling the cameras for the same price. I bought two Soviet cameras from another Iraqi with through-the-lens light sensors for $10 each. *Love to negotiate.* I had bought one of the lens and cameras for Nick Passino, my best friend in Huntsville. He was watching my home and had a PhD in Optics from Arizona State University.

On one of our last visits, Dr. Ra'ad gave us a personal tour to the Ibn Haytham Missile Research and Development Center. He had been addressing me most of the time. Then he requested that we join him for coffee in his large office along with many of his key staff members. He asked me to sit next to his desk. Further away chairs were occupied by Azad and Boris. His staff of about 15-20 were standing along the wall. I knew he was building up to something, so did his staff. He asked, "How long do you think it will take us to complete development of our new missile?" I knew it would be a mistake to provide my opinion therefore responded, "That depends on the ingenuity of the Iraqis." Everyone in the room laughed including those who claimed not to understand English. *Life can be fun.*

The team flew into Bahrain for discussions and needed to return to Baghdad for about two weeks. I was told to immediately call Teledyne Brown Engineering, my employer. I was instructed to return home immediately or I would not have a job because the US Army agency in Huntsville had not paid for my effort as promised. I stated that was not possible because two more weeks were required to complete the mission. Knowing it was impossible for anyone else to complete the mission, I said, "I am going back to Iraq." Later after returning home, I learned the Chairman of the Joint Chiefs of Staffs, General Colin Powell, had called a general in Huntsville and ordered him to pay for my time immediately. *May have saved my job.*

We completed our mission in Iraq and finished our final report back in Bahrain. Azad and Boris were headed to Moscow and I was headed to the USA. When Azad and I said our goodbyes with a big bear hug we both choked up. *I would have never considered this a possibility because of the Cold War. Our countries had been enemies for decades.*

Going through customs at the Orlando Airport, an agent reviewed my declaration showing that I had been a WMD inspector in Iraq and the list of several Persian carpets. The agent said wait here. I then saw him chatting with another official. He returned and said, "Go through that door." Being concerned I asked, "What is through that door?" He said, "I said go through that door." Turns out it was the exit. After Janie picked me up, we stopped at a carpet store. I asked them to provide an approximate value of each carpet. His estimates were about four times what I had paid. Years later, a carpet expert in Huntsville worked with Sotheby's to provide an appraisal that confirmed the higher value.

After arriving home in March, I discovered the Cowboys had won the Super Bowl, that in February 1993 the World Trade Center had been bombed, and several significant events including some at work.

To say getting to see and talk with children and grandchildren was the best part of returning to sanity would be an understatement. I had missed each of their unique personalities including their joy and smiles. *Life is great. I am still the luckiest person in the world.*

Back at work I resumed my duties on the TWGSS program. Don Martin filled in for me while I was in Iraq. Within a few months I was loaned to Teledyne, Inc as a management consultant to visit half of the Teledyne companies to evaluate their performance and submit a report of my assessment and recommendations to them and Teledyne. For five plus months I typically got on a plane on Monday morning and returned home on Friday. The companies were located throughout America and Canada. They consisted of small and large companies including dental equipment, manufacturer of the largest casting in the world, aircraft, electronics, high tech and much more. I was able to witness many different types of businesses. It was an exceptional experience. Most of the companies I visited on my own, but when visiting the larger companies, I was accompanied by two key individuals from Teledyne, Inc. They became good friends and were appreciative of my contributions.

When first arriving at a company, a meeting was set up with the company officers to inform them of the purpose of the visit. We were able to have a confidential meeting with anyone in the company. At the end of the review the officers would be briefed on findings and the report was submitted to Teledyne, Inc. All but one of the company presidents were supportive and grateful for the assessment and suggestions on improving their company. The large company president's ego resented us even being there. He certainly did not appreciate our suggestions, although his staff did.

On my second visit to San Diego I invited Paige to join me. Her children's ages were 2, 4, and 6. I knew she needed a break. We stayed at the Marriott Marquis San Diego Marina, thereby allowing Paige to visit USS Midway Museum and Seaport Village, walking distance from the hotel. Of course, the hotel had beautiful grounds and swimming pools for her relaxation. High school friends, now living in California, provided additional entertainment. During our time together we visited the San Diego Zoo, Balboa Park, Old Town and more. *It was special time with Paige.*

August 25, 1993, on a visit to Nashville, Tennessee, I met two Teledyne colleagues for dinner. Returning to the hotel, I was using both hands to lock my car doors (the car was designed this way to prevent keys being locked in the car). I had set my briefcase and computer (the rare portable computer was larger than my briefcase) on the ground. When I turned around to pick them up, I was facing a 9 mm Glock pistol about 10 inches from my nose. The badman said with force, "M.... F.... give me all yo' money." Within a nanosecond I handed him $300 from my front pocked. I had received a $300 advance expense cash for the business trip. Credit cards were rare in those days. Because he was so well groomed and dressed my immediate thoughts were that he would not risk leaving a witness. I knew my life was over. He firmly said, "Give me your wallet." I had mistakenly left it at home that morning. I said that and put my hands up and turned around so he could check my rear pockets. He patted my cheeks and when I turned back around, he was gone. I looked around the car to see he was climbing into a car without plates and escaped. My briefcase and computer permanently were in the wind. I was calm when going into the hotel lobby when asking them to call the police, who grilled me until after midnight. Two days later my hands were shaking from the adrenalin and other chemicals released during the event, even though I was otherwise calm. Teledyne, Inc told me to buy the best Apple portable computer, portable printer, and peripherals that were available and any software desired. Having no backup, it took me about two months to re-create the critical data lost. Other data was simply gone forever.

Near the end of my time with Teledyne, Inc the position of Teledyne Hastings president came open. I was told that if I would throw my name in the hat the position likely would be mine. After visiting a company in Canada and retuning home on a Friday I stopped by Teledyne Hastings in Norfolk, Virginia for an informal tour of the company. They had no idea why I was there. I met individuals throughout the company. The competence of all individuals at every level was impressive. The company was in a good financial position, had very good research and development of new products, marketing approach and exceptional manufacturing capability in their product field. I also noted the staff at all levels were much younger than my 55 years. The plant was located in an unimpressive area of Norfolk. After a few days it occurred to me that I would be leaving family, friends and my church and starting a new life by myself. The younger staff would not likely be helpful in starting a new social life. In spite of a significant advancement in my career, I decided not to throw my hat in the ring. Upon returning to TBE full time, I continued with the TWGSS program.

Family changes during 1993 included Chad and his family moving to Minnesota to complete his and Angel's education. Angel's paternal family was from Minnesota.

During the last week of December of 1993 Bonnie, Alan, Janie and I traveled to Jamaica for a grand week. This would be the last time Bonnie and I would spend a whole week together. Scuba diving was not as good as at Grand Cayman. We enjoyed many other activities and the company and sharing of old family tales. *Great way to finish a busy and unusual year.*

Chapter XVIII - 1994–1995

In January 1994 the United Nations invited me to present a paper at a February meeting. Iraqi president, Saddam Hussein had agreed to inspections he had resisted before. TBE did not have funds budgeted for such tasks so I approached Jim McGovern, TBE president. He provided the funds. At the UN headquarters in NYC in February, I was seated at a large donut shaped conference table with microphones at each position. Several countries had two representatives at the table. I was the only one not representing a country. Each country presented a paper starting on my right, making me the last to present my thoughts. At the conclusion, the UNSCOM Chief of Operations, Nikita Smidovich, sitting directly across the large table from me, said, "Thanks for all the contributions; they confirmed our thoughts. We heard only two new ideas that we had not considered, those came from Skipper Colin. Thanks Skipper. They were important and we will incorporate them in our WMD inspections." *It still amazes me that I was on the world stage contributing to history.*

In June, Janie moved to Huntsville from Florida. During the summer, I would find myself having a third neck operation to remove a disc. Not the best way to spend a summer. Must give Janie credit for taking care of me as she did in 1982 with my first two neck operations with love in her heart, my love was also on board. *It seemed like déjà vu.*

In September 1994, I was asked to be the Chief WMD Inspector in Iraqi. This time I signed a private contract with the US Army and took a leave without pay. I had saved enough vacation to use a day per week to keep my benefits. This was important for insurance purposes and to keep retirement benefits growing. The substantial private contract did not provide benefits. As usual the UN would cover all expenses. Later I would be walking around in Baghdad (3.5 million population) with a fanny-pack containing over $10,000 expense money and no one within a quarter of a mile radius was as tall, with a white bald head and no mustache. That amount of money would support a family for many years. The exchange rate of Iraqi dinars relative to American dollars was significant. There simply was no safe place to store the money. The mission was to last three months. However, my time in Iraq would be extended to five months because they were unable to find a suitable replacement.

The WMD Chief of the Chemical Team, Sergei, a Russian, and I were the only passengers on the UN C-160 cargo plane flying to Iraqi from Manama, Bahrain at the end of September. Arriving at the Iraqi airbase, we visited with Ambassador Ekéus, the director of UNSCOM for about 30 minutes, before he headed back to Bahrain on the same plane. He said that his meeting with the Iraqi hierarchy was the worst ever and he expected something bad would happen. After a few days the "October Crisis" started. Saddam Hussein began sending a large military force (Two Iraqi divisions of the Republican Guard) to the Kuwait border. The US countered with a large force known as "Operation Vigilant Warrior" that gathered in Kuwait and included a staff in Riyadh, Saudi Arabia. This military operation began October 8th and continued to December 15th.

The UN staff had left the Sheraton Hotel and moved to a fenced complex, Canal Hotel farther from the center of Baghdad. The converted Canal Hotel was located on the east side of the Tigris River in Baghdad near the Army Canal which ran northwest to southwest. Although it contained stagnant water it had large, multi-lane highways on each side. Converted for the UN Headquarters in Baghdad, the highways afforded easy access to the converted building, which supported several UN sub-organizations, of which UNSCOM was the largest. This was the same hotel shown on TV, when, on 19 August 2003, a suicide bomber truck quickly drove past the guard at the gate and into the building, killing UN Special Representative Sergio Vieira de Mello, and 21 others in the hotel.

After a tour of the facilities and meeting the staff, I retired to a one-star hotel, the al Hyatt (not to be confused with the Hyatt chain) near the Russian Mission. Nothing had changed from a security standpoint. The UN offices, vehicles and hotels were bugged. I was to room with John Hollstein from the Denver area. He was a former Airborne-Ranger in the Army before going to college and became an Air Force officer, American engineer, attorney, mountain climber, skier, aviation instructor, mountain climber, Col. in the Air Force reserves (an Intelligence unit), a fellow Episcopalian and also single. Great man full of integrity and competence, who took no prisoners. For about two months he and I would be the only Americans in all of Iraq. Sanctions prevented Americans from being in Iraq. John's task was to install and maintain cameras at key locations in Iraq. He was a true asset.

The rest of my team arrived about one week later, October 6th, from several countries. That first week allowed me to get the lay-of-the-land and prepare for inspections. During that week, because of the October Crisis and being a WMD Chief and spokesman for the UN, I was required to grant an interview to any media in the world. An international news organization, Reuters, was the first to interview. Being new as a spokesman, I was concerned that this dude might make a fool of himself. John, who was listening, said it was a very good interview. Much later I was informed by UN headquarters that the full interview was impressive and broadcast worldwide except in the US. After CBS interviewed me, their broadcast showed me crossing a parking lot and they put the opposite spin on the facts I provided.

During our surprise inspections, as the chief, I was accused of killing children and much more. I would listen with a calm poker face until they ran out of gas. After several weeks having received no reaction from me, they stopped. At times when we used a helicopter for our mission, we collaborated with the helicopter used by a photo team. Mike and his team took surprise photos at locations. Our collaborations would confuse the Iraqis making for more effective surprises.

On one helicopter surprise mission to northern Iraq near Mosel, to the north and the Kurd area, I told the Iraqi minder that he would have to ride on the Iraqi helicopter that always followed us. The Iraqi minder, a high-level engineer, had ridden with us as a courtesy. However, I was informed that morning from UN headquarters not to extend the courtesy starting today. The minder was very upset and refused to go on the Iraqi helicopter. He stated no facility would open the gate without him present. We lifted off without him. At the large missile site I had chosen for the day, the site manager would not let us in the gate. I said we were going in regardless. We were surrounded by Iraqi machine guns that were there (theoretically) to protect us. He begged for 10 minutes to call Baghdad for permission. He said, "I will be fired or worse, and my family will be dealt with severely." After 10 minutes he said, "I could not reach Baghdad." I had brought along a communication tech with a satellite phone that he set up about 20 feet from us with good reception. I told the site manager, "If you do not let us in, I will call NY and this will cause an 'International Incident,' which Baghdad will not like." He still refused. Team members suggested we hang-it-up and go back to Baghdad. Knowing this would set a terrible precedence, I lead my now nervous team through the gate. After inspecting the first building by myself (which I knew would have nothing of interest) then exiting the building, everyone settled down. On future inspections to this site they had a new manager. The previous manager who had always been present at several surprise inspections was no longer seen. *I can only imagine his fate.*

One ordnance base we inspected was so void of safety practices and equipment that we made a quick inspection and escaped. Reportedly many people had been killed in this facility. Obviously, I did not schedule this site for inspections often.

One of my duties was to have meetings at night with about 30 of the hierarchy of Iraq WMD and negotiate open issues since the end of the Gulf war. I would always attend the meetings by myself, and occasionally ask our interpreter to join me. General Hossam Amin was the head of the WMD and attended all meetings. He was to be on the list of "Deck of Playing Cards." The list of cards was created after the 2003 invasion of Iraq of those with the most bounty on their heads. Many of the others in the meetings were on the list.

At one of the large meetings, I informed General Amin that our team would arrive at a large facility that had a Chinese radar, previously undeclared, and would supervise its destruction. Iraq had agreed to a 150 km (90 miles) range missile capability at the end of the Gulf War. This radar had a range of 750 km or miles (do not remember which unit). I instructed them to provide an appropriate crew, a tracked vehicle, an acetylene cutting torch and a concrete truck. I had asked our interpreter to accompany me to the meeting to ensure no misunderstanding. He was very good at reading Iraqi body language and other signs when they were less than honest. The destruction took three days.

The morning started with informing the Iraqis of the plan to destroy the radar. They were to remove the large radar dish which was mounted on a large pedestal on a large low-boy flatbed trailer. The tracked vehicle then ran over the dish several times. The many pieces were then thrown into a pit dug by a bulldozer. The accessed covers were removed from the pedestal and thrown into the pit. All electronics were removed from the pedestal and the military support trailers, smashed and set on fire. The remains were thrown into the pit. The support trailers were gutted, and their contents thrown into the pit. The ring gear on the pedestal was cut with the acetylene cutting torch in several places. The pedestal was then laid down in the pit. The concrete truck then poured loads of concrete in the pedestal openings and filled the pit. They were not going to reverse engineer the radar. During the process the site manager kept requesting to save some items. Some requests were ridiculous, such as a cheap pressure gauge. He asked me several times to allow them to keep a very old, limited capability computer (it belonged in a museum). Knowing I needed to remain friendly with the Iraqis, I agreed to contact the UN headquarters and ask their permission not to destroy the computer. That night I sent a secure fax asking them to send me a fax telling me to destroy the computer. These three days were my most emotional days spent in Iraq. On the last day of the destruction the Iraqi minder was escorting us back to Baghdad. Before departing, the minder came back to my vehicle and asked if we would wait five minutes while he went into the site headquarters. I agreed. I asked our interpreter what that was about. He said the minder was going in to beat the hell out of the site manager. In his eyes the site manager had dishonored Iraq by begging. The minder came out with a grin and said he was ready to go.

I would visit shops some evenings. One was not to talk about why he was visiting until after drinking their strong coffee or tea and making small talk. To skip this hospitality was considered rude. There are more than a thousand carpet stores. My favorite shop was owned by Princess Amal, who would insist on providing a meal first. Typically, I would have a hamburger. You had to ask for beef, or you got mutton. After a fashion we would talk carpets. For two months I negotiated for a specific carpet before purchasing one in the afternoon. I had to pay in Iraqi dinars, not dollars. This required several heavy backpack trips to transport the dinars. Because it would be stolen from my hotel room, the Princess Amal kept the carpet until I was to go home. That night, I dropped by about 9:00 pm to take another look at the carpet. The biological team had arrived that day to perform about one week of inspections. They were in the shop. The chief, a female doctor from Minnesota, loved the carpet and offered me twice what I had paid. No sale! *Still is my favorite carpet.*

At another carpet shop, I became friends with the owner's father who was at least in his 80's. He was very wealthy and considered one of six carpet gurus in Iraq. Any dispute over a carpet value, quality or origin was ruled on by these gurus as the final word. One evening he had the flu and asked if I could get aspirin. Because of the sanctions, medicine was not available. I returned to my room and filled a small bottle with part of the 1,000 bottle of aspirin brought from home. He thanked me profusely and said if I had an interest in any carpets in Baghdad bring them to him for evaluation. I did. He was a great source of knowledge.

Before leaving Baghdad, the son of the Iraq Ambassador to the US, who had been stationed in the US for 10 years, offered me two carpets he wanted to sell that night. The Ambassador's son was the best friend of the son of Princess Amal. He was going to slip out of Iraq the next day. His father had been recalled from the US and had a mysterious auto accident in which the auto was totally smashed, but the father had only a hole between his eyes. The Shah of Iran years earlier had given the father two carpets for a favor when the father was in the Iraq Ministry of Foreign Affairs stationed in Iran. I picked one of the carpets for a modest amount. I would learn later the other carpet reportedly sold for $28,000 in Jordan. *Should have selected the other carpet.*

From time to time, individuals visited Baghdad from UN Headquarters in NYC for a variety of reasons. Azad from my first tour in 1993 was visiting for 2-3 days. The day he arrived he was in the UN HQ lobby at the Canal Hotel when we returned from an inspection. He ran across the room, gave me a Russian bear hug and handed me a fantastic congratulation card. I was surprised and a bit overwhelmed. One time, Nikita Smidovich and several others arrived to have high level meetings with Iraq. I attended the meeting as the WMD Chief. At one point in the meeting, it occurred to me that we were making history. *I considered pinching myself to see if I was dreaming.* How did this farm boy from the White Mountains of New Hampshire and student of ENMU come to be participating in a historic meeting? *Still a mystery.*

On Christmas Day, John and I attended a large Catholic Church and it was filled with Christians not afraid to go to church. Although the nave was large it was filled with well-dressed, middle class worshippers. There were several large Catholic Churches in Baghdad. Each of the churches provided a service on the hour starting at sunrise and continuing services, finishing at dusk. The churches would empty after each service to make room for the next group. The Catholic service was similar to the Episcopal service, so John and I were able to follow the service even though it was in Arabic. We did recognize "Alleluia." When leaving the church, we noticed an Iraqi sitting on the sidewalk selling very small Charlie Brown Christmas trees. The trees were void of needles. I purchased one anyway for our room. The few handmade decorations from scrap and junk I put on it were as bad as the tree. Paige's children, Jason, Patsy and Joseph had sent some colored sketches they had made with love and sent via the UN Embassy courier mail system. They were placed underneath the tree along with a bottle of cognac Nikita had given me for Christmas. I still have the attractive empty Otard XO bottle on a mantle. Current price is $139.99 a bottle. The church service, the tree and presents made my Christmas. Sharing the day laughing with John about the tree was also memorable.

My only coat was stolen from the hotel room. I casually mentioned it to someone in the UN office in NYC. They reported that to the UN Security Council. My "Members" jacket unwittingly became a historic topic. I looked at street vendors and shops for a jacket to keep me warm when I had a free moment. Apparently, all jackets had one sleeve shorter than the other or otherwise unacceptable. By holding out I got sick. *Stupid me once again.*

One night at my meeting with the 30 hierarchy of Iraq, the topic was a missile they were developing. They had supplied crucial data necessary to calculate range. Our team had been constantly inspecting the development. General Amin claimed the missile had a range of only 150k (90 miles). According to standard calculations the range was significantly longer. We had been debating this for two weeks. I said to him, "We both know you are a very good engineer and that back of the envelope calculations would be closer to the correct range." I had anticipated that challenging his pride as an engineer would not allow him to continue the charade. He paused then said, "You are correct." He then provided data they had been withholding and agreed to stop development. *Will always enjoy negotiating.*

I had become good friends with James, the doctor from New Zealand, who headed up the medics and the infirmary at the UN Canal compound. All the medical staff were Kiwis. Great people. James had been requesting going into the field with us on a mission. Not supposed to happen. One day we were going to witness a missile engine test at the al-Rafa Test-stand rather than conducting a surprise inspection. The engine fuel was hydrazine-based hypergolic propellant which was the same fuel used on the Titan-II that I had a year of experience with in 1962-3. I knew how dangerous it was and that if one witnessed an orange cloud it was "time to get out of Dodge." I instructed the team and James to observe from the upwind side of a chain link fence surrounding the test-stand and run upwind as fast as they could, should there be a problem. James was excited to have joined us. When the attempt was made to fire the missile engine, I realized it had failed. An orange cloud was forming quickly, so I hollered "run" and took off running upwind. James said, "This will be my only trip to the field." Later I was told UN headquarters viewed a video from one of John's cameras. Someone asked, "Who is the one running the fastest and out in front." Then said, "Oh that's Skipper, he obviously knows what he is doing."

At the conclusion of a surprise inspection of Iraq's largest development and manufacturing facility, the site manager (he spoke good English, but feared becoming too emotional, if speaking in English) asked the minder to ask me if I could obtain a specific medicine, Silver Sulfadiazine. His toddler son had pulled a pot of boiling water from the stove and badly burned his back. The doctors had explained without the medicine the son's survival chances were not good. Because of the sanctions, the medicine was not available. I said, "I will try." Back at the UN compound, the minder waited outside the gate, at my request, while I found James in the infirmary. James had an adult container of Silver Sulfadiazine that he gave me. He said, "This is very expensive, they owe you big time." *Not my concern.* I asked him for necessary cleaning and application supplies not knowing what the Iraqi doctor had to work with. I then asked him for instructions necessary for cleaning and application. Returning with an armload of supplies and the medicine, I gave them to the minder and told him the instructions to be used. He carefully wrote them down in English, then asked me to repeat again so he could write them in Arabic. After the exchange I turned and headed for the gate. After about 10 feet I turned back around and said, "I will pray for the boy." Without waiting for a response, I headed for the gate. The boy would quickly recover with minimal scarring.

That night I was again in a meeting with the 30 hierarchy of Iraq. About midway into the meeting, there was a pause when changing subjects. General Amin said, "What you did today brought the UN and Iraq closer together more than anything to date." While that was not on my mind, it was great to hear and appreciated. This reconfirmed in my mind that Iraqis respected you for your competence and practicing your religion. They reportedly did not care what your religion was.

On one occasion Nikita came from NYC to conduct a surprise inspection of a specific building at a small army post. He was alone and asked my team to join him on the mission. The Iraqis were very upset when we arrived and at first refused to let us on the base. We found nothing but cobwebs, old army mattresses and emptiness. The next day I flew via the UN C-160 cargo plane to Manama, Bahrain. As soon as I landed, very good high-altitude photos were shown to me that had been taken the previous day. They showed large trucks at the next building soon after we left the base. Information I was not to share at the time.

The Russians on the team asked if they could stay at the Russian Mission, a stone's throw from our hotel. I knew they had lost all income and a pension when the Soviet Union collapsed. They needed to save the UN per diem to survive. I quietly allowed this to happen, even though it was against policy. When any team member was to rotate-out, the Russians would prepare a good meal and an unlimited supply of vodka for all team members. The large dining room at the mission was located on the second floor with a very long table. After finishing the meal everyone was relaxed and talkative. The Chemical Team Chief, Sergei, a great guy, sat at one end of the table and myself at the other. Following the meal, I moved to Sergei's end of the table so we could solve world problems. The windows were open. At one point, I realized I had been hearing automatic gunfire in the alley below. I also observed, no one seemed to care, including me. Conversation was not interrupted. We had gotten so used to hearing gunfire that we ignored it. *Strange!*

Jerry at the UN NYC Headquarters was responsible to randomly select an approved Iraqi missile system by serial number to ensure they had not been upgraded. They were to be gathered by Iraqis from all parts of Iraq and moved to one location. My team would join Jerry at a location near Basra to conduct the inspection of each missile. Good news, a day I did not have to write a SITCOM for UN headquarters. Nikita and Scott had previously told me my daily SITCOMs were the best they had received and that the headquarters staff looked forward to reading my SITCOMs each morning because I was thorough and provided interesting information they needed, and they enjoyed my various experiences. My SITCOM reports contained info from the surprise inspections and my take on the evening meetings and other observations.

One day I received word to be prepared to fly to Bahrain to meet with staff from NYC headquarters. They were sending a UN C-160 plane to pick me up. The plane lost one of its two engines on the way to Iraq and returned to Manama airport. They would have to wait for an engine from Germany. They needed me sooner, so they arranged for me to fly on a UN Russian cargo aircraft similar to the US C-160 aircraft. The Russian Antonov An-12 flew me and young Danish soldiers who had been stationed in Northern Iraq to protect UN personnel who were distributing food and more. The Iraqis custom agents (the custom facility consisted of a card table setup in the sand on their largest military airbase) searched the others from one end to the other and their belongings. *Don't ask about the restroom facilities.* The goal seemed to be to make life miserable. They were not allowed to touch me or to search my luggage. The Russian UN plane flew me to Kuwait City after a brief stop at a remote airstrip in Kuwait. Without a passport, I was not allowed into the Kuwait City terminal. My passport was locked up in Bahrain UN offices. A UN representative, after 30 minutes of *debating*, succeeded in getting the Kuwait customs to allow me into the terminal and finally on board a commercial flight to Bahrain. At Bahrain the same problem occurred without a passport. I was not allowed into the country until the UN *debated* for thirty minutes again. *It had been a long day.*

At the evening meetings, I had been pressuring them to deliver to us a large number of gyroscopes (they were much too accurate for the missiles they were allowed to have) delivered to them after the Gulf War, by a less than honorable UK citizen. They had been denying knowledge of the gyros. I had the serial numbers of all the gyroscopes. They finally confessed and said they had been thrown into a canal and therefore could not be provided. Iraq had constructed a canal between the Tigris and Euphrates rivers. I asked which canal and the location of the dumping. They reluctantly provided the info, at which time I told them to have dredging equipment (generically called a steam-shovel) and crew at the location the following morning. They recovered a number of gyroscopes in the mud on the first day that matched the serial numbers. I assigned one member of our team to monitor the operation on following days so we could continue our surprise inspections. He was not a happy camper watching the Iraqis dig through many piles of mud. This solved other problems I had with this individual. Never found all the gyros.

My roommate John returned to Colorado but would return several times after I headed home. John had become a good friend, whom I am still in contact with. He returned to Iraq, with several other UN inspectors, immediately after the 2003 invasion of the country, a head of the eventual 1,400 inspectors assigned later. He noted to me that Ibn al Haytham, the fenced complex of large buildings where missiles had been developed, had been looted and was reduced to cement foundations only. The Saddam billboard of many (64) teeth I had observed countless times at the site was nowhere to be found.

Media personnel were escorted directly from the Jordan border by the Iraqis to a specific hotel in Baghdad. They were not allowed to leave the hotel without an escort, allowed to point their camera, or talk to any Iraqi that had not been selected by Iraq. A famous Washington Post journalist wrote a piece not disclosing the limitations. They staged several situations Saddam wanted the world to think was happening in Iraq due to sanctions, all propaganda and not true. I had personally observed the locations where the plight of starvation and begging supposedly occurred. It never occurred anytime I was at those locations.

I had been averaging 14 hours per day for nearly five months and realized, for the last month, I was making small physical and mental mistakes. John had told me before leaving that I was like the point man on an army patrol, behind lines. The point man was rotated out after two hours because of a tendency to become exhausted and make mistakes. He said there was no one to relieve me. I knew it was time to go home before making significant mistakes. Two weeks before I returned home my replacement arrived, thereby providing a seamless continuance of the long-term inspection team. My team had been the first long term WMD Inspector team. A surprise "going away party" was given for me along with speeches and a fancy brass tankard with my name and position engraved. It was difficult saying goodbye to good friends I would not likely see again.

On my stop in Bahrain, I approached Col. Dave Underwood (chief of the Bahrain UN office) who had become a good friend. He was a retired Air Force colonel, who had served on the close staff of the Chairman of the Joint Chiefs of Staff, Colin Powell, before Dave retired. I had accumulated a lot of baggage that would certainly exceed airline limits. He said not to be concerned, someone will pick up you up at the hotel and walk you through customs and the airline counter.

A handsome young man, Mohamed (he was a member of the royal family) arrived in a large Mercedes with a gorgeous girl in the passenger seat, obviously his evening date. At the airport he asked for my passport and ticket and said he would meet me in the VIP lounge. A bit later he returned my passport and a boarding pass and said all I had to do was board. I asked how much did the extra weight and baggage cost. He said that was not my concern.

I returned home via Washington, DC. Arriving at Dulles Airport late at night, my significant quantity of luggage was the last to arrive at the baggage claim. All fellow passengers on the 747 aircraft had been gone awhile. With the baggage loaded head high, I pushed it to the customs agents. I picked the oldest of the two remaining. I had been told the oldest was not as eager to make a name for himself as were the younger agents. He asked, "How are you?" I said, "Tired." He took my declaration form and placed it on a stack of them without looking at the form. He said, "Have a nice evening."

The next morning, I met with an Army civil servant for breakfast at the hotel. He had visited Baghdad and I had given him a tour. His first question was, "How did customs go?" After telling him how, he asked me to describe the agent. He said you picked the toughest and meanest agent at Dulles. *Luck is underrated.* He then escorted me to several agencies in the Washington area to be debriefed.

The joy of arriving home in March was beyond words. It took me three weeks to realize how exhausted I had been. I did not want to go back to a structured environment. Looking around, many of those retiring at 65 were hobbling around. I wanted to climb mountains and travel when retiring. Paige and Chad were long ago out of the nest. Being a single widower, I was responsible for only myself. So, I retired from Teledyne Brown Engineering on March 31, 1995 after nearly 33 years. *Serving with UNSCOM was an honor and privilege and a great experience to top off a career.*

Chapter XIV - 1995–1999

Finding myself, on April 1, 1995, retired at 57 was a real blessing, not an April Fool's joke. Janie, who was teaching in Huntsville after moving from Florida in June 1994, before I headed to Iraq, would help me assimilate back into a normal routine. However, soon I would wonder how I ever had time to work.

I had loved Colorado when living there twice in the early 1960s. Patsy and I had planned to live there before ending up in Huntsville in 1963. I planned to buy a ranch in a favorable location and after about five years, sell lots to "Baby Boomers" when they retired. The plan was to raise livestock to help with a mortgage. I did a lot of research on land for sale and headed for Colorado. Some of the properties simply would not meet my goals. I spent about a week in a beautiful small town, Salida, (population 5,000) to see what it would be like to live there. It had one theater that reportedly was only open on Saturdays and showed the same movie for 2-3 months. In a cafe I frequented, the patrons chatted mostly about cattle, sheep, hogs, hunting, etc. I realized Huntsville was where family, friends, and church were and had a lot to offer. Besides that, I was about five years too late for the "Baby Boomer" idea to bear fruit. *The car headed home.*

My beloved Gold Wing motorcycle, having no members of the fairer sex's interested in climbing aboard, ran away. The good news was the new owner offered more dollars than the purchase price five years earlier. *Good news, bad news.*

I missed seeing Chad and family, and being retired, Mahnomen, Minnesota was on my radar. We had a great visit. Only problem was a speeding ticket in Louisville, Kentucky on the way to Minnesota. Returning home was much better, routing through Grapevine, Texas to visit Bonnie and Nancy.

July 4th Eunice High School reunion beckoned me annually along with the opportunity to visit Patsy's folks, Ebb and Lucille. Getting to visit Jim and Mardy Manes, Calvin Craig, Tony Pearson and Irvin Smith was pure enjoyment. Visiting Irvin's remarkable folks was always my first stop in Eunice. Being with those friends in Mom's generation was always a highlight. They never failed to tell me stories that revealed the conditions before New Mexico was a state and its early years. As always, my car found the way home via Carlsbad,

Cloudcroft, Ruidoso, Santa Fe, and Colorado.

Having been without a beloved Apple Macintosh since retiring and needing a computer, I purchased a Mac and would always replace computers over time with Apple's latest.

In August Janie and I visited George Washington University where Jackie was a student. Janie moved in with me in September. Neither of us had lived with someone other than children since our spouses had died decades earlier.

Paige attended her 10-year reunion at Grissom High School with a class of 600. She was voted most beautiful in her class. This Dad always thought she was exceptionally beautiful. She was proud of the honor, *especially having had three children.*

After Chad purchased a small farm near Mahnomen, Minnesota, I returned to lend a hand. I traveled to the farm and installed power and fixtures in five of the seven outbuildings while Chad was at work. The temperature during those first two weeks of October never got above *minus* nine degrees. I will never forget trying to install a small screw in a flood light fixture in 45 mph wind at the top of a ladder. Fingers being numb made that task nearly impossible. *Loving one's children is a challenge at times.*

During much of the school year of 1996-7, I enjoyed watching Jason, Patsy and Joseph on Monday, Wednesday and Fridays from the time school was out until about 5:00 pm. These energetic grandchildren, at times, required some discipline, resulting in facing a corner after scuffling got out of hand. Most of the time they were all well behaved. Joseph had a habit of not raising the seat despite trying to persuade him otherwise. On one occasion, I told him that was the behavior of rednecks. Problem solved. *Sorry Joseph, could not resist telling that story.*

In 1996, I decided to add a screen-sun room to the house. I wanted to make it appear as part of the home's original design. With some creativity this was achieved. *Always wanted to be an architect. My engineering aptitude saved the day.* In May 1996 I would pour the concrete foundation and flooring for the screen-sun room. One day John, Paige's husband, helped me install the roof rafters. The short brick wall around the exterior was installed by a brick mason. I would perform all other work on the project. In hindsight, installing the terra-cotta tile floor should have been farmed out. My fragile neck hurt for many weeks. I used tongue and groove cedar for the cathedral ceiling and the low interior wall. I had designed the screen openings to be the same size as sliding glass door panes. This approach reduced the glass price to one third the price of custom glass. *The engineering blood was always present.* An air/heating duct was conveniently located allowing the sunroom to be heated and cooled.

My heart was set on climbing all 63 fourteeners in America. Colorado had 58 of the peaks over 14,000 feet. Janie and I headed to Colorado in July. We spent many days at 9,000 feet and higher to become acclimated to the elevations. We visited a friend of Janie's in Estes Park. We climbed the Twin Sisters Peaks (11,428 ft elevation) in the Rocky Mountain National Park near Estes Park. The trail was difficult and rated strenuous. *Nice challenge.* We visited several cities, parks and villages before meeting John Hollstein, my roomy in Baghdad. John and I climbed two fourteeners, Grays Peak and Torreys Peak. John was a big help teaching me many tips of do's and don'ts. When I reached Grays Peak, there were several *younger* climbers already resting at the top. I received a big applause. *For the first time I felt old.* Janie and I continued our journey to other parts of Colorado and New Mexico.

In November 1996, Janie and I knew living under the same roof should not continue. Much as we loved each other, in *my* opinion, our temperaments were not compatible. She would move to Jacksonville, Florida in February 1997. We continued to see each other through most of 1999. At that time, despite love, it was in both our interest to move on. I would never regret having her as part of the 18-year adventure we shared. I would always think of her and her family as part of my family. After all, her mother was my Mom's best friend (I grew up calling her Aunt Sparky) for many decades. Paige and Janie still remain close, vacation together and more.

I purchased Reunion genealogy software in January 1997 to catalog my family history. In a period of about two years I would spend 2,500 hours or more on genealogy. I also included Patsy's family to provide our children with a complete picture of their ancestors. Starting out I did not even know my Dad's parents' names. Dad's death certificate in Santa Fe revealed their names and that they were from Canada. Discovering his mother was a McCabe led me to become aware of a McCabe reunion that occurred every five years in Truro, Nova Scotia. August 1997 was on the calendar. I would travel to Nova Scotia to conduct genealogy research across the province. At the reunion, I found that nearly all the 200 attendees were engineers, they were built like me and their temperaments and mannerisms were similar. I had discovered where my engineering aptitude originated. They said their engineering aptitude did not skip a generation. Another aptitude was art or music, but occasionally skipped a generation. *I should have raised my hand at that one.* I do love art and most music but creating them is not in my DNA. I am still collecting fine art. In my opinion all music written before about 1960 is good, afterwards not so much.

Janie and I attended Jackie's graduation in May 1997 from the Elliott School of International Affairs of George Washington University. She graduated Summa Cum Laude with a major in Eastern European Affairs. She would go on to serve with the Peace Corp in Siberia, Russia.

A bonus of retiring was to rarely miss the ballgames of Jason, Patsy and Joseph. They started out with "T" ball and progressed through baseball, basketball and football to the high school level. Typically, each one was among the best on the field or court. It was a privilege to watch them.

Most of 1998 was spent on genealogy, traveling to Jacksonville, Minnesota, my annual trip to New Mexico and of course attending grandchildren's ballgames.

In March 7, 1999, I awoke to the smell of electric smoke. I did not readily discover the source, so I turned off the power and called the fire department. They responded in about five minutes. They found the squirrel cage motor in the HVAC system had burned. Smoke had gone through the whole duct system. The insurance company replaced ducts, the heating-air-conditioning unit, cleaned carpets, drapes and much of the furniture.

I toured Ireland in May 1999 with 30 individuals from church. One of our priests, Reverend Jack Wilson, had been an Episcopal monk for several years before moving to Huntsville. He planned a great trip to visit several monastery ruins. We learned a lot of history. We did visit many other venues during the trip. Pubs were not excluded. *Great memories.*

Another research trip was necessary to add to my genealogy base. We flew to Boston and rented a car to drive to Canada to provide more flexibility. Janie and I explored Nova Scotia after arriving on the ferry from Portland, Maine to Yarmouth, Nova Scotia, a 12-hour night crossing. Normally I would spend days in archives while Janie explored towns or cities. We moved on to archives in New Brunswick and Quebec. One day we popped down to a small village in Maine to spend no more than an hour at an archive and return to Canada. We crossed the US border, no thanks to "Barney Fife," (*think Andy Griffith TV Show*) the US customs agent. He discovered copies of documents I had copied in archives in Canada that I had not declared (who knew this was an issue). He all but strip-searched us and our vehicle while a lot of traffic backed up waiting to enter our great country. We did not even have to stop when going back into Canada. After leaving Quebec we drove through New Hampshire to visit my boyhood farm.

Richard Hamner and Gaines Watts had formed an Episcopal Cursillo reunion group and asked me to join them. My first reunion group was great but had not met in years. We meet once a week for spiritual discussions. A few years later Jack Little joined our group. Twenty years later we still meet weekly. The group has grown. Gaines and Jack have since died and will always be missed for their contributions, intellect and love.

Chapter XV - 2000–2019

The year 2000 would be more than interesting. Each month, for many years, my closest friends (Nick Passino, Frank Vann, Billy Barnes, Don Martin and I) would meet for lunch. In January on a Thursday, at lunch, Billy suggested I consider asking out a lady, Nancy, from my church. I thought Nancy was married, but she was not. I attended an adult Sunday school class that she was teaching that Sunday. Nancy was obviously beautiful and intelligent with a sense of humor. That evening I called her home. Her adult son Will answered the phone. The caller ID showed me as Ernest. He said she was not available. She called me back in about five minutes apologizing for not taking my call. She knew me as Skipper not Ernest. After small talk, I asked her to the Broadway Theater League performance of *Chicago* the coming Friday, January 28th at the Von Braun Concert Hall. I had season tickets for decades in the third row, dead center. She agreed. On Friday leaving the performance I noticed an opera, *Manchurian Candidate,* was scheduled the following night at the Von Braun Playhouse. She had never been to an opera but agreed to be my guest. About one week later we dined at a nice continental restaurant, Pho's Fine Dinning. A week later we dined at the Fogcutter Restaurant & Lounge.

I received a phone call from New Mexico and was told that if I wanted to see Joe, Patsy's only sibling, to head for New Mexico. He was in the last stage of colon cancer. I would stay with Ebb, their father and drive him from Hobbs to Eunice every day to visit Joe. I stayed six weeks before Joe was gone on April 1st. During that time, I communicated with Nancy daily via email. This was like an old-fashioned courting approach when writing was a method of getting to know someone. This was also an opportunity for Nancy to *vet* me in Huntsville. We both treasured those emails.

Joe's doctor, whose practice was in Hobbs, would climb on his Harley with his nurse and make a house call to check on Joe in Eunice. *Love New Mexico.* I played golf with 90-year-old Ebb once during this stay. *Never again, it was embarrassing.* He was playing with an assortment of clubs from the 1950s, worn-out and split golf shoes, and his pull cart with rattling wheel bearings. Lucille, Patsy's mother was on her last legs in a nursing home. Driving to visit Lucille one day, I got mad at Patsy for the first time after her death. I thought, "Damn it, Patsy, you are supposed to be here for your mother." Lucille died in August. Ebb had lost his family. When departing for home I left my new clubs, a new cart and shoes behind the bedroom door. He would not have accepted them. When I arrived home, Ebb called to tell me I had forgotten something. I said I had not and had purchased a new set. I actually had immediately done so in order not to lie. His game improved. He had been wining golf tournaments, which he continued to do until he was 101 years young.

I must tell a little of Nancy's story, after all she has put up with me for 20 years and has added to my foundation, shaped my future and made me a better man. Nancy was born in Nashville in 1948 and moved to Huntsville in 1958. She graduated from the University of Alabama in 1970 with a major in history and minor in Spanish, then married and had three great children; Lovell, Will, and Michael. Later, Nancy would go on to be Executive Director of Huntsville's only hospice for five years, vice president of United Way, allocating funds not raising money, for 18 years, and director of the Alabama ALS Association for three years before retiring. When I met Nancy, she was on 12 to 14 nonprofit boards plus serving on several committees in our church and the Episcopal Diocese of Alabama. She was the first female president of the Diocesan Standing Committee. *That was a big deal.* She has served as Chairman of several boards including the Huntsville Symphony Orchestra. She is widely known, respected, loved in Huntsville and beyond. After retiring, she became just as active as a volunteer. The main difference was she no longer received a paycheck. All the above is just the tip of the iceberg. I would soon learn she was loved by all and easy to love.

In June 2000, Michael would marry Summer Mann at the Episcopal Church of Nativity, our church. They had met at the University of Alabama in Tuscaloosa. Like me, Nancy was a cradle Episcopalian as were all our children.

I would head to Eunice for the annual Eunice High School reunion on July 4th. Following the reunion, I picked up Nancy at the Midland International Air & Space Port for a journey through the Rockies from Southern New Mexico to Canada. We checked out many fine art galleries, museums and of course several National Parks. We climbed Wheeler Peak (elevation 13,167 feet, the highest peak in New Mexico) at Taos Ski Valley. We returned to Huntsville with visits to the Badlands National Park in South Dakota, Iowa, Missouri, and St. Louis. Columbia, Missouri was meaningful because Nancy's mother, who had been valedictorian of her class, graduated from Stephens College. Nancy still thinks this was our best trip of all our travels.

In September we were part way home from a wedding in Nashville when Nancy received a call that her daughter, Lovell, was going into early labor. She asked me to hurry home so she could go to Atlanta. I said, "We are headed to Atlanta now." Cutting through several back roads we hit an Interstate freeway to the hospital arriving in time for the premature (2 lb.-13 oz.) birth of Miller. Not to be outdone, Summer gave birth to Tucker about six weeks later in Huntsville. Both are now in college. *Time does fly.*

In May 2001, Nancy and I toured several European countries: Germany, Denmark, Austria, Italy, Switzerland, Liechtenstein, and France. Nancy thought the country that she would like best was France and last of all Germany. At the end she reversed that assessment.

Chad and I would meet in Colombia, Missouri and head to Colorado. We spent the first night with our old friends, Bobbie and Gene Sanmann. It would have been great to have spent more time with them, but we headed to Fairplay, Colorado to climb four fourteeners nearby. The following morning, we climbed Mt. Democrat (14,148) then proceeded to climb Mt. Cameron. On the saddle between the two I started early signs of altitude sickness, so we headed down to the trailhead. *I know, it was dumb to try and climb before getting acclimated to the altitudes.* We went on to Aspen and climbed more peaks. It was great to spend significant time with just Chad for the first time in many years.

In January 2002, Nancy and I wanted to travel some place for a week during the week of Valentine's Day. After a few discussions, she said, "You plan the trip and surprise me." I planned a 10-day trip to Rome. I told her to pack for a climate on the coast of the Carolinas. At the Huntsville airport, I asked her to wait back from the counter so as not to reveal the surprise. I presented our tickets and passports while blocking the view and advising the agent of my intent. At the Atlanta airport we had a five-hour layover, so I suggested we wander over to the international terminal to have lunch because the food was better. After dining I noticed the marquee only showed a flight to Brussels, so I suggested killing some time by walking down to that gate. Then I suggested we sit a bit at that gate. I thought she could not see the Rome gate. I asked if she would like to visit Brussels. She said sure with modest enthusiasm. After sitting there awhile out of site of the Rome gate, I handed her a wire bound book I had created for the Rome trip. The enthusiasm was increased several fold. We did not miss anything in Rome. Great place to celebrate Valentine's Day. After returning to work she was telling her friends at United Way about the trip, when one friend asked if Skipper had a brother.

In October, during fall break, I offered to take Jason to London and Paris. When he declined, 13-year-old Patsy said he was crazy and asked if she could go. We had a fantastic time spending five days in each city and traveled on the high-speed train between the two. Each day we started at 8:00 am and ended late at night. She slept well and had to be roused each morning. *This old goat had more energy than Patsy.* It was a remarkable journey with a delightful granddaughter. We shared so many adventures that will never be forgotten.

During January 2003, Nancy and I ventured to Bemidji, Minnesota to visit Chad and family. We would go to the headwaters of the Mississippi and cross on foot. The snow was deep, fresh and beautiful. Chad, Spencer and Denver took us ice fishing on Bemidji

Lake. The boys each got nibbles. *You guessed right,* Nancy and I got nothing.

In March 2003, Nancy and I were hit head-on by a 1992 Lincoln Town Car (a tank) that was southbound doing about 70 mph on I-65. We had just stopped for a jackknifed 18-wheeler truck in our north bound lane. Nancy was taken to the local hospital in Cullman, Alabama. My faithful car was totaled. At the time, I thought I had escaped injury. Not so lucky, I would need a fourth neck operation. This would end my joy golfing with Harry Butcher since retiring.

In March we also found a house that we loved. I presented an engagement ring that thankfully was accepted.

In July 2003, we were at the hospital in Atlanta when Myers was born and joined Miller in Lovell and Jonathan's growing family. Lovell and Jonathan would later adopt two loving children, Anna and Bella, in China.

I walked Nancy down the aisle in the Episcopal Church of the Nativity in January 2004. I knew I was emotionally in trouble, when standing at the back of the church I saw more than a hundred of our closest friends and family faces radiating love. There were eight priests counting those in the congregation. *They must have wanted to send the message that this was going to work in the long run, or else.* Three were conducting the marriage. Retired Rev. Emile Joffrion blessed the rings, Rev. Steve Bates conducted the marriage and the current Rector, Rev. Andy Anderson, assisted. During the vows, tears flowed down my cheeks. Later I was told that Paige shed tears also. My sister Nancy and her daughter, Charlotte, who both lived in Texas, attended the service. Our children and Nancy's siblings and families attended. Nick Passino and Buddy Little were my best men. Donna Rush and Maggie Little were the bride's maidens. We had four official witnesses. *Buddy being the Presiding Judge of the Circuit Court was going to make sure we would stay legally married, or else.* We now had a loving blended family that actually liked each other. We hosted a lively reception at The Ledges Country Club. We were to be the first wedding reception at the new club house but ended up being the second. We honeymooned in Hawaii at Maui, Kauai, and Oahu. We toured the first two islands with rented Mustang convertibles, rode a bicycle from the highest point on Maui, rode horses, toured on a helicopter and attended festivals. We joined a day tour for Oahu that included much of the island and visited the Arizona Memorial.

Cannot imagine a better honeymoon or someone better to share it with.

In June, our church, along with St. Thomas, would send a group of volunteers to a small village in the mountains of Honduras that had no water, electricity or medical care. I would join the medical mission as one of the volunteers each June for two years. We provided doctors, a pharmacy, dental and veterinarian services. I primarily worked in the dental clinic and had opportunities to pull teeth. I had a ball with the children. I remember when we were walking up a hill to the church for a service on the last day. A little boy walked up to me and gripped my hand for the journey. My eyes became wet. *I received more from these missions than I ever gave.*

In July 2004, Nancy and I toured New Mexico, Colorado, Kansas and Missouri. As a result of this trip, we placed visiting all presidential museums on our bucket list. We have since visited many but have a few to go.

In June 2005, on a genealogy trip to Indiana, New York, DC and Virginia, we discovered we might be related. We both had ancestors from Nansemond Co, Virginia near Norfolk, that lived there at the same time in the early 1800s. The population of the county was about 100. Detailed records were not available because they had been moved to Richmond during the Civil War to protect them from being burned by the Union troops. Later the records were destroyed by the Union troops when they burned Richmond. We will never know if indeed we are related.

In August we flew to Anchorage, rented a car and toured

Alaska. I had now visited all 50 states. We visited Fairbanks and several of their National Parks and even attended the Alaska State Fair in Wasilla. I had the pleasure of flying in a small plane in the copilot seat to the glaciers near Mt. Denali. On our return home, we detoured through the San Francisco airport. Harlan and Jan Averitt picked us up and hosted us for four days. Nancy thought I must be crazy to visit someone for four days, not having seen them in 40 years. We had a blast and would meet in Santa Fe for many years to come. In October 2006, I drove to Los Alamos and surprised Harlan at his dad's memorial service. Harlan had spread his brother Deryll's ashes at a small park on the way to the ski area of Los Alamos because Deryll enjoyed the view towards Santa Fe. Harlan would always share a beer with him when visiting the area, pouring one where the ashes were poured and drinking one himself. I wanted to share a beer with Deryll. Family members attending the service from far and wide joined us to do the same. *Special time.*

December 2005 would start with the birth of Jacks, son of Summer and Michael. Jacks would entertain us for years as a fine athlete, arguably the best on the field or court. More importantly, he is a great student with a warm heart.

During the next few years, we would attend high school graduations of my grandchildren, Patsy and Joseph, from the large

Grissom High School. Patsy, despite being the shortest player on the court, would be the varsity basketball captain her junior and senior years. Joseph would be captain of the football team his senior year. He also played basketball. Joseph attended Auburn University and Patsy attended Calhoun College. I rarely missed attending ball games of Paige's children.

Chad's children, Spencer and Denver, being in Minnesota meant we only attended one high school wrestling tournament. We would travel to Bemidji, Minnesota to attend grandsons Spencer and Denver's graduations. Spencer joined the Minnesota National Guard and served a tour in Kuwait. Denver is making the US Army his career as an Explosive Ordnance Demolition (EOD) expert. He has served three tours in Afghanistan and received many awards. Once again, he is serving with the Special Forces somewhere in the Middle East in 2019-2020. I also attended their bootcamp graduations.

In January 2007, Nancy found a possible grant source "Save America's Treasures" when searching the internet. The National Park Service of the Department of Interior awarded these grants once a year. I encouraged Rev. Andy Anderson to pursue having someone prepare an application. He put a committee together that prepared a good application. The grant was not awarded. No surprise because no grants were awarded on the first try. Typically, three attempts would be necessary before the possibility of an award. The following year I modified and resubmitted the application. Still no award, but they reported it was a very good application and that it should be submitted the following year. So, I tweaked the application and submitted it again. They announced that we had been awarded a grant for $432,216 in December 2009.

In 2007, while serving on the Building and Grounds, I prepared a statement of work and specification for restoring the stain glass windows then acquired three proposals. In December, Building and Grounds committee approved awarding a contract knowing funds would be available from the recent capital fund raising campaign. I would continue to oversee the project.

A five-year project at church was started in January 2008. The Episcopal Church of Nativity sanctuary was completed in 1859. It is the only building in Huntsville that is a National Historic Landmark and only one of three in north Alabama. The Hellen Keller home in Tuscumbia is another. The church had raised funds to cover the cost of several projects that would be implemented by the Capital Campaign Implementation Board (CCIB). The Restoration Project was separate from each of the other projects such as adding a ramp to Bibb Chapel, adding a children's playground, updating the computer system and the organ, and removing the Huntsville Health Department building purchased by the church. I lobbied along with others to have Loch Neely become chairman of the CCIB. I believed he had the best background and a great passion for the church. In my mind, this was to be my only contribution to the projects. Not to be, Loch persuaded me to join the board. Later I would become the Manager of the multimillion-dollar Restoration Project.

The Restoration Project included re-leading the stained glass windows, repointing the brick with lime mortar on the church and Bibb Chapel, repairing external doors, exterior painting including the 160 year old cast-iron fence, repairing lime plaster and repairing wood on the interior, and replacing roofs with copper shingles on three large buildings. I would spend many hours conducting research on materials, building methods, identifying qualified contractors and vendors, and learning the details of the Ecclesiological Gothic architecture incorporated by the original architect, Frank Wills. The first restoration project I started was re-leading the stained-glass windows and replacing hundreds of panes. I would follow the National Park Preservation Briefs on all restoration projects. The good news is that Loch was always available to bounce ideas off of, to review statement of works and specifications prepared, and to fill in when I was not available to oversee contractors. He was a huge asset to me and the CCIB and, as always, to the church. The CCIB would meet once a month for the duration of the projects.

I did cartwheels for about 30 seconds after we were awarded the grant in December 2009. Then it dawned on me that I would have to incorporate government regulations in our statements of works, specifications and would be following specific government bidding and award procedures. Having dealt with the government concerning these areas over the years was a big help. Also, Elaine Hamner with her government experience was an invaluable resource. The award was the only one awarded to Alabama that year and the third largest in the country. The grant required the approval of architects in Washington, DC on all specifications, statement of works, and contractors selected. The Alabama Historical Commission (AHC) in Montgomery was now required to review and approve the detail specifications. I had already traveled to Montgomery to advise them of our plans. I also gave presentations to the Huntsville Historic Preservation Commission (HHPC) seeking approval of our plans. The AHC commented that no one had ever been as prepared. They gave their blessing on the detail plan. The HHPC also gave accolades on the information supplied and approved our application.

In September 2009 we were blessed with a granddaughter, Mary Ceil, thanks to Michael and Summer. She has been a blessing. Later in September, Paige and I drove to Bemidji, MN to attend Denver's wedding to Shiree. They would bless us over time with three great-grandsons: Talen, Casteil, and Thorin as well as a great granddaughter, Everlyn.

The main double doors and bell tower double door frames were infested with termites. As a result, I had to reverse engineer the heavy deep door frames including the arches. We used a Virginia company to mill the many oak pieces. Loch and I traveled to Virginia to verify the design and be assured the manufactured pieces were acceptable. We arrived in Huntsville with the pieces and then assemble and install the frames. The original oak doors had to be disassembled and rebuilt. Loch, Frank Vann and I would provide all the labor (over 2,500-man hours) for the door project. Maggie Little, local artist and good friend would match and stain the new oak frames to match the 160-year-old oak doors.

I would take some of the tracer sections from the church home to repair and refinish. I have a well-equipped wood working shop. Nancy gave up her spot in the garage while I had fun. *She is a winner.* The church was closed for five months while the interior restoration work was conducted, and the nave roof replaced. Scaffolding was erected to the ceiling to allow plaster and wood repairs to be accomplished.

There were no funds identified to repair four crosses in and on the church. So, I anonymously funded their repair and/or replacement. In the late 1950s when the steeple was rebuilt, a simple stainless-steel cross was installed on the top of the steeple. I knew this did not resemble a cross that the original architect, Frank Wills, would have created. An old blurry picture of the church cross appeared to be a budded cross. I studied the 13 remaining churches and the cathedral he designed. They had budded crosses on their steeples. I could not in good conscience leave the stainless-steel cross atop the steeple, even though there were no funds available. I designed a budded nine-foot cross (the cross would be seen far away on the 154-foot steeple including the cross) and had it manufactured in Germany. They had the experience to properly apply gold leaf as well as the skills to build the cross. I repaired and refinished the external cast iron Floury cross (at rear peak of the nave). I paid to have the external copper Tulip cross (located at the front peak of the nave) repaired. The interior sculptured cross (located at the apse, the peak of the chancel inside the church above the altar) was missing about one-third of the sculpture. I hired an art professor at Alabama A&M to repair the cross.

There are many stories and details that occurred during the restoration that I would love to share but will not in this book except for one that I will always treasure. One day a young couple was standing on the sidewalk and asked if they could go inside. I escorted them inside and they each said it was the most beautiful room they had ever been in. According to Nancy's calculation, I spent 8,000 man-hours over a five-year period on the project. I thoroughly enjoyed working with Loch, Frank, contractors, church staff, and getting to know many church people that before I had only known by sight. The project was a lot of fun and it was an honor and privilege to be part of the CCIB program.

The rest of the story—the project would go on to win two international awards and one local award. The presentation of the first international award, North American Copper in Architecture Award, was presented on the exterior steps of Bibb Chapel. It had been at least three years since the award had been given to a project in the US. I invited the mayor, city council, local architects and church members. Of course, the local press attended. We had a good turnout. I had the honor to introduce the presenter. *Pride can be a sin. Oh well, I am almost perfect.* I traveled to San Antonio for the next international award. The National Roofing Contractor's Association (NRCA) at its 126th convention hosted the award banquet for about 1,000 individuals from countries around the globe the winners were announced. NRCA 2013 Gold Circle Awards presented an Honorable Mention for Innovative Solutions: Re-roofing. The Huntsville Historic Foundation presented an annual award to the church for its restoration project. Loch graciously accepted the award for our beautiful historic church.

Nick Passino, my best friend for 35 years, had retired as

President of Teledyne Solutions in 2002. He was still full of energy with a big heart. Tragically, he would have a fatal head injury that caused his death on March 1, 2011. He and Marylin were in southwest Florida. I would pick up their son, Matt, in Birmingham and drive to Charlotte, Florida. Their daughter, Uta asked if I would like some private time with her dad. I would. Knowing he was going to die within hours, I bawled and bawled. I would be in the room with Nick's children when he died. Suspecting they did not want to leave Nick, I asked his children if they would like me to go to the hotel to get Marylin. She had planned to be gone only a short while. I told her she needed to return to the hospital. I did not want to tell her why. She asked if he had died, I reluctantly said yes. After the family had returned to their homes, I walked the beach for a few days to reflect on our friendship. *He was the best of the best.* Later Marylin would tell me that Nick said for her to call me if she needed anything.

Lois Watson, the widow of our boss (decades ago) and great friend, Dr. Harry Watson, had asked Nick and me to be Durable Power of Attorney, health care proxy of her Living will, Executor of her Estate and subsequently trustee of a trust set up from the will in 2003. She had no children and all relatives lived out of state. Nick was the primary individual in the above documents with me filling in when Nick was not available. She now had Alzheimer's and the courts had ruled her incompetent. Nick and Marylin had gone above and beyond to take care of her finances, preparing her home for sale, attending doctor visits, picking up her medicines, etc. To date, I had only filled in when they were out of town. Now I had the responsibility. Marylin pitched in with a wealth of history concerning her health and personal needs that helped beyond words. Marylin would also purchase clothing, toiletries, etc. *Not my strong suit!*

The first task I performed was signing the sales contract and later closing documents concerning Lois's home. Over the years I managed her financial affairs such as paying bills and managing her substantial assets which were spread over several accounts. Making decisions concerning her medical care were constant. These tasks resulted in such things as signing documents allowing surgeries, being called at 9:00 pm while attending an event to go to the ER for several hours and sitting with her at a local hospital on Christmas morning. That morning our home was full of family waiting for me to arrive so the turkey could be served, etc. These typical events were just a tip of the iceberg. At no time did I feel inconvenienced. I always considered it a blessing and honor to be with her. I cannot imagine Christmas morning sitting with her in the hospital being more meaningful. Later, in November 2017, she had been released from the hospital to hospice care at her nursing home. I would be in her room when she died. *She was a great lady!* I arranged a graveside service conducted by a preacher from her church. Family came from parts of Georgia and Texas. Many of the family had not seen each other in years. Nancy prepared a reception in our home to provide the opportunity for the family to tell stories about Lois and catch up. I enjoyed the opportunity to get to know her family. *As usual Nancy outdid herself.* I am still settling her estate and managing the trust I set up per instructions in Lois's will. I expect to manage the trust for years to come.

In April, Joseph and I traveled to Minnesota to attend the baptism of my great-grandson, Tysen, Spencer's son. We made several stops on the trip such as touring two John Deere factories, Chicago, and a VIP tour of the Corvette factory and museum. This last stop was Joseph's favorite. *Surprise! Great time thanks to Joseph.*

Nancy's son Will was engaged to Tess (an anesthesiologist). In October 2011 the family journeyed to Jamaica for a week to attend a very special beach wedding. They both are super nice people. They have since blessed us with two grandchildren, Katelyn and Rhett. They reside in St. Simons Island, Georgia. Will is a stay at home dad, although he still works part time from home for a NASCAR team. Speaking of NASCAR, for Christmas, Nancy gave me a "Ride Along" at Talladega Racetrack knowing I was a great fan. I wanted to go more than 175 mph, but the professional driver said he was not allowed to drive faster. *Damn!*

I flew to Jacksonville, Florida to be with my children on Pearl Harbor day in 2017. It was very special to be with Paige and Chad on the 40th anniversary of Patsy's death. *She has missed so much that life has to offer, although she was with us this day.*

My sweet sister, Nancy, was in the final stages of cancer and had moved in with her daughter, Charlotte in Midlothian, Texas under the care of hospice in April of 2016. Luckily, I arrived a few days before she died and had some great visits with her and her children: Charlotte, Shannon and Eric. She left behind exceptional children that I will always love. *Nancy, being eight years younger and a female, was supposed to live longer than me.* Months later my wife Nancy and I would meet my sister's children and families in Carlsbad, New Mexico to attend the burial services officiated by the priest from Grace Episcopal Church where I had served as an Acolyte in my early years. Nancy's ashes were interred at our parents' burial plots.

Other losses over the last •several years include many good friends and my lunch buddies: Frank Vann, Billy Barnes, Don Martin and of course Nick Passino. I had the opportunity to visit Frank in the hospital after he had a stroke. He was unable to speak. His daughter and granddaughter were present. They said, "Now we can put a face to the man Frank talks about. He likes your management style." Without thinking I said, "Like taking no prisoners." I was just trying to be *humorous*. They both responded in unison, "That's it, that's it." *Really!* Frank's wife, Mary, told our priest that she wanted me to conduct the whole funeral service. *Really again.* As for Billy, I have him to thank for suggesting that I should check out Nancy. Don and I go back to 1964 soon after I came to Huntsville. Early on, he was my boss, a class-act and always had my back. Six of nine of my Episcopal Cursillo, a reunion group that I met with weekly, have died and two of my current reunion group have died. I miss them one and all. Here I stand with the physical and mental capacity to love, worship at a church I love, a loving blended family, good friends and ability to continue my financial consulting business. *Go figure! I still do not understand what people saw in me that made me part of their lives.*

I am very aware how lucky I am to have the chance to continue to check things off of my bucket list. We currently have a trip planned in May 2020 to Norway and Sweden. Travel will always be a pleasure to me. Another pleasure I have indulged in is the collection of art. I swore off collecting additional art, but it keeps finding its way to our home. The latest painting arriving was painted by our good friend, Maggie Little, a widely known artist with many awards. *It is a treasure.*

One of my treasures during adult life has been enjoying discussions with people from all walks of life. I am amazed, frustrated and amused concerning the changes that have occurred during the full life I have lived. Dramatic changes have occurred in families, politics, technology, fashion, acceptable speech and behavior. I have gone from a large crank phone on the wall in my childhood home to smart phones, clothes lines to dryers, ringer washers to spin washing machines, slide-ruler in college to a home computer on which I am typing, radios to televisions, vinyl records to digital music & movies, cash to credit cards, checks to automatic electronic payments, one family auto to multiple autos per family, milk delivered to your door to online shopping, encyclopedias replaced by Google, men delivering ice to your ice box to refrigerators, medical advances that could not be imagined, etc. Many family structures have changed and so have daily routines; a family dinner is now the exception for most families. Politics always change but there does seem to be fewer real statesmen at work. Life expectancy was 59.7 years when I was born in 1938 and is 78.7 in 2019. *Nice to beat the odds.*

Cost of Living Changes During Skipper's Lifetime

Item	1938	2019	Change
Average Income	$1,731.00	$46,800.00	2,704%
New House	$3,900.00	$315,000.00	8,077%
New Car	$960.00	$37,185.00	3,873%
Movie Ticket	$0.25	$9.26	3,704%
Gasoline	$0.10	$2.50	2,500%
Postage Stamp	$0.03	$0.55	1,833%
Average Rent per month	$27.00	$1,450.00	5,370%
Tuition to Harvard per year	$420.00	$95,470.00	22,731%

Nancy and I have shared more than one can expect to have the opportunity to enjoy. We have visited Russia, China, Canada, Mexico, the Caribbean and nearly all countries in Europe in addition to my trips to Honduras and the Middle East. We have also enjoyed many trips in this wonderful country of ours. I have enjoyed a full life with expectations of many years to come. The joys and any successes I have experienced were based on a wonderful family, remarkable friends and faith. *It is still a mystery how fortunate and blessed this Dude has been during this adventurous journey.*

Nancy and I always have each other's back and so much more. I am grateful to wake each morning knowing her love, generosity, intellect, humor, integrity, all she brings to the table and will always be there. After 20 years Nancy is still the joy of my life.

I love you Nancy.

Ernest "Skipper" Colin

From a small farm in rural New Hampshire where he began life, to New Mexico through his college years, Ernest "Skipper" Colin moved to the Rocket City of Huntsville, Alabama in 1963. Skipper has navigated around the United States and the world stage with a skill that would have made his parents and his forebearers proud. He retired in 1995 after nearly 33 years with Teledyne Brown Engineering. He is enjoying his retirement years with his wife Nancy, keeping busy with travel, family, and friends and is always up for the next big adventure.

Acknowledgements

Without my lovely wife, Nancy George Colin, whose encouragement to write my story, her love, support and editing, this story would not have been written.

Many thanks to Mardy and Jim Manes for reviewing the entire book during different phases plus encouragement to continue.

Thanks to Christine Brown and John Carson for their exceptional editing talent, guidance and patience.

Others who deserve recognition for reviewing various chapters or providing guidance are John Holstein, Donna Rush, Ed Seigler, Manfred Segewitz, Chuck Whaley, Hugh Morgan, Bonnie Sudbrock, and Caroll Crawford.

Made in the USA
Columbia, SC
05 May 2020

96103353R00135